(Inter)views

Cross-Disciplinary Perspectives on Rhetoric and Literacy

Edited by
Gary A. Olson
and
Irene Gale

Introduction by
David Bleich

Afterword by
Andrea A. Lunsford

SOUTHERN ILLINOIS UNIVERSITY PRESS
Carbondale and Edwardsville

*To Fred for making so much possible,
and to Charlotte, Annette, and Charlotte*

Copyright © 1991 by the Board of Trustees,
       Southern Illinois University
All rights reserved. All material contained herein is reprinted
by permission of the *Journal of Advanced Composition*.
Printed in the United States of America
Edited and designed by Gary A. Olson and Irene Gale

4 3 2 1   94 93 92 91

Library of Congress Cataloging-in-Publication Data

(Inter)views: cross-disciplinary perspectives on rhetoric and literacy
    edited by Gary A. Olson and Irene Gale; introduction by David Bleich;
    afterword by Andrea A. Lunsford.
        p.   cm.
   Includes bibliographical references.
   ISBN 0-8093-1737-0 (alk. paper)
   1. Rhetoric. 2. Literacy. 3. Written communication.   I. Olson,
Gary A., date–   II. Gale, Irene.
P301.I58 1991
808—dc20
                                                   91-17653
                                                       CIP

The paper used in this publication meets the minimum requirements of American National Standard for Information Sciences—Permanence of Paper for Printed Library Materials, ANSI Z39.48-1984. ∞

Contents

Preface
  Gary A. Olson and Irene Gale ix

Introduction: Do We Need Sacred Texts and Great Men?
  David Bleich 1

Mary Field Belenky

Composition, Collaboration, and Women's Ways of Knowing:
  A Conversation with Mary Belenky
  Evelyn Ashton-Jones and Dene Kay Thomas 27

Politicizing the Composing Process and Women's
  Ways of Interacting
  Elizabeth A. Flynn 45

Dueling with Dualism: A Response to Interviews
  with Mary Field Belenky and Gayatri Chakravorty Spivak
  Marilyn M. Cooper 51

Noam Chomsky

Language, Politics, and Composition: A Conversation
  with Noam Chomsky
  Gary A. Olson and Lester Faigley 61

Response to "Language, Politics, and Composition:
  A Conversation with Noam Chomsky"
  James Sledd 96

Language and the Facilitation of Authority:
  The Discourse of Noam Chomsky
  Robert de Beaugrande 100

Jacques Derrida

Jacques Derrida on Rhetoric and Composition:
A Conversation
    Gary A. Olson 121

Jacques Derrida on Teaching and Rhetoric: A Response
    Sharon Crowley 142

"Where Have You Come from, Reb Derissa, and Where Are You
Going?" Gary Olson's Interview with Jacques Derrida
    Jasper Neel 145

Paulo Freire

History, *Praxis*, and Change: Paulo Freire
and the Politics of Literacy
    Gary A. Olson 155

Freirean Pedagogy in the U.S.: A Response
    James A. Berlin 169

A Response to Gary Olson's Interview with Paulo Freire
    C.H. Knoblauch 177

Clifford Geertz

The Social Scientist as Author: Clifford Geertz on Ethnography
and Social Construction
    Gary A. Olson 187

The Somewhat Unitary World of Clifford Geertz
    Linda Brodkey 211

Clifford Geertz on Writing and Rhetoric
    Lisa Ede 219

Richard Rorty

Social Construction and Composition Theory: A Conversation
with Richard Rorty
    Gary A. Olson 227

Response to the *JAC* Interview with Richard Rorty
  Kenneth A. Bruffee 236

On Personally Constructing "Social Construction":
  A Response to Richard Rorty
  John Schilb 238

Gayatri Chakravorty Spivak
Rhetoric and Cultural Explanation: A Discussion
  with Gayatri Chakravorty Spivak
  Phillip Sipiora and Janet Atwill 243

Toward a Productive Crisis: A Response
  to Gayatri Spivak
  John Clifford 255

Talking Differently: A Response to Gayatri Chakravorty Spivak
  Thomas Kent 261

Afterword
  Andrea A. Lunsford 267

Preface

(Inter)views: Cross-Disciplinary Perspectives on Rhetoric and Literacy is a collection of interviews with major scholars from outside the discipline of rhetoric and composition whose work has had an influence on the field. Each interview is followed by two short response essays from notable composition scholars. Originally published in the *Journal of Advanced Composition*, these interviews and responses constitute a dialogue about language, rhetoric, literacy, and other topics relevant to composition theory. Because rhetoric and composition is an especially interdisciplinary field, much of its scholarship depends on the work of scholars from other disciplines. The careful application of these scholars' work is essential. Thus, the scholarly interviews in this collection function as a *primary source*, in that they are direct, focused opportunities for these internationally prominent scholars to address key intellectual questions in our discipline's scholarship.

This collection includes interviews with psychologist Mary Field Belenky, linguist and philosopher of language Noam Chomsky, French deconstructionist Jacques Derrida, international literacy scholar Paulo Freire, distinguished anthropologist and fellow at Princeton's Center for Advanced Studies Clifford Geertz, philosopher Richard Rorty, and cultural critic Gayatri Chakravorty Spivak.

Mary Field Belenky and her coauthors gained instant acclaim for their *Women's Ways of Knowing*. Along with Carol Gilligan, Belenky is the feminist scholar most often cited by composition scholars interested in feminism. In the interview, Belenky speaks at length about the nature of collaboration, the writing process, and ethnographic research. Following the interview are responses from two compositionists well known for their work with feminist issues: Elizabeth Flynn and Marilyn Cooper.

The interview with **Noam Chomsky**, eminent linguist, philosopher of language, and social critic, covers a wide range of issues, from deconstruction to feminism to social construction. He explores literacy, paradigm shifts, and his own writing process; and he has much to say about rhetoric, propaganda, and indoctrination. On many key subjects, his views stand in sharp contrast to the current preoccupation with social forces and the rejection of innateness. In fact, he's especially critical of how meaning and the mind are now studied. James Sledd and Robert de Beaugrande provide rigorous critiques of some of Chomsky's positions.

The conversation with internationally prominent philosopher **Jacques Derrida** reaffirms his conviction that the intellectual "tradition" is important.

He discusses literacy, writing across the curriculum, the role of composition instruction in higher education, and rhetoric and composition's place as a discipline within the structure of the university. He even describes how he himself learned to write, and he outlines his views on rhetoric. The responses to this interview are by two compositionists closely associated with deconstruction: Sharon Crowley and Jasper Neel.

Paulo Freire is world renowned for his work in literacy theory and "liberatory learning." His work has had direct and significant influence on composition scholarship. In this interview, Freire discusses a range of issues relevant to composition studies, including the politics of literacy, feminist theory, and critiques of his own work. James Berlin and C.H. Knoblauch respond to this interview.

Clifford Geertz's work is cited frequently in composition scholarship, usually in relation to social construction or the role of ethnography in composition scholarship. A fellow at the prestigious Institute for Advanced Studies, Geertz is one of the most important anthropologists of our time. Geertz discusses the nature of interpretation, rhetoric, and persuasion, as well as the role of ethnography and other research methods in both composition studies and the social sciences. Linda Brodkey and Lisa Ede provide insightful, constructive critiques.

Richard Rorty is perhaps the United States' most important contemporary philosopher. Social constructionists in composition such as Kenneth Bruffee have drawn heavily on Rorty to argue for what James Berlin calls a social-epistemic view of writing and rhetoric. This interview reveals that some compositionists have misinterpreted crucial parts of Rorty's work and that Rorty himself is not especially sympathetic to some of the ideas that often he has been said to champion. Rorty speaks disparagingly of composition and defends E.D. Hirsch's call for a renewed cultural literacy. The two responses to this discussion are by Bruffee and John Schilb.

Cultural critic **Gayatri Chakravorty Spivak** provides an articulate response to numerous questions relevant to rhetoric, composition instruction, and deconstruction. This interview is an excellent counterpart to the Belenky in that these two thinkers represent two divergent "feminisms." John Clifford and Thomas Kent contribute perceptive analyses of Spivak's positions.

This collection also includes a critical introduction by literary theorist and composition scholar David Bleich, and an afterword by Andrea Lunsford.

Needless to say, these seven intellectuals' perspectives on matters of epistemology, writing, rhetoric, and literacy are diverse and, often, in direct opposition to one another. Yet, as heterogeneous as their views may be, all seven share an abiding passion for language, for rhetoric, for discourse. If these interviews illustrate anything, it is that the study of discourse (and, therefore, those issues of special concern to rhetoric and composition scholars) is of paramount importance to some of today's most influential thinkers—a propitious sign for the future of rhetoric and composition as a discipline. We hope that the conversations between compositionists and others in this text will widen and enrich the ongoing dialogue in composition theory by clarifying positions and opening new issues for discussion.

We would like to thank those who helped make this project a success: Tom Ross for sustained moral and financial support; Kenney Withers for encouragement and understanding; Richard Preto-Rodas for wit, perseverance, and companionship during the odyssey to Brazil; Fred Gale for assistance in conducting the Derrida interview; Reed Way Dasenbrock, John Schilb, and Phillip Sipiora for contributing questions for the Derrida interview; Libby Allison and Marilyn Alfred for expert editorial assistance; and Evelyn Ashton-Jones for friendship, inspiration, and careful editing.

Gary A. Olson
Irene Gale

Introduction: Do We Need Sacred Texts and Great Men?

DAVID BLEICH

When I was in training for the academy, interviews were not a part of scholarly inquiry. During a newspaper strike in New York in the mid-1960s, the *New York Review of Books* was founded, and it published interviews with distinguished figures. Recently, scholarly journals also have begun using interviews in an attempt to expand the traditional styles of discourse in academic work. The conversational format is definitely an improvement over the declarative monotony of the formal essay. As Deborah Tannen and other sociolinguists have suggested, conversation is becoming for many an especially fruitful source of social understanding, a preferred way of learning, of thinking with others, of testing received thought. Conversations help to promote the feeling that, yes, there *is* a heartbeat on the pages of our intellectual lives.

In the pages of this volume, for example, one sign of its heartbeat is the fact that while the interviewers tried as hard as possible to work from common starting points in each interview but still to let the conversation go spontaneously, the collection of interviews is, euphemistically, "uneven." Some interviews are richer and more interesting than others. Some are short and casual, others long and thoughtful. In this introductory essay, however, I want to consider each interview (with its own respondents and in comparison to what other contributors have said/written) to have something valuable to teach. The collection in aggregate gives an especially interesting picture of many issues in the study of language and writing, and it provides some guidance about how we might change our approaches to our subject, to one another, to students, and to widely discussed political and social agendas in the academy.

In my reading of this volume, the Chomsky interview best poses the most problems of writing, language, and social relations, Robert de Beaugrande's angry, impatient commentary notwithstanding. The Belenky interview, to me, presents the most in terms of new, useful proposals for what might now be done in school and university classrooms.

Of all the work by Chomsky that I have read, this interview is definitely the richest, most interesting, most fertile statement. Early on, Chomsky says/writes,

> I have two full-time professional careers, each of them quite demanding, plus lots of other things [such as correspondence].... I discovered over the years that probably my only talent is this odd talent that I seem to have that other colleagues don't, and that is that I've got sort of buffers in the brain that allow me to shift back and forth from one project to the other and store one.

While most of us will agree that Chomsky's political work is about as demanding as his work in linguistics, few of us have taken his political writings as belonging to a "full-time professional career." But now that he describes them in this way, it rings true. His livelihood as a thinker and public figure does in fact come from both of these sources. His sense of their equivalence, so to speak, brings out the problem of his total enterprise ever more strongly. His explanation suggests why it is a problem. He says his "only" unique "talent" is that he has "sort of buffers in the brain" which enable the frequent shifts of attention his work demands. In casual circumstances, we might pass over the "buffers in the brain" as duly metaphorical. But because the brain as an entity and a concept plays such a key role in his reasoning about what language is, his saying that his talent is his possession of these buffers makes me want to think about it more.

Talent is unmeasurable and it has no fixed structure. Chomsky's claim of any talent at all is given modestly, since most who would acknowledge his talent would definitely consider it in grander, value-laden terms that are more related to imagination and intelligence than to anything physiological. Chomsky's articulation poses a problem in that while he maintains a rigid separation between his linguistic and political work, his statement implies that his talent is *reducible* to "buffers in the brain." Later on in the interview, he similarly suggests that because human beings have come to consider slavery immoral, there is some sense in searching for the "innate basis of moral judgment": there may be, he implies, something innate (genetic? physiological?) about opposition to slavery. Similarly, the "move away from patriarchy" is "a step toward understanding our true nature." Such statements suggest that he strongly separates his two careers because of his private sense that his political work may be taken to be less authoritative because it is unscientific. The separation between linguistics and politics in his thought, which I think ought to be explained as the exercise of values, Chomsky longs to explain as being due to "innate" physiological endowment. He seems to tacitly authorize his political activity on the basis that the *views themselves* as well as his removal of them from his work in linguistics may be rooted in an "innate" condition.

Because of this longing, the two careers seem always distant from one another, seem to represent a conflict of values which, in my reading, reflects the classic conflict of values in the academy: there is "real" work, science, and there is other work, necessary, important, yet ultimately fluid and definitely unpredictable—politics, humanities, the search for a just society. Chomsky's separation of the study of language from this other work represents his participation in the values which his political efforts oppose. Nevertheless, he seems quietly to want these efforts to be ultimately justified by the same standard (innateness) he claims authorizes his linguistic work. Toward the end of the interview, he says/writes,

> But let me tell you what my own choices and priorities are. Like any human being, I'm interested in a lot of things. There are things I find intellectually interesting and there are other things I find humanly significant, and those two sets have very little overlap. Maybe the world could be different, but the fact is that that's the way the world actually is. The intellectually interesting, challenging, and exciting topics, in general, are close to disjoint from the humanly significant topics.... The use of language to impose authority ... [as a topic] has no intellectual depth to it at all, like most things in the social sciences. Also, it's of marginal human significance as compared with other problems.
>
> People often argue, and I think this is a real fallacy, "Look, I'm a linguist; therefore, in my time as a linguist I have to be socially useful." That doesn't make sense at all. You're a *human being*, and your time as a *human being* should be socially useful. It doesn't mean that your choices about helping other people have to be within the context of your professional training as a linguist. Maybe that training just doesn't help you to be useful to other people. In fact, it doesn't.

I think these passages give a good sense of how Chomsky appropriates a traditional cultural prejudice to conceal the meaning of his own choices and priorities: the prejudice is the sense that the intellectually significant and the humanly significant are "disjoint." What seems to follow from this is his general deauthorization of work in the social sciences. The particular kind of social science most emphatically deauthorized is the study of the use of language as a political instrument. This belief tries to conceal the possibility that his *own use of language in the presentation of his linguistic program may also be political or moral* in the senses he uses these terms. He presents his own separation of values as a fact: "The fact is that that's the way the world actually is." He reasonably suggests that one may *make* a separation between the intellectually and humanly significant; but he also seems to maintain, in the strongest possible terms, that this separation is a rigid fact about how the world "actually is." He maintains that the category "human being," to which we all belong, is the one from which we make choices that are morally and socially motivated. He says that this does not necessitate professional categories also leading us to such choices. But then he also says that professional training "in fact" doesn't help you to be socially useful. Wouldn't it be more reasonable to say that professional categories are some of many "human-being" categories?

We should remember in this context that within Chomsky's well-known linguistic program, an identical separation takes place: that between competence and performance. Performance is part of the "human" context and as a phenomenon, he often characterizes it as "mysterious." It is also separate and distinct from his concept of what is scientifically approachable. This separation permits the investigation of competence as an innate component of human (genetic? physiological?) materiality. The concept of competence permits us to think of language as a thing, an object of investigation in the Newtonian sense, like a planet or a blueprint. Moreover, Chomsky seems to want language to emerge in our understanding *more* as a planet or a blueprint than as a social entity. This perspective leads him to the very strange, ungainly (and to me *false*) view that there is a rigid separation between the "intellectually interesting" and the "humanly significant."

I suppose that one can consider his opinion to be self-serving in the narrow sense: it is adduced to justify his own early insight that there is something very interesting about the fact that "John is easy to please" is quite different from "John is eager to please." But I don't believe this is a fair thing to say, since all our views and opinions, if they were not self-serving, would not serve to include ourselves in the discourse of public values. So let us admit that a "self-serving" opinion is what we all hold in one degree or another. But Chomsky's opinion about the separation of values is, in my judgment, a point of view linked to values that I think he rejects, as can be seen in his approach to politics. In spite of his wish to "push" his moral and political opinions into the realm of the innate in order to buttress his "intellectual" views, these opinions, particularly in their informal dimension, seem to me to release a quality of mind in him that his former student, Robin Lakoff, has actually made the basis of an influential, successful, professional life, while nevertheless continuing to be a linguist in a sense that I think is richer than Chomsky's.

This quality of mind makes the distinction in the interview between greed and power-hunger. Chomsky says/writes,

> I'm very much in favor of corruption. I think that's one of the best things there is.... I think it's a wonderful thing. I'd much rather have a corrupt leader than a power-hungry leader. A corrupt leader is going to rob people but not cause that much trouble.... I think we all ought to applaud corruption.... Power-hunger is much more dangerous than money hunger.

De Beaugrande calls this opinion "the most cynical sophistry in the whole interview." He then points out (to Chomsky? to us?) that "money is power." I think, however, that Chomsky's formulation demonstrates the style and depth of human imagination that ought to be working in his linguistics and that actually does work in Robin Lakoff's linguistics, one of whose contrastive sentences are "Oh dear, someone has put the peanut butter in the refrigerator again" and "Shit, someone has put the peanut butter in the refrigerator again." Chomsky's distinction does away with the formulaic identification of wealth and power common in naive Marxist thought. Chomsky did—can I really say this?—the *empirical* work of thinking about actual political leaders and *discovering* how, in some instances, greed might be a hedge against fascism, the ultimate enemy of human social life. His implication is that for most normal people, it is enough to be rich—certainly a view that any good Marxist will accept. Although some people will try to get rich illegitimately, their aims will still be partial in that only *some* power will accrue from this wealth. De Beaugrande does not see that Chomsky is concerned mostly about a different *kind* of power that individually is psychological and socially is absolute. It is this kind of power that is actually to be feared, Chomsky suggests. Because this power thinks of itself beyond the pale of human life (and is therefore not primarily avaricious), it perpetuates itself by murder rather than by just theft. (I suppose one of the "socially redeeming" features of the violence-porn film *Goodfellas* is that the hero, himself surrounded by power-hungry murderers, seems to confine himself to stealing and stops short of murder.)

One of the attractive features of Chomsky's own discourse in this interesting (do I mean *intellectually* interesting or just *humanly* interesting?) passage is his sense of humor, something de Beaugrande does not really respond to, unfortunately. "I'm very much in favor of corruption." Here in his discussion of politics, Chomsky calls on the memories of his working-class family, members of which were cultivated and mentally active even though they were unemployed workers. I take seriously Chomsky's citation of his childhood experiences, since they seem familiar to me, having had similar ones myself. The vote in favor of corruption—both the discourse and the substantive opinion itself—comes from this soil. For those who don't recognize it, it is (at least) Jewish wit (also known as gallows humor), and it consists in advocating in an exaggerated way the lesser of two evils. Ghetto life of Jews appears in conversation and in Yiddish literature as bad in every possible way; thus, the joker will say, "I'm in favor of paying higher rent; it means the landlord will not evict me." Chomsky transposes this local style of wit into the public arena in order to argue that in the larger context of world affairs, energy ought to be spent opposing fascism more than (but not instead of) it should be worrying about swindlers.

Chomsky makes a characteristically rigid distinction between greed and power-hunger, but because the *context* is informal, conversational, and reflective, one can hear the distinction as pragmatic and empirical, something one cannot do for the distinction between competence and performance, which Chomsky presents under the rubric of "scientific" theory. In addition, the "human" side of his intellectual life emerges in his sense of humor, his spontaneous use of ironic exaggeration, and his involvement in the conversation.

This last point is of particular importance for this volume and for our consideration of discourse, writing, and language use. Chomsky says that he never particularly thought of himself as a writer: "In fact, most of what I've published is written-up versions of lectures.... Most of the writing I do is probably letters." For Chomsky, as for many other thinker/scholars who appear frequently in public, there is no serious distinction between the oral and the written. The sharing of thought, of oneself, may just as easily be spoken as written, and neither carries any more authority. While writing is convenient as a marker of certain speaking events that others not present can then learn about, it is not a significant change of form with respect to the *human* contribution of the speech event.

Chomsky presents his writing habits in a way that sends a message beyond the description of how convenient it is to be able to move between speaking and writing easily. This message is something like saying he is able to "dictate" his writings: whatever I say is worth writing. Appearances to the contrary, this attitude is the opposite from the attitude we might want to teach in writing classes which urges students to emulate the human voice in their writing projects. The actual "etiology" of Chomsky's approach is that if you occupy an especially respected social position, anything you say may be taken up by publishers and converted into a salable book. For most people it is not easy to speak in public. It is not easy for these same people to write because of their correct perception that when you write, you ought to have something to "say" that is important enough to write as well. To teach people to write is to teach them how to understand the importance of what they have to "say." Since Chomsky already feels that what he has to "say" is important, he can function according to the principle of the identity of speaking and writing.

Chomsky's feeling of his own authority, manifest in the interview's premise that "a journal editor will now interview a 'towering eminence in linguistics and the philosophy of language,'" exposes the "human" dimension of his mind, and actually derives from his quite rigid approach to work and thought in linguistics. His early ideas about language—deep structure, generative grammar, linguistic competence, transformational rules—have acquired authority as science in the model of physics, and not as humanities in the tradition of philosophy or philology. At MIT, where I was once an undergraduate, the term "interesting" was routinely used to designate issues and problems that were considered scientifically significant. When the term was used by an individual scientist, it always *appeared* to have a personal cast but was more importantly meant as an expression of the scientist's judgment of what ought to be pursued as a scientific project. What was happening then, and what is happening in Chomsky's use of "interesting" in the interview, is the *identification* of personal judgment with scientific worth. In other words, the scientist "dictates" what issues shall be studied. Chomsky's separation of the "intellectually interesting" from the "humanly significant" is his attempt to claim that *his real source of authority—his theory of language—is not subject to challenge on "human" grounds*. Moreover, it is not subject to the same political analysis he offers in this interview about the role of intellectuals. These intellectuals, "submissive" insofar as they collaborate with an oppressive political ideology, are those from whom he distinguishes himself through his political activism. True, Chomsky is different in this regard from most American academics. The problem arises in his wish to insulate the concept of language and his theory of language and mind from the attention of social and political analysis.

In a sense, Chomsky conceals his implication in traditional scientific ideology, which, in my view, is androcentric and narcissistic. An oblique piece of evidence for this view is his begging off answering his former student's view that he "never really understood what the feminist movement is about." He intellectualizes part of his response by saying that there is no single feminist movement (perhaps, but that is not germane to the student's real comment), and then he says, "I'm not the person to judge." Of course, he "supports" women's search for social equality (how can he not do this?). But it is revealing that he will not engage this challenge. I believe this student was referring, at least in part, to his acceptance of the traditional style of scientific work in which a scientist acquires a kind of authority that is insulated from political scrutiny *merely by virtue of its being science*, and then exercises personal authority as if it were scientific. As I have discussed in "Sexism in Academic Styles of Learning" (*JAC* 10, 231-47), this is a characteristically masculine social trope, one that describes Chomsky's work and place in linguistics, and one that undercuts his important political, "humanly significant," work.

Bearing in mind my reading of Chomsky's use of "interesting," what can be made of his statement about Derrida and deconstruction that he just doesn't "find it interesting." His reason is that there are two parts to language and, therefore, to claim its indeterminacy is only half true. On the one hand, a "definite structure of concepts and of meaning" just grows in people's minds. On the other hand, the use of these concepts is indeterminate. We recognize his original distinction between competence and performance, where only competence is "interesting." Given this view, it would be accurate to say that Derrida's perspective finds only performance "interesting," and as a result locates the issue of language totally in the matter of usage. It is not my opinion that "both views are valid," or that the issue of language ought to be divided as Chomsky divides it or treated as Derrida treats it. I do think, though, that Derrida shares a speech/writing accent with Chomsky: to isolate a perspective, stick to it, and consider as germane (or interesting) only those views that speak within that perspective. The Derrida interview, while revealing the "human" character of the individual, also shows the sense in which the thinker is fully caught up in his characteristic project.

Where language in its "competence" state is the fundamental perspective for Chomsky, writing in its totally inclusive (and thus indeterminate) state is the fundamental perspective for Derrida: "I am unable to dissociate thinking, teaching, and writing." So "yes and no" is his answer to the simple question, "Do you think of yourself as a writer?" Given our own rising politics of tolerance, Derrida at once seems to give an attractive, appealing answer. But as we know, the "yes and no" is already a feature of an intellectual dogma that suggests some necessity for hedging every hint of certainty, especially to the common question posed by Olson. In that same answer, Derrida also says that his "yes and no" derives from his view that "writing to me is the essential performance or act."

Those of us familiar with Derrida's work understand just how wide a range of new ideas have emerged from this simple and appealing consideration. These ideas add up to a comprehensive philosophy of interpretation that emphasizes the endless *possibility* that language use has, and that this limitless range of human opportunity has been suppressed in the history of philosophy and in Western intellectual life since its beginnings in classical times. From this standpoint, the search for an "innate" basis of linguistic competence can seem quite uninteresting.

There is no doubt that as we come into contact with Derrida the person as with Chomsky the person, these persons overwhelm the interview scene with views themselves, and there is virtually no "inter" to be seen. Nevertheless, I have the feeling as I read the interviews with both people, I am getting what feels to me to be the truth. Here, for example, is Derrida's account of his training:

> Instruction was very hard and heavy, very demanding according to classical norms. I was trained in those very classical norms. And probably people who read me and think I'm playing with or transgressing norms—which I do, of course—usually don't know what I know: that all of this has not only been made possible by but is constantly in contact with very classical, rigorous, demanding discipline in writing, in "demonstrating," in rhetoric. Even if I feel, or some of my readers think, that I am free or provocative toward those norms, the fact that I've been trained in and that I am at some level true to this classical teaching is essential.

Most of us reading "theory" in the last two decades well know that Derrida's work is one of the bases of the now-routine opposition to "essentialism" since his thought helped to overturn the sense that words have fixed "essential" meanings. But here we see that in the human context of this interview, writing is an essential act, and Derrida's training in classical norms is likewise essential to anyone's understanding of his philosophical project.

Derrida's use of "essential" is symmetrical to Chomsky's use of "interesting." They are terms that each person's work rejects in some important ways, but which each uses in what I think is a relatively personal appropriation in order to enhance the authority of their claims as thinkers trying to tell the truth. Just as the authority of science is appropriated by Chomsky, the authority of tradition, "classical norms," is used by Derrida to bring to bear a fixed and traditional standard of *value* on what many have taken to be new and revolutionary systems of thought and knowledge. Derrida says that as a teacher he starts with *the tradition*: "If you're not trained in the tradition, then deconstruction means nothing. It's simply nothing." He then elaborates:

> I'm in favor of the canon, but I won't stop there. I think that students should *read* what are considered the great texts in our tradition—even if that's not enough, even if we have to change the canon, even if we have to open the field and to bring into the canonical tradition other texts from other cultures. If deconstruction is only a pretense to ignore minimal requirements of knowledge of the tradition, it could be a bad thing.
>
> In fact, according to the privilege you give to one or another aspect, deconstruction may look conservative. I'm in favor of tradition. I'm respectful of and a lover of the tradition. There's no deconstruction without the memory of the tradition.

We don't need to quarrel with his approval of the canon, but we might want to wonder about a phrase like "minimal requirements of knowledge of the tradition." Here Derrida takes his own training and background as a guide to something he implies that none ought to question: "minimal requirements."

In the same way that Chomsky puts aside the subjective or phenomenological experience of language, Derrida takes for granted a fixed, presupposed sense of minimal requirements, referred to by Derrida as "the tradition." The question we ask is this: "Minimal requirements for *which people*?" Or, "*Whose tradition?*" If, for example, what he refers to as requirements are, rather, something like "received cultural materials," this already has a different sense from requirements, and it definitely plays a different role in any school situation. "Received materials" can be different for different groups of people. Even each individual may have "received" something different in school, even though these different works were all treated as canonical. Furthermore, if we assume that each person may have received something different, it no longer is too urgent to "deconstruct" what people received. The question of "canonical" works may then be referred to specific school curriculums, to standardized examinations. The question of fixed teachings being recursively presented as authoritative is transferred to the practical institutions that are used to certify students and to declare them "educated." In this way, Derrida's viewpoint puts aside the active social forces and histories that students and any other "writers" carry into their language situations, scenes, contexts, and relationships.

Like Chomsky, Derrida cannot but express sympathy with feminism, but he also takes some pains to "answer" the question of feminism by claiming that it cannot be just one thing:

> Sometimes feminism replaces phallogocentrism with another kind of hegemony. I wouldn't say that all women do that, but it's a structural temptation. It's perhaps inevitable at some point that they try to reverse the given hierarchy, but if they do only that—reverse the hierarchy—they would reinscribe the same scheme.

While this answer may seem sympathetic from one standpoint, it would not be responsive to Sandra Harding's claim in *The Science Question in Feminism* that the hierarchy of sciences *ought* to be reversed. Furthermore, it would not be surprising to read of how feminists might use deconstruction as a way to deliberately reverse the traditional hierarchy of other social situations, beyond the academy. In Derrida's short commentary, the issues raised by feminism are themselves not engaged—especially the thought that reversal may *not* "reinscribe the same scheme." I get the feeling from the limited character of this discussion in the interview that Derrida is not terribly interested in whether deconstruction can, as Olson asks, "help bring about the goals and aspirations of feminism." In this case as well, Derrida's style is similar to Chomsky's in exercising what seems like "intellectual privilege" analogous to Chomsky's scientific privilege. In both men's discussion, there is a de facto reduction of the issues in feminism. And it is possible that in both cases Olson, the interviewer, collaborated, however inadvertently, with each interviewee by not marking their lack of interest in this topic.

It is noteworthy how much more animated and detailed are Derrida's discussions of logocentrism and of how deconstruction is practiced by "followers" of his such as de Man and Miller. It is even a bit embarrassing that he speaks of Cixous as "a very old friend of mine who I admire deeply" and who is "one of the greatest writers in France today," but he does not mention these personal views as he engages the work of de Man and Miller. And in addition to the relatively brief interest in feminism, Derrida finally gets to claim that logocentrism is a "universal structure." Both he and Chomsky continue to work under the traditional ideology of science in which single thinkers consider it their responsibility and their aspiration to establish "universals," believing all the while that they are merely discovering them. But if such projects are viewed as creations of academic ideology, and if the feminist critique of this ideology is used as a different way to understand it, Chomsky and Derrida seem more similar to one another than different. Their lack of "interest" in one another's work suggests more that they are thinking in "either/or" terms about themselves as language philosophers than as co-workers on the common project in which many perspectives may have something valuable to contribute, and where a "universal" truth no longer counts as the ultimate achievement of research into language.

After forcing myself, as a young man, to think of the intellectual styles of Chomsky and Derrida as exemplary in some sense, the voice of Geertz definitely offers relief. I suppose if you study anthropology long enough, you forget about trying to find universals; in that field, universals are what you start with—the human race—difference is what you find. So now, many of us, and especially teachers of writing, can't say enough about "thick description." What has been going on in writing classes for decades now emerges from anthropology as legitimate research. The search for detail and accuracy in teaching first-year students how to describe something now comes as a "method" of work by "grown-ups." From the interview, it looks as if Geertz, taking his education seriously, following his "human" and "ideas and values" side rather than a more abstract intellectuality, studied a subject that "interested" him in the subjective sense—as opposed to the Chomskyan sense. Because of his own skill in writing (he "wanted to be a novelist and a newspaper man," and so he "majored in English"), and his obvious pleasure in it, writing has entered the sacred halls of method.

In his review (alluded to in the interview) of three works on feminism and science, Geertz shows himself to be more devoted to this idea of method than we might imagine. In writing about Donna Haraway's *Primate Visions*, a work whose diffuse character and aggressive liberties with language seem to make Geertz nervous, he says, "Her lack of method fails her. The genre [of primatology as part of feminist theory] doesn't appear"; the politics of being female "remain unformed" (*New York Review of Books* 8 Nov. 1990: 23).

His review ought to be read in light of claims made in the interview which suggest, as do Chomsky's and Derrida's interviews, a presupposed support for the feminist movement. The review raises questions as serious about Geertz's perspective as the interviews raise about Chomsky's and Derrida's. I think it is a question of his own discourse, which is as clearly declarative as any traditional masculine academic, myself included. Perhaps more than any of those interviewed, Geertz's discourse shows just how difficult it has been and continues to be for feminine and feminist concerns to join the men's association of academic work. I don't know if Haraway is my cup of tea either, but that is not the issue. I think the issue is more how we will welcome the new forms of discourse offered by feminism. At least one of the forms is the habit of persistent questioning. In his review, Geertz notices that the essays in the volume *Feminism and Science,* edited by Nancy Tuana, has many essays whose titles are questions. To this fact Geertz responds, "Framed by nervous, questioning titles . . . the book is an anthology of dilemmas, conundrums, puzzlements and worries, which, taken together, give an arresting picture of great intellectual commotion without much in the way of a definitive sense of where it is that it might be heading" (19). Who needs to know "where it is heading"? Why are the questions described as "nervous"? The nondeclarative modes in feminist inquiry make up one of its characteristics, one of its clear contributions to scientific inquiry. But Geertz responds badly to the "commotion" and the riddles posed in this inquiry, rather than accepting them in the traditional way: these scholars do their work in a way I haven't done mine; what can we learn from it? The result is that Geertz seems to me to be patronizing and vaguely ironic, even in titling his review, "A Lab of One's Own." "Feminist looking," he writes, is "still tentative, limited, and internally troubled" (19). But why in the interview does he not say similar things about Kuhn's book, a "watershed work." It is quite easy to see why he does not say that. Since "Tom's a good friend of mine," and since Kuhn's book is written in the familiar declarative style we men are used to, it seems clear to me that the difference is that feminist discourse and the politics it promotes are threatening to even the "humanist" anthropologist that Geertz is. Why aren't the masculine "revisionists" of scientific philosophy described as "internally troubled"? Why wasn't the debate between Einstein and Bohr ever described as "nervous"? What Geertz does not engage is the fact that feminist thinkers understand how much higher the stakes are now than they were when only men were setting the discursive pace. Feminism has insisted on including the heretofore nonscientific questions of the social ostracism of women into the discussions of what science is to begin with. For Geertz, this poses a "riddle" or a "conundrum." For some feminists, it is less a riddle than an attempt to enter the discourse in polite and respectful ways, since there can be no question but that the feminist programs, of whatever stripe, are insisting on change in the population of scientists, in the style of discourse, in the ways money is appropriated, spent, and distributed for scientific research, and finally, in the way questions of science are posed to begin with. I do not see how anyone reading in feminist epistemology can avoid seeing with clarity the feminist insistence on change in all of these areas. These are definitely not "nervous" or otherwise "internally troubled" voices. In my reading, they are politically agitated and, in many cases, just plain angry.

Lisa Ede's response to Geertz suggests her own discomfort with the apparent complacency of Geertz's discourse. She asks about his endorsement of pluralism: "Couldn't it also mask the agreement to disagree politely, rather than to confront differences?" While she writes that she has no answer to this question (she obviously does have at least a provisional answer: yes), she also says that she simply wants "to point out that Geertz's genial, liberal approach may have the limitations of, well, genial liberal approaches":

> The questions that Geertz has clearly given much thought to—whether fields like anthropology and composition studies can be too diverse, the benefits and dangers of pluralism—are questions that we must continue to ask. We must also recognize that terms like "pluralism" themselves require critical scrutiny, lest we rely upon commonsensical (and hence unexamined) understandings of their meaning.

"Questions that we must continue to ask." This formulation describes the questions found in the Tuana book. As a rule, continuous questioning has not been part of academic discourse. The interrogative voice in the academy is always overshadowed by the declarative. Geertz wants the closure and clarity offered by the declarative. In describing his own writing, he reports that he does not write while he is in the field: "So for me at least, it's a fairly divided life. I don't write in the field; I write after I return. Mostly, *here* I write and *there* I research." Of course, boundaries do matter and are not to be done without. And *we* are not in a position to say how writing shall be done by any individual. But to make the division as clear and comfortable as Geertz does suggests the division he sees between writing and experience: is it "emotion recollected in tranquility"? "Facts" recollected in tranquility? "Culture recollected"? After all, emotion recollected in tranquility is what Wordsworth said poetry was, and it's how the would-be novelist Geertz now produces science, "after the fact." While Geertz and others of us seem quite open to change, is our discourse, declarative and after the fact (and the way we endorse teaching it to others) already resisting the change we say we endorse? Not according to Richard Rorty.

This is what Rorty says about "freshman English":

> I think the idea of freshman English, mostly, is just to get them to write complete sentences, get the commas in the right place, and stuff like that—the stuff that we would like to think the high schools do and, in fact, they don't. But as long as there's a need for freshman English, it's going to be primarily just a matter of the least common denominator of all the jargon. Besides, I don't see how freshman English teachers are supposed to know enough about the special disciplinary jargon.

What emerges in this short interview with Rorty is what many may have suspected from reading his work but could not quite pin down: it does not matter to him what happens in school. His own discourse is so distant from issues of writing raised by Olson and usually treated in *JAC* that he is unable (or, more likely, unwilling) to make any connections between his own writing and teaching experience, and those who, like Kenneth Bruffee, try to make his thought play a role in how we think about language. The brevity of the interview suggests that the occasion itself was of no interest to him; he could not see it as in any way contributing to his work and thought, and there is no sign that he wished to contribute to the project undertaken by Olson. The interview situation did not suggest to him that *those teaching first-year English* are thinking of this subject differently from how he is thinking of it. Worst of all, the whole question of teaching seems permanently separate from thinking and writing as he conceives them. Rorty's answer to the opening question of the interview, "Do you think of yourself as a writer?" gives the best explanation of how Rorty sees himself in relation to the questions posed by this volume: "I enjoy writing, but I have no idea of what the effect of the style on the audience is. I think, like most people in this line of work, I write to please myself." The pragmatic Rorty sees no point in concealing either his contempt for the question or his narcissistic thoughts. (Schilb, in his commentary, reminds us that the "lone figure" of Rorty is pictured on the front cover of his new book.) Let him please himself. Is that his final contribution?

Rorty's interview shows most clearly of all how a purely declarative discourse stands in the way of social change, both within the interview conversation, and in American society ("I still think of America as a spectacular success story"). The advocate of "conversation" seems unable to participate in one, and the appearance of self-absorption, reasonably concealed in the Chomsky, Derrida, and Geertz interviews, inhibits discussion in this case. Freire's interview, while retaining the declarative style and some of the tropes of individualism, suggests how departures from individualism may take place for those of us who have social and professional "momentum" in the declarative mode. Here, first, is the end of his interview:

> What I would like to say in closing, though, is that I feel happy. I have had the privilege in life, while still alive, to receive recognition from institutions, from the universities, and from many people. That is, history is not waiting for my death in order to say, "That man existed." So I am happy. These things don't make me arrogant, but undoubtedly they make me happy as a human being. You cannot realize how beautiful it is for me when in different parts of the world I am recognized—when, for example, a young man or a young woman working in a shopping center asks me to write an autograph in one of my own books which they happen to have in their pocket.... Scenes like this I have had all over the world, and it is for me a reason to be happy, but not to be proud.

Freire is the only one of the interviewees to mention how old he is: close to seventy. Repeatedly, he refers to his having come out of an obscure part of northeastern Brazil to take a place both on the world scene and in the education establishment in São Paulo. Those of us thinking about narcissism and self-involvement may wish to consider Freire's habit of including his own personal experience whenever engaging Olson's questions. When I read the interview for the first time, I wondered, do I care if Freire is "happy"? Well, I suppose I didn't at first but then I did especially because I found myself surprised at his striking this note in the interview—an announcement of personal satisfaction with his life and work *as if it mattered*. Then it seemed to have mattered only because of the "stroking" one feels when recognized and honored by strangers. But finally I thought it mattered because the interview itself, more than most of the others, told a story of learning and change, not just of success. In a sense, Freire feels recognized for *what he learned* as well as for what he taught. He comes across as much a student as a teacher.

Where Chomsky told of how the history of linguistics was marked by the great turning point of generative grammar, where Derrida told of how he mastered the tradition in order to deconstruct it, Freire told of how, in spite of the march of technology, he believes in his "hand, in the pencil, and in the white piece of paper before me." He describes how his co-workers in the United States "know how to use the machine [the computer], how to put it at their service. It's fantastic. They do much more than I because they use a very good instrument.... Maybe I will start [to use a computer], because I believe that in the last analysis there's always time for us to learn."

Freire's story is not the success of doctrine or dogma, or of a particular program of teaching; it's how a series of "maybes"—possibilities—were pursued and converted into experiences marked by publication, rather than publications that were the experiences themselves. He describes "speaking" a book with partners in conversation, in contrast with Chomsky's simply transcribing his lectures. He tells how he arrived at this thought about ten years ago: "I asked myself, 'Why not start *speaking* books instead of exclusively *writing* them?'" The point here is less that this is an answer of sorts, than that it was just a new idea, a way to be responsive to some of the ideas which were first announced in the traditional declarative—and in *Pedagogy of the Oppressed*, even declamatory—style. The interview seems to depict a history of growth as well as an acute consciousness of his own history and juvenile motivations:

> Perhaps the moments which challenged me and invited me to think of a much more participatory education in relationships between educators and educatees were the moments in which I did not understand the teacher but nevertheless lacked the courage to ask questions because I felt myself inhibited vis-à-vis the arrogance of the teacher, the authority of the teacher. Maybe those negative moments challenged me and invited me to think of that *more* than the positive ones. At least, this is what I could tell you now.

I cite this passage because it too contrasts with the accounts of the others that emphasized almost exclusively professional experience and aspiration of the individual. In Freire's case, the classroom situation is the event he recalls, the fear that he felt and most students today still feel, of asking questions and appearing ignorant. While strongly presented, his recollection remains tentative: "Maybe those negative moments..." There are, in this interview, variations in discourse that admit the subjunctive, the conditional, the possible, and the questionable, even as the clear sense of his own self-awareness and memories are brought forth as elements in his scheme of motives and purposes.

It feels to me that the person who announces at age seventy that he is happy is the person who lived in social fear a great deal when younger, stronger, and more intense, but who has found important new social means of defeating that fear. It is noteworthy how *un*radical Freire really is, how much his project is itself much more decisively pragmatic than is Rorty's, which is only pragmatic in a doctrinaire, individualistic sense. Rorty's pragmatism is purely scriptural and removed from collective human experience.

Freire says/writes that "the authority of the teacher *has* to exist." He describes the necessity of balance between pedagogical authority and the freedom of students, and he implies that at every moment new means are to be sought which promote and strengthen that balance. This is not a doctrine or an ideology but a principle through which education as an institution is to be guided.

At least one of the fears that played a role in Freire's life is the fear of changing the traditional masculine identity. He explains that "when I say I am also a woman,"

> I am first of all expressing my solidarity with women in their struggle, and I am also saying that scientifically it is true. This point is that to a large extent I became able to overcome the fears the culture had imposed on me, and I am not afraid that people say, "Ah, look,

> Paulo does not know yet whether he is a man or a woman." ... I don't feel bad because I recognize in me something which could be characteristic of men but also characteristic of women.

While we may not be certain of differences between Freire and the others discerned through their discourses alone, two items in Freire's interview are different from the others' endorsement of feminism: his announcement of biological participation in being female, and of his participation in men's cultural fear of being a woman. Perhaps it would be right in this instance also to say that Freire "learned" to defeat the fear. Who can say, really, what their origin is, and do we need to determine any origin at all? The point for us is that they are *announced*, and the announcement is a different level of contribution to the discussion of feminism than is found in the interviews with the other men. It is undoubtedly the case that for most men who unconsciously associate themselves with "men," the fear of being woman-identified is strong. Having predicated his work as a teacher on the fear created by economic oppression, it is not a long step from this fear to the fear instilled by the masculine hegemony *in other men*—by the muscular over the weak, by the armed over the unarmed. It is this fear among men of other men that lies at the root of fascism and terrorism, and it is the fear that Chomsky only indirectly alludes to in his distinction between greed and power-hunger, the latter being the origin of the fear men have of other men. To me, Freire's endorsement of feminism is less consequential than his willingness to announce forthrightly the fear on which the historic masculine hegemony of civilization is founded. He is speaking for men, as he is most authorized to do.

More than all the other men in the interview situation, Freire's discourse is clearly moving toward a simultaneous political and social self-knowledge. Even what appears narcissistic ought to be understood as a historical and social self-awareness. It is noteworthy, I think, that Freire's answers to Olson's questions are short like Rorty's, but they engage the question. His answers are like Geertz's in their humane and personal quality, but they are more courageous. His answers are like Derrida's and Chomsky's in that they are serious and willing to engage challenge, but they are more forthright even as they are less declarative. We men who are serious about discovering more about how to contribute to social change would do well to think about Freire's perspective.

One of the strangest features of Freire's perspective to many men and all privileged or established social sectors may be the envisioning of professional programs as unalterably unfinishable. Freire's "happy" conclusion may easily be taken as a statement about how individual fulfillment marks the success of a project. One reason the other four male figures I discussed don't offer such a personal reflection on their own lives is that the vision of personal happiness is more a part of their unacknowledged ideology. For

Freire, it is a piece of luck that he was happy to learn that someone reads his books. For the others the personal *sense* of success is so tied to the ideology of text production that it is considered bad form to take any personal pleasure in it in public. Rorty, the least obviously happy of the four also appears as the most complacent, the most convinced that he/his-work has produced a public closure of sorts on a set of received issues. Freire's personal happiness is an acknowledgement of what one can accomplish within the limits of mortality; but his formulations about what is and what is not "the case" in education, society, and the history of ideas are more tentative than any of the others.

The foregoing observation is meant, in part, as a preface to Spivak's contribution. From a traditional perspective, Spivak's orientation might be seen as something like "dissatisfaction with everything." She opposes *both* hierarchy and balance; many of us who oppose hierarchy, however, have in fact substituted balance as the reasonable next phase. But I don't know that we ought to be reading the perspective of "persistent critique" as a doctrinaire endorsement of dissatisfaction. Balance, she says/writes, "doesn't really do away with privileging but only creates a new privilege." There is an instance in my own experience in the Rochester City School District that suggests how this might be the case. One might expect that white teachers in a mostly black school can introduce literature by black authors in hopes of "balancing" the curriculum and thus win the attention of the students. In general, however, this does not work, because the students' high drop-out rate is less a response to the curriculum than to the conditions of their lives: whatever the white teacher proposes—in this case, a "balanced" reading list—is viewed more or less as privileged, and while more black students may be more responsive to a more familiar literature, very little will change about the underlying premises of schooling for these students.

Spivak's attention is on the university rather than the schools but similar reasoning applies, I think. She says/writes,

> I think we should make use of the fact that our institutional system of education emphasizes committee structures, and, therefore, we should open and reopen these questions [of theory and practice in composition studies] constantly. It's a great waste of time, I know, but, in fact, we should think of it as a spending of time rather than a wasting of time. It is also true that the ... constitution of our student bodies changes. It is also true that the nature of departments and their emphasis on service, and so on, quite often change with different hiring practices and philosophies of chairs, and various roles of chairs—as for example, the chair as first among equals rather than a somewhat imperious director.

This description applies well to the changes taking place where I work, at the University of Rochester. Analogous to the race-relations issues in Rochester City Schools are issues of teaching philosophy at the university. There are those who wish to "establish a writing program" of thus and such nature. There are others who wish to create a structure that will take into account the complexity of change that Spivak describes. As a matter of ideology, what Spivak describes seems quite bizarre to traditionalists, but it seems quite sensible to younger faculty, women, and minority faculty involved in discussions of how to "open up" the writing program. What Spivak brings out is an awareness of the great changes now taking place in school populations, changes which reflect the unending pressure for both social justice and intellectual flexibility emerging from the constant need to include more and different groups of people in institutions that previously were meant only for the privileged. Her own status as a "Third World" native is only a faint marker of the changes in discourses and values she is advocating. "Persistent critique" is less a philosophy of dissatisfaction (though in many ways it is just that) than a desire to include the openness to change in all institutional and intellectual practices. By and large, the university practices and intellectual styles to which I was introduced in college and graduate school in the fifties and sixties cannot really accommodate what Spivak advocates. Those who sense this deep level of incommensurability stiffen their positions—like Hirsch and Bloom—in the process remarginalizing figures like Spivak.

The committee meetings alluded to by Spivak represent challenges as much because constant questioning is alien to university functioning as because those always on committees cannot publish enough to get tenure. This only means what most of us in "research" universities have known for a long time: publication is the fastest and surest way to get tenure; teaching and service alone will never get tenure, though publication alone usually will. But is publication what Spivak means by "persistent critique"? Perhaps so, in part. Mainly, though, it is a politically active way of functioning in the university that has no normal status in the vast majority of postsecondary institutions. The politically active groups or individuals are almost always marginal. In extremely few cases are duly constituted critical voices (such as faculty councils or senates) influential in the daily business of university life. Seriously critical voices often have a forum in classrooms, but provided the classroom format continues in the traditional competitive-individualistic structure. The confinement of critique that "means business" to publication (of such essays as this) is the university's way of resisting change while seeming to endorse academic freedom.

The Belenky interview discloses just how fully academic ideology is committed to resisting changes that I and others consider necessary for the long-term welfare of higher education. The interviewers asked her how collaborative research and writing should be evaluated by university tenure and promotion committees. She says/writes,

> In the academy, collaborative work is demoted, but it should count *double* in faculty evaluations. If a work is embedded in a collaborative process, the writers goad each other into endless revisions. For example, in our study there's hardly a page that wasn't rewritten fifteen or twenty times. No one working alone can do that kind of intensive revision, nor can they benefit from the extensive redrafting that takes place in conversa-

tion. The kind of reflection and revising enabled by collaboration brings a quality of depth and scope to a work. Collaboration may only produce two-hundred or three-hundred pages of text, but perhaps they're more enduring than the two- or three-hundred pages of a single voice.

At the University of Rochester, doubt was cast on the work of a recent tenure candidate because most of the list of thirty or so publications had more than one author. The deans seemed to imply what many teachers imply about their students' efforts at collaboration: it is a form of cheating. The candidate finally won tenure in this case, but the fact that this question was raised at all is a typical occasion for which the approach of "persistent critique" is appropriate. In the foregoing citation, Belenky's point is that collaboration takes more work than individual effort, but, obviously, much more is involved than how much work an individual ought to be doing.

Belenky's issue is related to how fully one can associate collaboration with women's abilities, interests, and welfare. From this perspective, the downgrading of collaboration in the academy is yet another form of opposition to women. Belenky is fairly clear in her view that women take to collaboration more spontaneously than men do. She cites research which suggests that women are less comfortable in competitive situations because one person's "winning" usually necessitates someone else's "losing." A zero-sum game "is no way to live." Consistent with Gilligan's findings, women's more culturally characteristic (not innate or necessary) ethical posture finds justice more in meeting the needs of all parties to a conflict than in finding a principle by which some people's claims are declared more worthy than other people's. As a principle of work in the academy, therefore, collaboration moves toward finding a way for each individual to contribute a "voice" in a collective project, to present a "sound" that is substantively unified but is just as decisively dependent on the various individual contributions of several or many, as in an orchestra.

The structure of academic life—that is, the path toward tenure and promotion as well as the traditional classroom style of competition for grades—is clearly governed by competitive (and comparative) individualism. It has been noticed that in this context many women "fear success." (Can such a fear be ascribed to *any* of the five male figures interviewed in this volume?) Belenky judges that "where doing outstanding work is embedded in a collaborative relationship, women don't seem to have problems with the idea of success at all." In other words, the academic situation promotes in women *both* fear of failure and fear of success. She points out that

> We wouldn't have to spend any more energy teaching collaborative processes and creating forms to support them than we do creating and teaching competitive processes. On the whole women work better in collaborative situations, and women can teach us how to do it, how to teach it. When we do make the educational environment more collaborative, I think we'll *all* be happier in schools—men as well as women.

This is to me a convincing argument, and in general (should I say this?) a *true* one. But this raises the point that Marilyn Cooper addresses in her reflection on Belenky's contribution. While Belenky is circumspect about claiming any universal truths about either women's ways of knowing or about the stages of knowing for all people, she nevertheless is substituting an ethic of "balance" for the prevailing ethic of hierarchy. I agree with Cooper's citing Spivak's opposition to "balance" at this point. "Persistent critique" will admit argument in the traditional sense to the public forums of discussion. Cooper, perhaps more self-consciously than Belenky, advances this point:

> Our belief in the value of pluralism and in the social constructedness of all knowledge (which are not the same thing) does not prevent us from saying that in particular situations ideas can be adjudged not only false but also pernicious; nor does it prevent us from wanting to discredit those ideas in the pursuit of knowledge. That race is not a predictor of intelligence, that individualism is not necessarily a good basis on which to build a society, that women are not inherently more nurturing than men—these are arguments we want to win in our current situation, and ones we have good social reasons for wanting to win.

Unlike Cooper, Belenky tends to avoid *saying* that she wants to win an argument (except in a friendly context, as I will later cite), though it is clear that she hopes to "win" in the sense of her trying to get her vision to materialize on a more widespread basis. She says, rather, that "hard-nosed conversations" are what regulate and guide thought toward what ought to be advocated. When Cooper says that "a perspective conceals at the same time that it reveals," she is working toward a *discourse* that is inclusive and varied but *not* toward a discourse that excludes oppositional stances, particularly because so much opposing is going on right in the advocacies of Belenky and others we feel share our interests. Cooper seems concerned that a *purely* collaborationist ethic may *conceal from ourselves* the moments when an argument is indicated and necessary, moments, put more brutally, when we want to yell, "Throw the bums out." Was it fair, in other words, for Dr. Jean Jew at the University of Iowa to have to spend nearly twenty years of her life in litigation (*Chronicle of Higher Education* 13 Mar. 1991: A15-16) in order to nullify a sexist slander which did continuous material damage to her life? Discourse must be able to oppose the derogation of discourse. The availability of this option is what Cooper wants to include in Belenky's discussion.

As I think about Belenky's and Cooper's remarks, I notice how I start to understand their perspective as *paradigmatic*, and I immediately wonder if this is already a misunderstanding. The paradigmatic (actually, perspectival) thinking discussed by Ludwik Fleck in 1935 and later elaborated by Kuhn in 1962 has also already become a formula for identifying almost any movement for changes in thought styles and collective values. I find that I must reject thinking about their work in paradigmatic terms, or even calling the orientation they represent something like "post-paradigmatic." These terms try to establish "schools," however transient they turn out to be, which, when presented to students, always seem much more rigid than they really were to those who first used the terms. Students then accept the apparent fixity of these terms, and it then takes a great deal of undoing to reestablish just how fluid they are. At the same time, it is the not-so-secret wish of many traditional academics to originate the vocabulary that others are to use routinely. This is the kind of power that is often sought in the academy. Few challenge the wish for such power. Some people really do want to be the "word giver," the agency which "names the world": some want to accede to the "power-magic," to accede to a promethean role and to be thus publicly recognized as having changed discourse. Can there be any doubt that, in spite of Freire's authentic retrospective pride (it is pride because he denies he is proud) in his achievements, part of this pride is the fulfillment of his own wish to "name the world"?

So let me set aside my impulse to speak of paradigms (readers of this essay may remember just how seriously I used the term in my earlier work) and consider how else we may relate to this comprehensive difference in viewpoint we see in the discussions of Belenky, Cooper, Spivak, and others, like Evelyn Keller and Sandra Harding, whose work is perceived by even Geertz, the "good guy," as "nervous" or "internally troubled."

I believe that a helpful way of thinking about their discourse is to understand its partial character. Embedded in every sentence is the potential for other things to be said at the same time. I felt that each sentence *requires* another sentence, perhaps an addendum from me, perhaps from the author, perhaps from other readers. I feel that the discourse *invites* conversation, and, only sometimes, opposition. If I listen to Chomsky and Derrida, I immediately want to argue. I want to say yes, but. I feel that if I agree with them, it will be met with a kind of complacent satisfaction, with sentences like, "That's what I've been saying all along," or "Yes, I first pointed that out twenty years ago," sentences which all sound like, "I'm glad you've finally seen the light that I've been shining for so long." Of course, these figures are different from one another. But it is striking how few times, maybe none (I did not do an exhaustive check), the interviewed figure asks the interviewer anything, hardly even for clarification. The so-called "nervous" questions that make Geertz nervous sound to me more like invitations to collaborate. They are "why don't we consider" questions. They are calls for more voices that are falling on ears which expect only declarations that provide opportunities for (masculine?) listeners to contribute counter-declarations. Geertz is so used to "this is how it is" titles, that a truly open-ended question in the title appears to him like a black six of hearts and a symptom of insecurity. Too few of us really understand just how to participate in an academic conversation. And Rorty's interview suggests to me that he doesn't care to participate in a conversation at all. Against this background, we have Belenky's description of how her group went about writing their book:

> We had a month-long pajama party at a cottage on the shore, a big rambling mansion on the ocean. We spent a month trying to frame the book and talking through the process of writing it; by the end of the month, we had a reasonably firm view of its shape, so we sketched out a table of contents....
>
> It wasn't always clear [how much of a sense of individuality each of us felt]. At times someone would write something so gorgeous that you would think it needed to be in your own chapter and you'd fight for it. Sometimes I found myself winning one of those fights and integrating into my own text a beautiful perception from someone else's text, their words and my words. This process is really very sensuous. It's so loving to have that mingling going on—knowing that these are stolen words in a way, words coaxed out of someone, but liking the closeness of having her words and my words all mingling right in there. Sometimes this feeling happened, too, as we worked with the interviews that we had collected from the women, I'm sure others have experienced this—for example, when they're putting a beloved mentor's words in a document that they're working on. In my teaching, I try to get students to cite a text and put that scholar's words and name next to their own words and name, and I try to help them understand that this is a way of making it clear that the two of them are talking together now.

Let me think about this passage in two ways, referential and invitational. What this refers to is generally censored in academic discussions, confined, at best, to the hallways at professional conferences. Can you imagine Chomsky explaining how he worked on generative grammar during a "pajama party"? Can you imagine any scholar of the traditional stripe including, as a serious explanation as Madeleine Grumet does, reference to the "sweaty socks" which surrounded the writing of her book? Can you imagine Geertz explaining how his electric bill is late while he is writing about himself "after the fact"? What might we think if Derrida referred to his reading of a paper as "sensuous"? And what about all that "mingling" that Belenky reports? The "coaxing"? The stealing of "gorgeous" words? The "beloved mentor"? How routinely, by the way, does this beloved mentor move in on his female students? How permissible is it to mingle the words of my mentor with my own without inciting the nervous titters of those who have sexualized the university classroom through the structure of authority but without any love or closeness? How appropriate does it seem to any readers of this volume that Belenky considers loving closeness a part of scholarship and research? What graduate student will think of, or admit to thinking of, the citation of a source as an intimacy between oneself and some unknown figure? What might it mean to think about citations in this personal way at all? How many suffering students could not announce the exhilaration of *feeling qualified to cite* an accomplished scholar's words as contributing to their own? How many of us feel we must act as if we had mastered a text a small part of which we wish to cite? How many try to show off that they found a "great man" whose "sacred text" somehow fits into their own work? How many grown people founded their total professional identity on their obsequious association with the name of a canonical figure?

Belenky's passage describes a situation that honors the public and private at once. Her description urges me to feel that no element in the experiential path to understanding ought to be censored beforehand as a contribution to understanding. She says that working together overcomes the enforced loneliness of traditional scholarship and research, that it provides a context for work that can and will lead to a more just workplace. It is also a description of what any group of collaborators may encounter. Those of us who have encouraged collaborative work among undergraduates know very well how much of the time is spent (wasted, we say sheepishly sometimes) in idle chatter "warming up" to the tasks. Yet when we inspect this chatter, it is just as pertinent to the undergraduate tasks as were the pajamas and the seashore to the tasks before Belenky and her colleagues. Collaboration, as described in the foregoing passage, *produces new forms of discourse* that are then eligible for inclusion in the research and scholarship that emerges. This I think is part of what Belenky's description refers to.

As an invitation. To announce a feeling of sensuousness in intellectual exchange *invites comment but not argument*. People don't often argue with you if you say how you are feeling. There are the "stolen" words and the "fight" among friends. This too is an invitation to us to test our own social relations and to perceive in Belenky's situation difference as well as similarity. It is true that Belenky spoke her description, but now it is written, and nowhere more in this volume is there more interest in the change-yet-lack-of-change of the transformation from the oral to the written. The oral discourse, by its inclusion in the volume, has become "authorized" in a new way. It has become admitted to a more public place. We see before us this process of admission, a process which itself invites our reflection and commentary.

But there is another, less sanguine, invitation in this passage. It is the invitation to challenge the pajamas and the New England cottage. Perhaps you are poor or otherwise ostracized because you are not white or privileged. Will you be able to hear Belenky with the same endorsement that I do? Will you look at the rest of this volume and wonder why none of your own ethnic background is represented? Will you then be able to feel the enthusiasm of intimate, professionally established peers at a safe and secure site, supported by a life of plenty and hope? Can this be your experience? Because I am already white and male, I can't answer these questions with authority. Does Belenky's idealism ring false to you? If you ask your secure white colleagues to enter *your* community, will they come? Perhaps Marilyn Cooper was thinking of you when she answered Belenky with endorsement but with some serious doubts as well. Perhaps Cooper is warning us not to be fooled by the promise of love and mingling into thinking that stern, tough opposition to social pain is no longer constantly in order, and in ways we are not eager to expect.

Cooper takes up Belenky's invitation by assuring us that it is appropriate to respond to Belenky's discourse with doubt and challenge. She is urging us to believe that our anger and impatience ought to continue to live in us even as we are coaxing and mingling. It is perhaps this troubling mixture of attitudes, attitudes that are made plain if we let ourselves include the physical, emotional details of our daily lives in the presentation of our work, that is so alien to academic work. This mixture carries the sense that whatever space we carve out for ourselves, it is still, and in the foreseeable future, a part of a privileged circle of thinkers and workers whose freedoms and satisfactions proceed as if others were not excluded, in pain, angry, and frustrated.

It is not enough just to announce an invitation to others. The discourse of teaching and learning itself must send that invitation on every occasion. The great man and his sacred text invite people only to worship you-know-who. And, yes, I do think it is the work of the teacher, the teacher of writing, but really any teacher, to teach how to write the unfinished paragraph, the incomplete essay, the challenge to the power-hungry, to write about the breadcrumbs and greasy dishes, the small talk, the sighs, and the sweat in the interviews we are about to undertake.

University of Rochester
Rochester, New York

Mary

Field

Belenky

Composition, Collaboration, and Women's Ways of Knowing: A Conversation with Mary Belenky

EVELYN ASHTON-JONES AND DENE KAY THOMAS

When Mary Field Belenky was a graduate student in psychology in the 1950s, she was told to use male subjects because women "mess up" the data. In *Women's Ways of Knowing: The Development of Self, Voice, and Mind*, a collaborative work written with Blythe McVicker Clinchy, Nancy Rule Goldberger, and Jill Mattuck Tarule, Belenky chose to ignore her graduate school advice and focus on women subjects. The results of that research, published in 1986, provide major insights for her own discipline of psychology, for other disciplines, and for everyone interested in the way gender influences knowing and learning. In an ideal world, the collaborative nature of *Women's Ways* would have dictated that we interview all four authors. Although that wasn't possible, Belenky serves as a superb spokesperson, exploring connections among *Women's Ways*, her own current research, and topics central to composition studies.

In the following interview, Belenky provides a rare opportunity for us to hear about how collaboration worked for the authors of *Women's Ways*. She describes a world of "pajama parties" that gave them the "luxury" of "sustained conversation"; feedback on drafts that was "excited and loving" yet "hard-nosed and critical"; and a "sensuous" intermingling of words and voices as they integrated each others' texts into their own. Belenky also relates how their research subjects contributed to this collaborative effort: their subjects were women from varied backgrounds who became both collaborating writers with the researchers ("It was also *their* words") and audience as the researchers drafted the text. As Belenky suggests, these women became "real participants in the project."

For Belenky, collaboration is clearly more than just a good way to get work done; it is vital to education and crucial to the survival of the world. She criticizes the current cultural emphasis on competitive models for learning, terming it "irrational," and she suggests that educational institutions today do reflect the values of both received knowledge and subjective positions, equally problematic perspectives because they preempt any possibility of real dialogue. In place of the current model, she envisions a dialogic pedagogy of cooperation and collaboration. The pedagogy she elaborates is not "soft" but, rather, allows for both "believing" and "doubting" activities toward cooperative ends. And it is this kind of pedagogy, she maintains, that alleviates the discomfort women often feel with the values of educational institutions.

While Belenky acknowledges that gender politics may influence collaborative interaction, she feels that this problem can be resolved by putting the issue on the classroom agenda. Foregrounding the politics of gender in classroom interaction, she believes, will prove advantageous for all students: women "will get more of a voice" and men "will get to be better listeners." She also acknowledges a "danger" that research into gender differences can reinforce traditional gender stereotypes and reproduce gender ideology, but she feels the more serious danger is in disregarding women's ways of coming to know, in *"not* trying to give voice to this whole range of human experience that has not been articulated and is not an integral part of the culture." Nor does Belenky consider *Women's Ways* "essentialist" in any way: "What we are really doing," she says, "is describing characteristics that women and men have developed in the context of a sexist and aggressive society."

Throughout the interview, Belenky attempts to show how the knowledge that she and her coauthors have constructed is illuminating for composition studies. She discusses several of the epistemological perspectives outlined in *Women's Ways*: silence, received knowledge, subjective knowledge, procedural knowledge, and constructed knowledge. *Silence* is experiencing the self as voiceless and without the capacity to receive or generate knowledge; *received knowing* is seeing knowledge as absolute and always in the possession of "authorities"; *subjective knowing* is distrusting authority and understanding knowledge as personal and originating within one's self; *procedural knowing* is perceiving knowledge as objective and rationally derived, though subject to multiple perspectives; and *constructed knowing* is understanding knowledge as "constructed," the knower acknowledging and taking responsibility for shaping knowledge. She suggests that because student reactions to education will be affected by their epistemological positions, compositionists should enrich their teaching strategies with research done by social psychologists. Belenky also firmly believes that while *Women's Ways* has been both praised and criticized for its exclusive focus on women, its insights are not limited to women: "We are not claiming that these might not also be men's ways of thinking." Women's ways, she asserts, are ultimately "human" ways.

To Belenky, writing begins in the private world of the expressive and moves from there into a more public conversation. Her philosophy is constantly presented through the personal experience of connecting with the known and moving on from there. Yet, she also sees her work as "steeped" in social constructionism, weaving together the personal and the social. Readers will not find disembodied theory, research, or practice in Belenky.

Instead, they will find connections that leave no place for adversarial methods where someone must lose. In this spirit, Belenky provides us with an enheartening view of our own discipline as she situates composition studies both "at the crosspoints" and "on the cutting edge."

Q. Do you think of yourself as a writer?
A. I do, and I'm very puzzled by it because I find writing so hard, so arduous, so painful. If you're engaged as I am in research that's embedded in interpretive-descriptive processes, your major research tool is trying to articulate clearly the understandings that you're coming to—and writing is integral to this process. Interpretive-descriptive research is very different from traditional research in the social sciences, which relies on statistical tools to communicate findings. In the research that my colleagues and I do, we're following in the steps of such social scientists as Piaget, Perry, Kohlberg, and Gilligan. They all are writing a story that grows out of conversation, and they savor the words of the people they've been interviewing, putting the words in a story line. The goal of their work is to understand and describe people's thinking, to try to understand the structures of mind, so the only tool they have is language: language for eliciting people's thoughts, language for trying to understand the deep organizing principles of thought, and, finally, language for articulating these things. So narrative has become a particularly important tool for social scientists who are trying to understand thinking. You know, Lawrence Kohlberg once told me that when he was conducting moral judgment studies at Yale in the late 1950s, several people asked him why he spent his time looking at verbal behavior. It has taken psychology a long time to notice that humans are meaning-making animals.

Q. *Women's Ways of Knowing* has received widespread and enthusiastic attention. How do you feel about its reception?
A. The attention surprised us. We had hoped somebody would read it, but we didn't anticipate that it would be widely read across disciplines, which I find so interesting. It's terrific. When you publish something and people read it with care, you can pick up with strangers just like we are in the middle of a long, exquisite conversation. It's interesting to see how it gets played out.

Q. One recent review criticized *Women's Ways* for excluding men from the research sample. What is your response to this criticism?
A. In the book, we say that we felt that the male template was so powerfully etched on our minds that it seemed very important to stand back from it and to find, to hear, the woman's voice. This is very hard work, and we wanted to do whatever we could to make it more pure, to hear it. Although we studied women and make these claims for women, we are not claiming

that these might not also be men's ways of thinking. Actually, I think most of what we say in the book applies to human ways of knowing, but it's important that someone listens to women and tries to see them in their own terms.

Q. Would you describe how you and your colleagues went about conducting research collaboratively and, more specifically, how you went about writing the book collaboratively?

A. Because the writing was part of a much larger project, I want to convey a bit of the project's history. For a variety of reasons, the four of us thought we might like to do research together. Although some of us had worked with each other before, on the whole we hadn't known each other very well. But we had all been developmental psychologists interested in intellectual and ethical development, interested in thinking more carefully about women. And so we had the first of what we came to call our "pajama-party" meetings at a motel in New Hampshire that was a midway point from where we all were living. In our conversations there, we kept going around and around, trying to articulate what our driving questions were and, also, what we perceived as the driving questions at the edge of our discipline. After this period of eating, swimming, and talking, we went home, wrote a proposal, and got funding from FIPSE. What we created at this first pajama party was an umbrella that framed most of our important questions, even though they were still vague.

Because we all lived in different places, the grant gave us financial support to hold one of these pajama-party meetings about every five weeks for three years. Very regularly, then, every five or six weeks, we were able to sit down together and work around the clock for three or four days at a time. I can't tell you how important it is to have this kind of time for working, sleeping on your thoughts, and returning to the conversation—without distractions from children and telephones. We all had raised families as well as having careers, and the luxury of that kind of sustained conversation was just terrific. The pajama party was very important to the process.

During the three-year period that FIPSE funded us, we developed a very broad conversation with women from all walks of life. The grant allowed us to visit a variety of institutions and talk with women about their life experiences—their histories, especially their intellectual development, and how the institutions they were in were supporting them. FIPSE had primarily charged us with helping the faculty at these institutions to understand their students and their students' development, and with encouraging the faculty to broaden their thinking about pedagogy—this was not an agency funding basic research. In the process of carrying out FIPSE's goals, however, we collected these marvelous interviews and had them transcribed. We were very much interested in the research questions, and working with the faculty on this development project brought a whole other group of people into the conversation. Our work was enriched because it was cast as an *action* project rather than just research.

Q. Are you positing a much larger group of collaborators than the four of you who coauthored *Women's Ways*?

A. Absolutely. The women we interviewed were themselves drawn in. A word that seems better than *collaboration* is *dialogue* because it suggests that our so-called research subjects were real participants in the project. In a very real sense they were also, much of the time when we were writing, the audience. Let me tell you about Lillian Rubin's *Worlds of Pain*, a study of lower middle-class marriages—a study that is, like ours, based on interviews. Rubin had a pact with the people that she interviewed: they would review and approve any writing she did before it went to publication. She notes that none of those people had much criticism of her writing, so she didn't change or reedit the work in light of it; but I believe, because she had this pact to give them the work before publishing it, that she wrote *to them* in a way—and it's a beautiful book. Rubin's book was a model for us, even though our sample was too large to promise everybody we would get their permission. But as our book was written, we very much had in mind that it would be read by the people we had interviewed.

Q. So the audience you had in mind as you were writing was a friendly audience, women who could benefit from the information as you organized it?

A. Absolutely. But the information wasn't just what *we* were thinking or organizing; it was also *their* words because we worked from transcripts of the interviews. In fact, when the book first came out many women said that we had given words to things they'd always thought. It seemed funny at first, a backhanded kind of compliment. Here we'd done this extraordinary thing. But giving words to these ideas was exactly what we tried to do, and that's a lot to do. Moreover, I think we ought to teach ourselves and our students that we can have real choices about audience. We all need to understand how writing the same material for different audiences changes the voice. That is very empowering knowledge to have.

Q. How did you coordinate the actual writing of *Women's Ways*?

A. We had a month-long pajama party at a cottage on the shore, a big rambling mansion on the ocean. We spent the month trying to frame the book and talking through the process of writing it; by the end of the month, we had a reasonably firm view of its shape, so we sketched out a table of contents. Then when we looked at the plan, it made sense that one person or another would write certain chapters. Certainly, some decisions were arbitrary, but for the most part we saw a clear and rational division of labor that made deep sense. We also made a decision which in retrospect I think was very smart: that we would not put our names on different pieces. I don't know why we made that decision, and I'm still not sure why that was so smart. But I think it was, and it's probably one of the reasons the book ultimately developed the one-voice quality that it has.

Q. What means did you use for sending drafts to each other?

A. We all got computerized early on, but we made a decision to send hard copy—and I think that's very important. I wouldn't want to send around disks and have people start changing the text. So we sent around drafts and we wrote all over them. On the whole, we were amazingly excited and loving of what went around and amazingly hard-nosed and critical. We said, "Does that really make sense?" and "Say more," and "Why would you say that?" and "Where's your evidence?" For the most part even the early drafts were interesting. It was exciting to get the chapters, and we worked very hard criticizing them.

Q. So you deliberately set a limit on the collaboration, allowing for a writer's autonomy with hard copy representing personal ownership?

A. That's right. We would each get the hard copy back, three copies with lots of writing all over the margins, and we would choose whether to follow the suggestions. If you send your disk around and people start changing it, your words and theirs get merged too fast; you need some sort of a balance. Writing collaboratively gets very confusing because, when you're really working together, when the dialogue really starts, ideas grow and change and no one has real ownership. Yet you have to keep, or you ought to keep, your own voice. Having comments on paper is wonderful because you keep all of the different voices separate for a while. Because of the way my colleagues each wrote in the margin, I always knew their handwriting, and so as I worked on redrafting I had their different voices to work with.

Q. When your voices ultimately merged, how much of a sense of individuality did you feel?

A. It wasn't always clear. At times someone would write something so gorgeous that you would think it needed to be in your own chapter and you'd fight for it. Sometimes I found myself winning one of those fights and integrating into my own text a beautiful perception from someone else's text, their words and my words. This process is really very sensuous. It's so loving to have that mingling going on—knowing that these are stolen words in a way, words coaxed out of someone, but liking the closeness of having her words and my words all mingling right in there. Sometimes this feeling happened, too, as we worked with the interviews that we had collected from the women. I'm sure others have experienced this—for example, when they're putting a beloved mentor's words in a document that they're working on. In my teaching, I try to get students to cite a text and put that scholar's words and name next to their own words and name, and I try to help them understand that this is a way of making it clear that the two of them are talking together now.

Q. Your collaboration was clearly rewarding. Would you say the collaborative effort was crucial to the writing of *Women's Ways*?

A. The book could not have been written by any single one of us, without this broader conversation. It has a scope that reflects a wide range of experiences in a wide range of institutions, and a single person couldn't have created that. I don't think a single person can get the kind of clarity that comes through working together to pull away the chaff and let the bold ideas come forth.

Q. People discussing coauthored works such as *Women's Ways* don't seem to have a conventional way to refer to collective authors. For example, they often refer to *you* as the author of this study, thus unwittingly diminishing the contributions of your colleagues. Do you have any solutions to this dilemma?

A. This is a serious problem. The people who've had the most interesting things to say about our work are also people who have figured out gracious ways of acknowledging its collaborative nature. Sometimes they've solved the problem in very conventional ways, like writing out all the names each time. Now, that sounds awkward, but when you're reading it's just a clump of text that registers the same way a single name does. Or they find another way of referring to us, saying, "the authors of *Women's Ways*" or "the collaborative" or "the research group." They never single out one person. We have to learn, and we have to find forms for naming collective authors or collaboration is not going to become routine. I suspect that we will find forms as constructive knowledge becomes more widely disseminated in the culture, more widely valued, as more and more we see that this is how our children have to be educated to become constructors of knowledge, as we learn to value the collaborative process. Sooner or later we're going to find forms to support and cultivate collaboration, and then we'll cut across all disciplines.

Q. How should collaborative research and writing be evaluated by university tenure and promotion committees?

A. In the academy, collaborative work is demoted, but it should count *double* in faculty evaluations. If a work is embedded in a collaborative process, the writers goad each other into endless revisions. For example, in our study there's hardly a page that wasn't rewritten fifteen or twenty times. No one working alone can do that kind of intensive revision, nor can they benefit from the extensive redrafting that takes place in conversation. The kind of reflection and revising enabled by collaboration brings a quality of depth and scope to a work. Collaborating may only produce two-hundred or three-hundred pages of text, but perhaps they're more enduring than the two- or three-hundred pages of a single voice. Of course, most work that's published under a single author is collaborative as well. Piaget's *The Moral Judgement of the Child*, a work that laid much of the foundation for our own effort, was based on his wife's study of the marble games, his wife's dissertation. If you get out a magnifying glass, you can see the credit in small print. There are similar stories for a number of the other central texts in our discipline.

Q. Sometimes it's difficult for students to work collaboratively in classrooms. What roles might gender and the educational environment play in this difficulty?

A. This is at the heart of a lot of gender differences. Some people are so imbued with the competitive spirit that it's hard for them to work collaboratively, and some people are so imbued with the collaborative mode that working competitively feels dangerous and painful. A classic study that helped usher gender work into psychology was Matina Horner's work on fear of success, an interesting study looking at men's and women's responses to stories she gave them about personal achievements. Two of the vignettes Horner used were about Jane and John, who learn, in their respective story, that they're at the top of their medical school class. Typically, women go on to finish the story about Jane by having her suddenly contract a terrible disease like leprosy and dying; it's a great calamity with death and destruction following in the wake of her success. But John, of course, lives happily ever after—the skies open up and it never rains. Subsequent research has shown that fear of success tends to be a problem for women only if they perceive the success as coming at the expense of somebody else. In a win-win situation, where doing outstanding work is embedded in a collaborative relationship, women don't seem to have problems with the idea of success at all.

And yet we irrationally design our educational institutions to make them more competitive. We pit students one against another; we teach competition; we create it; we take in students selected as gifted and we grade them on a normal curve. We assume, we predetermine, that some of them are going to flunk. Why do we do that? We wouldn't have to spend any more energy teaching collaborative processes and creating forms to support them than we do creating and teaching competitive processes. On the whole women work better in collaborative situations, and women can teach us how to do it, how to teach it. When we do make the educational environment more collaborative, I think we'll *all* be happier in schools—men as well as women.

Q. Why do you think women seem to be more comfortable in cooperative settings?

A. You go back to Chodorow's powerful argument, where she elucidates the fact that early childcaring is done almost universally by women. The growing child's first search for identity is encased in that primary relationship and differs because of gender. The little boy, as he starts to ask, "Who am I?" has to say, "Me, I'm different from her," and he separates himself out from his mother. The little girl says, "We're just the same," and she has a kind of continuity and striving to be with/like/the same. So Chodorow argues that women's early embeddedness in relationships comes from women being cared for by women. Another important source for making sense of this is the research on power relationships, and the findings are very consistent: powerless people do the kinds of things that women tend to do. But the explanation I'm most drawn to is that women are involved in raising the next generation. To be noncompetitive—to be connected, to care, to engage in dialogue, to draw out the other person—is a good way to be if you want to sponsor the development of others. This way of being, which Sara Ruddick calls "maternal thinking," grows out of being engaged in maternal practice, and it provides a collaborative stance toward the world.

Q. Several researchers in sociolinguistics have suggested that conversation is inscribed by and reinforces an ideology of gender. For example, Pamela Fishman argues that women do the "maintenance" work of conversation while men control topic and direction, and Don Zimmerman and Candace West suggest that men feel free to interrupt women extensively. Might not this kind of gender politics influence the dialogue of collaborative learning groups? If so, how might women overcome these interactional problems?

A. I think teachers should put the issue on the classroom agenda: comment on the power of interaction patterns, assign a student in each group to watch gender dynamics—to keep track of it and give everyone feedback—and really talk about how disastrous it is to live in a culture that teaches men to speak and women to listen. Both qualities should be joined in each person. So for each class session, one person is in charge of keeping track of gender dynamics, using research tools, making a report. And, in the end, I predict that women will get more of a voice and the men will get to be better listeners.

Q. Do you see the need for a balance between collaboration and competition, or do you see collaboration as overwhelmingly the preferred model?

A. I would say that collaboration is overwhelmingly the preferred model. Alfie Kohn has written a book called *No Contest: The Case against Competition*, which shows why competition is such a problem. I worry, literally, about the ability of the world to survive a competitive stance where it's about winners against losers and winners taking all. We have to figure out a way to live with everybody participating and everybody's needs being met. Kohn has examined one side of the coin carefully and accessibly, but somebody needs to do the comparable book that shows why collaboration is so productive of real creativity. In my mind the world should not—cannot—be construed as a zero-sum game. That's no way to live.

Q. You distinguish between two types of collaboration, the believing game and the doubting game, citing Peter Elbow's advice to writers to play the believing game by focusing on the creative side, and then to play the doubting game by applying the critical side. Would you elaborate on this?

A. Both games are of enormous importance for anybody who's going to do serious intellectual work. Moving between the believing and the doubting game means moving between one stance, where you actively try to immerse yourself in a body of work and feel your way around the perimeters and get inside of it and understand it, and another stance, where you stand at a distance subjecting the body of work to a range of critical analyses. Both are powerful tools.

Q. How do the believing and doubting games relate to cooperative and competitive approaches?

A. They relate to Horner's research on fear of success. I have been doing some informal research, a series of workshops using guided fantasy, in which I invite people to imagine environments where the believing game is played and where the doubting game is played. We do the doubting game twice. In one environment, people are in a zero-sum world where there are winners and losers; it's a nightmare and women hate it. In the other environment, people are in a win-win situation, where they play the doubting game not to win or lose but to clarify arguments, to develop ideas, and to do better thinking. Women have no problem with the doubting game in such a collaborative setting. You can be a marvelous doubter, and doubting can be life-enhancing if it takes place in the service of the clearest possible understanding of truth rather than in one-upping another. We associate competitiveness—winning—with the doubting game, but competitiveness destroys the doubting game; competitiveness makes it a poor game for getting at the truth. Winning an argument and achieving a more comprehensive view of what's true are not the same.

Q. The research into women's cognitive, intellectual, and ethical development that Gilligan and your collective are doing is exciting. But doesn't it have the potential to reinforce gender stereotypes and essentialist definitions of femininity? Can't research into gender differences ultimately reinforce cultural myths about gender, including gender hierarchy?

A. Of course, that's a real danger, and I don't know what to do about it. There's also a real danger in *not* trying to give voice to this whole range of human experience that has not been articulated and is not an integral part of the culture—you give away the whole ball game. Men continue to set the standard and perpetuate a world where individualism and competition take precedence over relationships and connections. They create a world where competition is practically the only game in town, and collaboration and cooperation are not cultivated. That seems more dangerous, and I don't know how to get around it. Of course, many people consider the four of us "essentialists"—that is, they classify us with those who see sex differences as immutably rooted in biology. What we are really doing, though, is describing characteristics that women and men have developed in the context of a sexist and aggressive society, a society in which the public and private spheres of living have been drastically segregated.

Q. Recently, an article in a popular magazine cited Gilligan's study to argue that since women are by nature nurturers and men are *not*, then women who want meaningful relationships with men will have to fulfill the nurturing role—men obviously aren't suited for it. What do you think of such an application of Gilligan's ideas?

A. This is a poor reading of Gilligan. Nowhere does she say that nature alone accounts for these differences. The most empowering aspect of Gilligan's work for both men and women is that she examines conventional morality and notes that the conventional woman cares only for others. The self is not an object of the conventional woman's own care because she doesn't see herself as a person equally worthy of consideration. Gilligan's work has been important to so many women because it has helped them understand that they can be caring and nurturing to others but full of self—that they don't have to be selfless. To be true moral agents, women have to take themselves into consideration; they *don't* have to choose between care for the self and care for the other. It's not an either/or situation. That has been a marvelous and important insight, and it accounts for much of why Gilligan has such a widespread audience. Those who argue that women must do the supporting to maintain a relationship haven't even noticed that a woman, to interact meaningfully with a man, has a self she must care for.

Part of the problem is that Gilligan mounted a very complex argument; some people can see part of it and some people can see other parts. Mostly, we have a rigid, dualistic way of structuring the world that makes it hard for people to understand that a voice can be associated with gender without being encased in gender. If you are like Perry or Kohlberg and you study men, it's just so easy to say, "These are *the* forms of intellectual development" or "These are *the* stages of moral development for people." Nobody ever notices. But if you study women, you have to call it "women's ways"; if you called it "people's ways," you would meet with criticism about generalizing beyond your data. But calling it "women's ways" is problematic, too, because then men will think, "Well, if women do it and I'm not a woman, then I can't be like that." It's very confusing because we're gendered, but we're also just human beings.

Q. In *Women's Ways*, you discuss the politics of talk in family life and family "rules" for communicating that govern interactional activities within the family. What implications might these family rules have for women faced with communicating in the academic environment?

A. If you apply our scheme to forms of communication that occur in educational institutions, you can begin to see patterns that uphold each of the ways of knowing. For instance, the framework of the received knower, who assumes that knowledge gets passed down from one person to another, is reflected still in the architecture of our educational institutions, with our lecture platforms and chairs all lined up. I recently did interviews with elderly Vermonters near the Canadian border, inquiring about their experience of "voice" as they were growing up. They told me that in the little one-room schoolhouses they had gone to at the beginning of this century they never remembered ever writing their own words. They were always copying other people's words. Taking in and giving out other people's words were the primary educational tasks even in writing assignments, so the books containing their writings were called "copy books," not composition books. They showed us their copy books and it was true. There were no original words.

Q. Do you feel that it's productive for teachers to use models such as yours and William Perry's to help them understand students' ways of thinking?

A. Absolutely. These theories can help teachers see some of a student's deep thinking and to understand where a student is coming from. A teacher always wants to start from where students are and then move along *with* them. I use these theories all the time, although I often find that I'm wrong, that I've misdiagnosed a student. But I don't think this matters. If you're wrong and you operate for a while on a perspective that turns out to be inaccurate, the student corrects you. This process is enabled by Rogerian feedback: "So what I hear you saying is. . . ." And, correcting you, the student says, "No, that's not what I'm thinking." And you hear it and you adjust. The struggle to understand students is very life-enhancing, even if you don't always get it right.

Q. How can a teacher respond to a student operating from a received knowledge perspective—a student, for example, who comes into a composition class where the model is one of creative or critical thinking?

A. A teacher can talk about looking inside for insights and words, and when somebody does look inside and develops a new insight, the teacher can say, "Oh, that's neat. What an interesting idea. You've helped me understand that." The student experiences creating an idea that the teacher writes down, learns from, and passes on to somebody else. This kind of response can really break a hole in the received knower's world view. Received knowers often describe this kind of response as a turning point out of received knowledge for them; they discover that they, too, can be an authority who has ideas worthy of teaching to others.

Q. We often think of shifts from one epistemological position to another as taking more time than you're suggesting here. Can the movement out of the received knowledge position occur just that quickly?

A. Somebody who has such an "Aha!" experience is probably somebody for whom that world view is already beginning to fall apart, whereas a person imbued with looking upwards for the goodies might not even be able to hear, "That's an interesting idea." But one of the wonderful things about writing is that people's ideas are put forth in a concrete form, so you can look at it and say, "Oh, there it is." People looking at a portfolio of their writings can reflect on their own constructions, trace how their thinking grows and evolves and changes, and see that the ideas grow out of struggle and thought—they don't just come out of the sky. You can teach students how to trace what's going on in their own minds, through their own writing, in their own papers.

Q. What theoretical and pedagogical issues are pertinent at the subjective and procedural levels of knowing?

A. I see a great shift in the culture, a broad cultural trend of moving from a received position to a subjective position, with the more privileged segments of the population being carefully tutored to be procedural and constructed knowers. Cognition is consistently governed by subjectivism in the culture because there's so little dialogue in our educational institutions. People are easily locked into their own world view because they're not being engaged in hard-nosed conversations in which they're asked to compare their view of things with external realities. Without such conversations, we don't come to understand that words can communicate truths and that ideas can be developed and shaped. The subjectivist world view is narcissistic and private, one that thrives only in a culture like ours where people work too much in isolation.

Dialogue can certainly be realized at the procedural level. In a way, that's what procedures are, encouraging the knower to make, record, and communicate observations. Procedural thinking requires a much more active stance and more participation in dialogue than the previous stages do. Procedures cannot be taught without lots of small seminars and lots of laboratory experiences where students are doing whatever it is that's done in that particular discipline. Teachers have to have students engaged in the craft because students don't easily develop procedures by passively listening to lectures.

Q. You seem more hesitant than Perry does about describing epistemological perspectives as a developmental or sequential scheme of growth. Yet from what you've just described, you seem to view them as a model of growth.

A. It's complicated. My coauthors and I don't always agree on the "stage" nature of the epistemological perspectives. Perry's research, based on interviews of the same Harvard college students every spring, year after year, was a study designed for making developmental statements. The developmentalist usually selects a small homogeneous population, where the least desirable approach would be to interview and collect data from, say, the first graders and the third graders and the eighth graders and the twelfth graders and then make statements about their development. To make developmental statements, the most desirable tack is like Perry's, where a researcher interviews the same students every year over a period of several years: a longitudinal design. Perry had good data for making powerful developmental statements. In fact, my coauthor Blythe Clinchy and her colleague Claire Zimmerman felt that Perry's claims were not strong enough. The data that Blythe and Claire collected at Wellesley, in a study following the epistemological development of students there, was so orderly that they were convinced Perry could have spoken in an even more powerful voice about the stage nature of his scheme. And even Perry doesn't call them *stages*; he calls them *positions*, and he conceptualizes "backsliding" as a normal part of development. Many classic stage theorists say, "It's onward and upward"; any incidence of regression forces them to throw out the whole thing. And, of course, they tend to make very bold statements about universality, which Perry doesn't do.

Conversely, our study is poorly designed for making such developmental statements. We had a wide range of people, ages, social classes, and institutions. In some ways this was terrific because we had such a breadth of voices, but we can't make developmental claims from our data. Further, I think all four of us feel a great discomfort with the developmentalists' tendency to assume that a particular sequence is universal. To us, that seems audacious, even immoral, and we want to distance ourselves from such a stance. Some of my colleagues found it hard even to argue that one of these positions is inherently better than another. Now, that boggles my mind, because each position seems so much more adequate and adaptive than the previous positions, at least in the context of this culture.

Q. So even though your study's design makes you hesitate to assert a developmental model, you feel that the *Women's Ways* model is developmental in some sense?

A. Right. But I'm not sure if, even in this society, people move from received to subjective to procedural positions in that order. I can imagine—and I have some evidence—that it might be possible for a person to move from a received to a procedural position without spending very much time in a subjective position. My students at Vermont have been collecting interviews of undergraduates, and it seems like a number of the undergraduates they've interviewed are doing this in two very different ways. In the university context, most of the shift from received knowledge directly into procedural knowledge is through the route of separate knowing and is still quite authority oriented. But we also see people in a dialogue-rich environment moving from received into connected procedures without spending very much time in the subjectivists' world view.

Q. So it might be a developmental model but not necessarily a sequential one?

A. Possibly. In the study that I'm currently working on, with very isolated women in a poor part of Vermont, we have longitudinal data on 120 women that's just now going into the computer. These interviews, all scored blind, were conducted at three different times, about nine months apart. So our data is spread over about a two-year period of time, and it shows *on the whole* that the movement is through the sequence as we portrayed it and is extremely orderly.

Q. Several feminist compositionists are exploring the implications of your research for theory and pedagogy in composition studies. For example, in

"Women's Ways of Writing," Marilyn Cooper explores the implications of your work for women, describing the benefits of communal journals in a center for battered women; and in "Composing as a Woman," Elizabeth Flynn discusses gender in relation to research in the field and classroom writing assignments. What are your thoughts on the kinds of writing that might be beneficial for students, especially women?

A. I love the idea of a collaborative journal, especially the computerized communal journal that Cooper discusses, and I'm anxious to learn more about it. I think journal writing and what Elbow calls freewriting are excellent because a lot of thinking starts there. But I'm also worried. There's a danger in a narrow focus on private journal writing and private freewriting that doesn't broaden into a more extended and hard-nosed kind of dialogue and thus keeps a person lodged in the subjectivist mode. While personal journal writing creates an open process that lets a person be free and expressive, collaborative journal writing lessens this danger because the exchange can keep on going until, like with the writing of our book, the collaborating writers get very, very hard-nosed with each other.

Q. Are you suggesting that encouraging private, expressive writing can do women a disservice? Are you encouraging more of a balance among different kinds of writing?

A. One problem is the way we define "male" and "female" modes of writing. We look at the male mode as being real, true, hard, and the female mode as being soft, fuzzy, loving. But that's not true. What are all those words? What is often called the "female mode" can be so much more complex because it's always trying to hold everybody's perspective. It allows for an extended dialogue and, thus, for coming to clearer, sharper understandings of the essence of things. Yes, we need to have a balance, and the image of the extended dialogue is a productive way of thinking about it. In collaborative writing projects, whatever they are, writers experience the dialogic work of going through draft after draft, many more drafts than a writer working in isolation can create.

Q. In "Embracing Contraries," Elbow emphasizes two necessary processes for the classroom teacher. On the one hand, the teacher must be a supporter and nurturer of students (much like your conception of the teacher as midwife); on the other hand, the teacher must function as gatekeeper, upholder of standards, evaluator. How can a teacher balance the duty to nurture and support students and the duty to uphold academic standards?

A. I'm going to answer by going back to that original pajama party, where my colleagues and I kept moving between trying to think about who we were as individuals and what the driving questions at the edge of the field were. In a similar way teachers have to start with who students are—including their perspectives on the world—and, from that start, help students articulate what their driving questions are. If they are to find a home in the world, it's important that students eventually merge their questions with the ongoing questions in their disciplines, and students need help in making useful connections between these two kinds of questions. To be engaged in upholding the standards of the field or the institution without ever noticing who students are and what their driving questions are—which I think is very common practice—is an unfortunate imbalance for men as well as for women and for the state of the society.

Q. There's an epigraph in *Women's Ways* from Nel Noddings' *Caring*: "It is time for the voice of the mother to be heard in education." But the role of the nurturing mother whose approval is unconditional may be problematic for women teachers at grading time. What is your view of grading?

A. The current grading system is fraught with problems because the traditional system places all the responsibility for evaluation in the hands of faculty. If you want to help people develop powers of evaluation and self-reflection, it's unwise to give this responsibility solely to faculty. Grading should be part of a shared process of dialogue and collaborative evaluation. If people are going to develop thoughtful, internal standards, they need to participate in these processes in schools as well as in the family. The maternal approach involves the hard work of trying to understand students—who they are, where they've come from, and where they're going.

Q. But doesn't the mother model place women teachers in a position that reinforces what society socializes us to believe about women—that authority and the feminine are incompatible? Susan Stanford Friedman, for example, expresses such reservations about the mother model of teaching.

A. I'm reminded of a collaborative study by Richardson, Cook, and Macke from Ohio State University, "Issues in Sex, Gender and Society: A Feminist Perspective." This study looked at teaching styles and identified two modes: a collaborative, maternal mode, involved in the discourse of the rhetoric of inquiry; and a more authoritarian mode, involved in the discourse of the rhetoric of authority. Students invariably liked the inquiry mode more, felt more benefitted by it, and made more progress with it than they did with teachers more involved in the authoritarian mode. Whether the teachers were men or women, students personally liked and felt more benefitted by the inquiry mode—but they saw those professors as being less competent. Furthermore, in the institutions these researchers studied, they found fewer and fewer professors who worked in the inquiry mode as they moved up the academic ranks. But I'll bet if you look at institutions deeply imbued with the constructivist view, you might find a very different pattern—that senior professors are the ones most involved in a constructivist, collaborative, inquiry mode.

Q. Do you think that a student's epistemological orientation influences the way she or he evaluates those teachers?

A. Absolutely. You have two things going: first, the students and their frameworks and, second, the institution and its overriding philosophy. These can differ. An institution tries to bring students up to the ways of knowing it understands and values. And you have schools that primarily see themselves as teaching received knowers, as bringing people into their way of knowing. You have other schools, some of them educational experiments of the 1960s and 1970s, that conceptualize a subjectivist view of learning. And then you have some institutions deeply informed by a constructivist paradigm.

Q. In what ways is your work informed by social constructionism?

A. It is steeped in the very deepest roots of constructivism. For all four of us and our work in social psychology, the starting point is somehow the work of Piaget. I'm not sure you would necessarily think of Piaget as a social constructivist, but he certainly is a constructivist. In his very early work on moral judgment, he says the development of morality requires only the company of one's peers. Piaget pitted himself against the received view, often looking at the forms of the child's knowledge that were idiosyncratic to the child. The child would tell him things about how the world was that would never have been passed down by an adult, that were so different from the way adults see the world. His whole emphasis was on the original thought of the child and not on shared thought. That helped many of us break out of the received view. Vygotsky, on the other hand, had a deeper understanding of the social nature of language and thought, exploring the role of language and community in the development of thought and how language operates both internally and externally.

The constructivists' stance is important on many different fronts, whether it's to articulate, as Mary and Kenneth Gergen do, the philosophical basis of the social constructivist approach to the world or whether it's to do empirical research to show which kinds of writing best sponsor the development of mind. There's a lot of work to be done, and a lot of people in your field, like Bruffee and Elbow, are doing it right now.

Q. Composition is a field that has shifted toward a constructivist paradigm in the past few years, and this shift has raised a number of political and epistemological questions. Perhaps not coincidentally, it also is a field where the percentage of women on faculties has been increasing dramatically. How do you view these changes of politics, epistemology, and gender?

A. Women in composition may be in just the right place. With the shift from received to much more complex epistemologies, there has been a great shift in the balance of attention from reading to writing. We're now much more interested in the creations that students can construct than in the knowledge that they can absorb. Donald Graves looks at the fact that in the past no federal monies were supporting research on writing; all of the monies were going into research on reading—taking in words—decoding.

But with this epistemological shift, there is also an enormous shift towards emphasizing writing, the kind of writing involved in the construction of knowledge. More than most disciplines, composition—the way it is now being taught—is a discipline involved in a pedagogy that's much more closely aligned with the actual processes involved in the development of mind. The way you are now teaching writing more closely approximates the processes that good writers actually use. In a world that is going to need everybody functioning as active thinkers, not just the privileged few, writing as a way to thinking should be taught to everyone.

Q. Composition has reached out to different fields in the last few years, to the extent that we sometimes question whether the discipline has a core, and we often debate what that core might be. Would you comment on this?

A. You're on the cutting edge. Look at history. The Renaissance occurred at the crosspoints of travelers, of communication. It is certainly not high status to be at the margins or the crosspoints in the academic world which is pushing toward specialization. But anybody who is involved in working across disciplines is much more likely to have a lively mind and a lively life. You may not get as many brownie points, but in the long run you probably make a better contribution.

Politicizing the Composing Process and Women's Ways of Interacting

ELIZABETH A. FLYNN

As I was reading Evelyn Ashton-Jones and Dene Kay Thomas' interview with Mary Belenky, I couldn't help but compare it with Gary Olson's interview with Richard Rorty published in volume 9 of *JAC*. That interview was a lesson in miscommunication. Rorty clearly knew very little about the field of composition studies, made no attempt to find out anything about it before the interview, and insulted us all by reducing the enterprise to tinkering with grammar and mechanics. The gap between Olson and Rorty was unbridgeable, hence Olson's astonishment that Rorty did not consider himself to be a social constructionist, that Rorty thought writing across the curriculum was a terrible idea, and that he was sympathetic to E.D. Hirsch's views on literacy.

In contrast, Belenky and her interviewers collaborated in the production of a wonderfully illuminating discussion of *Women's Ways of Knowing*. The interview itself illustrates the point that women are often connected knowers capable of working cooperatively toward a common goal. Clearly, Belenky had prepared carefully for the interview and was knowledgeable about and appreciative of developments within the field of composition studies. In turn, Ashton-Jones and Thomas asked exactly the right questions, allowing Belenky to provide fascinating information about the collaborative creation of the book and to address important questions such as, Why were men excluded from the research sample? Does the book reinforce essentialist definitions of femininity? Is the model of intellectual growth described in the book developmental or sequential? What is Belenky's view of grading? In what ways is Belenky's work informed by social constructionism? The interview will certainly become an important document within feminist studies as it extends *Women's Ways of Knowing* in very useful ways.

Two thoughts occurred to me as I was reading the interview. The first was that *Women's Ways of Knowing* politicizes the process of intellectual development and can be useful in attempts to politicize the composing process. The second was that Belenky's discussion of the collaborative process that gave rise to *Women's Ways of Knowing* is a wonderful illustration of how women can cooperate to achieve a goal. There is a dark side to women's interactions, though, that also needs to be explored. I'll discuss each of these topics in turn.

Politicizing the Composing Process

The composing process is too often discussed by compositionists as an apolitical process. Cognitivists usually speak of it as if writing were solely an activity involving inner mental processes; social constructionists, in exploring the social dimensions of writing, do not always emphasize its political dimensions and sometimes ignore process entirely. As a way of demonstrating the usefulness of *Women's Ways of Knowing* to an exploration of the composing process, I'll attempt here a feminist rereading of James Britton's conception of expressive writing and Linda Flower's conception of writer-based writing.

Expressive writing and writer-based prose are concepts that are by now quite familiar to compositionists. Both Britton and his coauthors and Flower derive the concepts from the work of cognitive and social psychologists such as Piaget and Vygotsky and see writing as sharing many of the same features as inner and egocentric speech: the absence of logical and causal relations, ellipticality, language that has personal rather than public currency. Both expressive and writer-based writing are described as enabling writers in the initial stages of the writing process because they free them of the constraints of audience-centered writing. Britton gives informal or exploratory writing a much more central role than does Flower. For him, it is the matrix out of which all other forms of writing, including creative writing, emerge. Flower makes clear that writer-based prose is not necessarily a stage through which a writer must develop (22), and her discussion of the concept has a slight negative cast to it in a way that Britton's does not. Reader-based prose is clearly preferable because it allows for communication with an audience. Writer-based prose, if it becomes a stage in the process at all, is valuable because it leads to reader-based prose.

The authors of *Women's Ways of Knowing* are not, of course, dealing with stages in the composing process in their discussion of the "ways of knowing" that they identify: silence, received knowledge, subjective knowledge, procedural knowledge, and constructed knowledge. Nor do they claim that the categories are developmental stages. Belenky explains in the interview that the study did not have a longitudinal component and was not designed to identify developmental stages. She nevertheless feels that the model of female intellectual growth described in the book is developmental, though not necessarily sequential. Belenky might say, then, that intellectual immaturity is characterized by silence and listening to the voices of others, whereas intellectual maturity is characterized by active construction of knowledge, an integration of the voices of the self with the voices of others. I would suggest that the stages identified in *Women's Ways of Knowing* may well approximate the processes many learners, regardless of level of intellectual development, undergo when they learn something new. The stages may be seen, then, as in some ways parallel to the stages of the composing process.

Women's Ways of Knowing, though, politicizes the process. Compositionists do not generally recognize that the starting point for the language learning of some may very well be silence rather than inner speech. Opportunities for conversation, clearly an important determinant of intellectual growth, vary according to the political situation of the learner. Women from impoverished backgrounds in which there was little conversation in the home will only mature intellectually if they are able to converse in another context, usually the school. The teacher of writing, then, may well have to do more than simply allow students the freedom to "express" themselves by lifting the constraints of audience and judgment for a time. She may have to coax students out of their habitual silence.

Women's Ways of Knowing suggests, too, that egocentrism is not always the starting point of the learning process. The learner's self may be effaced, submerged in the voices of others. The writer/reader/speaker/listener may have no strong sense of self, no ego upon which to build an identity. The process of creating a self may well be complex and difficult and will hardly be accomplished simply by encouraging writers to move from expressive to transactional writing or from writer-based to reader-based writing. I'm speaking here of deeply ingrained habits of mind that result from oppressive conditions that are themselves deeply ingrained historically and culturally.

Also, *Women's Ways of Knowing* suggests that the movement toward mature writing or mature intellectual development is not simply a matter of moving from self toward other, from writer toward reader, but of integrating the self with the other, integrating writer and reader. Britton says of transactional writing that the writer is concerned to "enmesh" with the reader's relevant knowledge, experience, and interests (94). Flower speaks of writing "for" the reader (34). Surely, though, the goal of the writer cannot simply be to please the audience, to eliminate unnecessary barriers between writer and reader. The writer cannot give herself over to the reader and cannot give up her right to express herself. Writer and reader need to become "enmeshed" in dialogue; the writer needs to write "to" the reader. Transactional writing, then, needs to remain expressive in some ways, and reader-based writing needs to remain writer-based to an extent.

Women's Ways of Interacting

Women's Ways of Knowing is especially valuable to compositionists because it focuses exclusively on women's ways of learning, an area that has been neglected in composition theory and research. As I have suggested, thinking about women's ways of writing changes the way we think about writing in general. I couldn't help but think as I read the interview and reflected back upon the book, though, that the very positive portrayal of women's connectedness to other women did not quite coincide with my own experience or with some recent feminist research and theory. Belenky's description of the collaborative process that produced the book, for instance, illustrates a predominant theme in *Women's Ways of Knowing*: the wonderfully cooperative way in which women can work together. It would seem that women are, in general, more cooperative than men, more connected to each other and hence more capable than men of collaborating successfully. At the conclusion of their book, Belenky and her coauthors claim, "We believe that connected knowing comes more easily to many women than does separate knowing" (229).

The work of Nancy Chodorow has most often been used in the way Belenky and her colleagues use it: to emphasize the connectedness of mother and daughter and, by implication, the connectedness of woman to woman. Surely, though, women do not always work together cooperatively and are not always good collaborators. Implicit in Chodorow's depiction of mother/daughter interactions is the suggestion that women's interactions with other women may also be problematic in patriarchal society. In "Guaranteed to Please: Twentieth-Century American Women's Bestsellers," Madonne Miner uses Chodorow's work to construct a twentieth-century white middle-class American "woman's story," one that emphasizes the enormous psychic tension that characterizes relationships between mothers and daughters. Her position is based on Chodorow's finding that "girls cannot and do not 'reject' their mother and women in favor of their fathers and men, but remain in a bisexual triangle throughout childhood and puberty" (140). Miner sees bestsellers as portraying women who are bound to their mothers by intense physical and emotional appetites and as appealing to readers bound by the same appetites. She sees *Gone with the Wind*, *Valley of the Dolls*, and *Forever Amber* as portraying aspects of a daughter's relationship to her mother: desire, denial, fear, anger, compensation (192).

Anita Clair Fellman in "Laura Ingalls Wilder and Rose Wilder Lane: The Politics of a Mother-Daughter Relationship" discusses the "uncomfortable proximity" of Wilder and Lane. According to Fellman, "Each woman needed but could not satisfy the other. Their desires and offerings failed to coincide" (536). Fellman speaks of daughters who come to repudiate attachment as a form of dangerous dependence and who are emotionally distant from their mothers (540). Such women, according to Fellman, may be drawn to an ethic of rights rather than an ethic of responsibility, to use Carol Gilligan's terms. Their sense of morality may be one of "noninterference" (540, 541).

Literary critics and theorists are also beginning to explore the complexity of mother/daughter relationships. For example, Sandra Gilbert and

Susan Gubar in volume 1 of *No Man's Land* speak of the ambivalence felt by twentieth-century women writers toward the "maternal" tradition they were beginning to recover. They speak of Virginia Woolf's "paradigmatic ambivalence toward female literary inheritance," and claim, "The love women writers send forward into the past is, in patriarchal culture, inexorably contaminated by mingled feelings of rivalry and anxiety" (194, 195). According to Gilbert and Gubar, for the literary daughter the powerful literary mother becomes the subject of both "matrophilial utopian and matrophobic dystopian meditations" (196). The literary mother becomes "a figure to whose primal relation with tradition the daughter obsessively directs her consistently ambivalent attention, at just the moment when it would seem that maternal potency ought to have healed daughterly dis-ease" (196).

If mothers and daughters are sometimes caught in webs of tension and misunderstanding, it is likely that women in other situations may be as well, especially when relationships involve power imbalances. Deanna Womack makes this point in "Conflicts Between Women at Work." After reviewing several studies, she concludes, "Women in positions of power equality may be less likely to engage other women in conflict than women in superior-subordinate relationships" (48). Evelyn Fox Keller and Helene Moglen, in their essay, "Competition and Feminism: Conflicts for Academic Women," analyze and interpret stories told by colleagues in the academy and conclude, "The fact is that women seem to experience different, deeper, and more painful forms of competition with one another than they do with their male peers," and they find that competition increases with the magnitude of the stakes (494, 507). Keller and Moglen claim that the morality of the women's movement, with its emphasis on mutuality, concern, and support, is difficult to implement in the real world situations of the current academic marketplace" (502). They conclude that conflict and competition are inescapable facts of both the inner and outer realities of women's lives, and they see value in acknowledging the fact rather than denying it (510).

The authors of *Women's Ways of Knowing* suggest that our educational structures have served to separate women from each other and from knowledge and that new structures must be found that allow for connected knowing. They say in their conclusion, "Education conducted on the connected model would help women toward community, power, and integrity" (228). They tend to implicate men and exonerate women in their analysis of barriers to women's intellectual development. In the section on subjective knowledge, for instance, they speak of incest and sexual harassment as problems women often face in the home that are damaging to them intellectually. At the same time, they speak of the positive value for such women of turning to people close to their own experience (such as female peers, mothers, sisters, grandmothers) for validation of their own experience. Men become the villains, women the saviors. If we consider, though, that women's relationships with each other are often highly troubled, then the problem of women's silence becomes very complex and the solutions to the problem equally complex.

Michigan Technological University
Houghton, Michigan

Works Cited

Belenky, Mary Field, Blythe McVicker Clinchy, Nancy Rule Goldberger, and Jill Mattuck Tarule. *Women's Ways of Knowing: The Development of Self, Voice, and Mind.* New York: Basic, 1986.

Britton, James, et al. *The Development of Writing Abilities (11-18).* London: Macmillan, 1975.

Chodorow, Nancy. *The Reproduction of Mothering: Psychoanalysis and the Sociology of Gender.* Berkeley: U of California P, 1978.

Fellman, Anita Clair. "Laura Ingalls Wilder and Rose Wilder Lane: The Politics of a Mother-Daughter Relationship." *Signs* 15 (1990): 535-61.

Flower, Linda. "Writer-Based Prose: A Cognitive Basis for Problems in Writing." *College English* 41 (1979): 19-37.

Gilbert, Sandra M., and Susan Gubar. *The War of the Words.* New Haven: Yale UP, 1988. Vol 1 of *No Man's Land: The Place of the Woman Writer in the Twentieth Century.* 2 vols. 1988.

Gilligan, Carol. *In a Different Voice: Psychological Theory and Women's Development.* Cambridge: Harvard UP, 1982.

Keller, Evelyn Fox, and Helene Moglen. "Competition and Feminism: Conflicts for Academic Women." *Signs* 12 (1987): 493-511.

Miner, Madonne. "Guaranteed to Please: Twentieth-Century American Women's Bestsellers." *Gender and Reading: Essays on Readers, Texts, and Contexts.* Ed. Elizabeth Flynn and Patrocinio Schweickert. Baltimore: Johns Hopkins UP, 1986. 187-211.

Womack, Deanna F. "Conflicts between Women at Work." *Women and Language* 11 (1987): 47-50.

Dueling with Dualism: A Response to Interviews with Mary Field Belenky and Gayatri Chakravorty Spivak

MARILYN M. COOPER

In reading Evelyn Ashton-Jones and Dene Kay Thomas' interview with Mary Field Belenky, I found myself experiencing the same mood swings I experienced in reading *Women's Ways of Knowing*: alternately I was pleased with ideas that accorded with my own way of thinking, and I was irate at ideas that neglected my perspective. This is not to say that I have mixed feelings about the interview or the book. In fact, these perhaps unsettling shifts are what make the work Belenky and her colleagues have done and are doing so stimulating to me as I try to think about the problems of teaching writing at the post-secondary level. What helped me understand this was the fortunate juxtaposition of this interview with the interview Phillip Sipiora and Janet Atwill held with Gayatri Chakravorty Spivak. What I want to do here is to use some ideas that came up in the Spivak interview to help explain my response to the interview with Belenky.

The work done by Mary Field Belenky, Blythe McVicker Clinchy, Nancy Rule Goldberger, and Jill Mattuck Tarule is situated in a field beset by two recalcitrant dualisms: the man/woman dualism and the cognitive/social dualism. Two commonplace reactions to such dualisms are to refuse the either/or view of the world they promote, and to suggest that they can be resolved, that the different perspectives they refer to can be balanced and the tensions between them dissolved. Spivak's suspicion of balance and mediation can be instructive as we duel with these dualisms—dualisms that are also central in the study of teaching writing. I do not believe that the most productive way to handle the differences that often separate us is to pretend that they don't exist or to negotiate them out of existence.

Competition/Collaboration and Critical Discourse

The man/woman dualism constructs itself through many related dualisms, both in the work of Belenky and her coauthors and in society at large. The particular expression of gender dualism that caught my attention in this interview was the opposition between competition and collaboration. In the context of Belenky's discussion, it is a moot point whether competition is associated with men and collaboration with women because of innate differences or because of socially constructed ones; the current pattern that she and her colleagues disclose is that women by and large prefer to work collaboratively and that because collaborative work is devalued and dismissed in institutions structured on the basis of competitive strategies (such as institutions of higher education) women's work is often devalued and dismissed. Belenky goes on to argue that competition is not only bad for women but is bad for everyone and that collaboration is to be preferred: "In my mind the world should not—cannot—be construed as a zero sum game. That's no way to live."

In many discussions of gender differences in scholarship, the differences between men's competitive ways of proceeding and women's collaborative methods are reduced to an opposition between conflict and accord, or disagreement and agreement. Women scholars protest "attacks" on their positions; men scholars protest that such protests are themselves based on the method of disagreeing that underlies the investigation of complex ideas. In such arguments, women tacitly take the position that conflict is incompatible with collaboration, and men tacitly take the position that all disagreement implies competition. Both groups, of course, also imply that good scholarship necessitates either collaboration or competition depending on their allegiances. What I'd like to argue is that none of these positions is plausible.

In their book, Belenky and her coauthors come close to this reductionist view of competition/collaboration when they equate women's collaborative methods with Elbow's "believing game" and men's competitive methods with Elbow's "doubting game." They observe that women are in general uncomfortable with the doubting game: "Few of the women we interviewed ... found argument—reasoned critical discourse—a congenial form of conversation among friends" (105). And they observe that "many women find it easier to believe than to doubt.... While women frequently do experience doubting as a game, believing feels real to them" (113). The equation of doubting with competition and conflict and believing with collaboration and accord is evident when they quote Elbow, who "says that while the doubting game requires a 'combative kind of energy that feels like clenching a muscle. ... the shape of the believing game is waiting, patience, not being in a hurry'" (117). The problem with these equations is that not only are women excluded in educational settings that depend on competitive practices, they are also excluded from reasoned critical discourse, which depends on the doubting game. While there are reasons to be suspicious of seeing "reasoned critical discourse" as the sole mode of knowledge, it is also difficult to see this kind of discourse as the sole province of competitive men and women.

Belenky offers a more complex view of the contrast between competition and collaboration in her interview, where she sees them as separable from, and interacting with, the contrast between doubting and believing games. Here she points out that "both games are of enormous importance for anybody who's going to do serious intellectual work," and she refers to some "informal research" she's done that indicates that women dislike the doubting game only within competitive situations. She explains:

> In the other environment, people are in a win-win situation, where they play the doubting game not to win or lose but to clarify arguments, to develop ideas, and to do better thinking. Women have no problem with the doubting game in such a collaborative setting. You can be a marvelous doubter, and doubting can be life-enhancing if it takes place in the service of the clearest possible understanding of truth rather than in one-upping another. We associate competitiveness—winning—with the doubting game, but competitiveness destroys the doubting game; competitiveness makes it a poor game for getting at the truth. Winning an argument and achieving a more comprehensive view of what's true are not the same.

Belenky here shows clearly how doubting can be seen as more than simply competitive and how, by implication, disagreement can be included in collaborative working situations. (Her descriptions of the collaborative work on the book are further evidence of the compatibility of doubting, critical discourse, and collaboration.) But she also tacitly argues that competition is incompatible with what she calls "serious intellectual work": "competitiveness destroys the doubting game."

Is it true that under competitive situations the doubting game amounts only to one-upmanship? We may agree with the final statement in the quote above but still argue that winning an argument contributes to knowledge just as much as does achieving a more comprehensive view of what's true. Our belief in the value of pluralism and in the social constructedness of all knowledge (which are not the same thing) does not prevent us from saying that in particular situations ideas can be adjudged not only false but also pernicious; nor does it prevent us from wanting to discredit those ideas in the pursuit of knowledge. That race is not a predictor of intelligence, that individualism is not necessarily a good basis on which to build a society, that women are not inherently more nurturing than men—these are arguments we want to win in our current situation, and ones we have good social reasons for wanting to win.

Now, I am not arguing that competition and collaboration are equally important to good scholarship. I'd have to think a lot more about the subject and analyze the current academic situation in a great deal more detail before I could make any such claim. Nor am I arguing that we should try to achieve a balance between collaboration and competition in our work, or that we should all try to be equally good at both strategies. What I am arguing is that the two sides of this dualism offer a productive check on one another; that they remind us that there is always something left out of our calculations; that a perspective conceals at the same time that it reveals.

Asked whether Aristotle's concept of *techne* could be seen to function as a middle term deconstructing the theory/practice dualism, Spivak points out that "the deconstruction of something is, of course, not a deconstruction of the binary." She refuses to conceive of the middle term either as privileging one or the other side of the dualism or as achieving a balance between the two. Instead, she argues for a productive unease:

> If the middle term is something that cannot be sure of itself as either theory or practice, but finds itself inhabiting a kind of productive "unease," and every time it settles into either the theory of rhetoric or the practice of rhetoric, something on the other side beckons and says, "Look here you, you know you are dependent upon me and you're ignoring it," then I feel that the discipline of rhetoric can be an extraordinary ally in, let's say, exposing the artificial distinction between literary theory at one end and creative writing at the other end of our divided terrain.

What Spivak is arguing here is that treatments of problems involving dualisms (or binaries) are often insufficiently dialectical (in the Hegelian sense), that they assume a resolution of the tension rather than a use of that tension.

Applying Spivak's suggestion to the discussions of competition/collaboration and critical discourse, I think we can see that the possibility of an exclusive association of critical discourse with competition calls forth Belenky's consideration of how critical discourse can be collaborative and, vice versa, that her exclusive association of critical discourse with collaboration calls forth my consideration of how critical discourse can also be competitive. The binary nature of this relationship does not allow the possibility of a merging of collaborative and competitive ways of working. Competition and collaboration are fundamental opposites. You cannot, for example, collaborate with someone whom you're trying to win an argument with; at least, you can't do those things at the same time. Furthermore, anyone who comes at critical discourse with a collaborative way of working will always be liable to misunderstand what someone who comes to critical discourse with a competitive way of working is up to, and vice versa. (I described such misunderstandings earlier when I mentioned the oversimplified discussions of the competitive/collaborative dualism.)

With regard to other manifestations of the man/woman dualism, Belenky understands the value of this dialectical method too, a method that allows us a more complex view of phenomena such as critical discourse or voice: "We have a rigid, dualistic way of structuring the world that makes it hard for people to understand that a voice can be associated with gender without being encased in gender." Similarly, I would say that critical discourse can be associated with collaboration without it being the case that collaboration explains everything about critical discourse that's valuable. I would also argue, and I think Belenky would agree, that though women can be associated with collaboration, collaboration cannot simply be explained as women's *way* of knowing—all of which makes any discussion of gender differences and critical discourse very complex indeed.

The Cognitive/Social Binary

I'd like now to turn to a very much briefer consideration of the other dualism I noticed in reading the Belenky and Spivak interviews together—the cognitive/social dualism—and I'd like to suggest that we deal with it in the same dialectical way. I was especially struck by the difference in perspective between Belenky's argument for the value of the developmental sequence she and her colleagues have described and Spivak's refusal to extend her analysis of the functioning of rumor within a system of colonial aggression to a general theory of rumor.

Belenky points out that their study was not designed in such a way that would allow them to claim validly that the positions they describe are developmental stages, and she notes that they also are uncomfortable with the assumption that any particular developmental sequence is universal. She then adds,

> Some of my colleagues found it hard even to argue that one of these positions is inherently better than another. Now, that boggles my mind, because each position seems so much more adequate and adaptive than the previous positions, at least in the context of this culture.

I think most would agree that Belenky's perspective, like that of most psychologists today (I'm simply ignoring behaviorists), is cognitive; that is, she investigates problems by asking questions about the way people (or women, or types of women, but not individuals) think. And though she often, as here, makes a nod to the idea that thinking takes place within a social context that may have a lot to do with how individuals think and with our evaluation of those ways of thinking, such considerations have little effect on what she feels she can validly claim. This, of course, infuriates me, because from my perspective the only thing that's valuable to explain about thinking is how individuals think in particular social situations. But though I am infuriated by the relegation of social context to an addendum, I realize that it is just because the cognitive perspective rules out the analysis of social context that it can analyze those aspects of thinking that are adaptive across a variety of situations, if not universally.

Of course, I still find Spivak's position much more comfortable. When asked to comment on the relationship of rumor to Western humanism and democracy, she replies (in part),

> Rumor could in fact be operative in insurgent efforts against the organized *logos*. But this requires situation-specific study. Just as people like Derrida say that they cannot speak of anything outside of Western metaphysics, I do not feel authorized to establish my critique of the imperialist field as a general theory.... [Still] it is quite possible to see the lineaments of what might gel into what we are calling the technical use of the word *rumor* in my commentary on the operation of rumor in a very specific case.

Spivak's perspective, like that of other Marxists, is social; that is, she investigates problems by asking about what forces are operating in the specific social situation. And though she acknowledges the usefulness of generalizing across situations, she does not see the possibility of making such claims as establishing the value of her work. (Perhaps this is what some people find infuriating about deconstructionists.) In fact, it is just by ignoring what holds true in all situations that scholars working from a social perspective can explain why a phenomenon occurs in one specific situation and not in another.

Finally, I would like to argue that the cognitive/social dualism cannot be resolved, that these two perspectives cannot be held at once or combined, despite the claims of "social cognitivists" and others. As Spivak says,

> I don't think that reconciliation is ever going to happen, frankly, because mediations are always interested. There is always a residue of either this or that side in the way in which mediations are performed.

Cognitivists may qualify their conclusions with remarks such as, "at least in this context," and social theorists may speculate on the implications of their conclusions for a general theory, but these remarks are best read, I think, as expressions of the "bad conscience" that dualisms produce, the voice Spivak hears saying, "Look here you, you know you are dependent upon me and you're ignoring it." Each perspective reveals something only by concealing what the other reveals; to pretend that master and slave are one, that social and cognitive perspectives are really after the same truth, is not enlightening but mystifying.

It is precisely this tension arising from the cognitive/social dualism that is productive in the field of composition research. Just as the tension arising from the competitive/collaborative dualism helps us explain the complex nature of critical discourse (among other phenomena), so the tension between cognitivists and social theorists keeps us from reducing the complexity of writing activities to a unitary, and therefore false, model. Just as cognitivists would acknowledge that their analyses of the structures of thought have little value in predicting an individual's thought process in a specific social situation, so scholars working from the social perspective acknowledge that their analyses of specific situations have little value as the basis of general theories. The relationship is not, of course, one of ecumenical bliss. Misunderstandings occur as scholars read research from the opposite perspective from which it was produced; and there is a fair amount of wrangling over which are the most productive, most valid, most correct methods of scholarship. But it is important that we see these misunderstandings, these conflicts, as positive, that we use them to define and understand our own perspective better, if we want to advance knowledge in the field of writing research.

Michigan Technological University
Houghton, Michigan

Noam

Chomsky

Language, Politics, and Composition: A Conversation with Noam Chomsky

GARY A. OLSON AND LESTER FAIGLEY

Ever since the publication in 1957 of *Syntactic Structures*, Noam Chomsky has been a towering eminence in linguistics and the philosophy of language; and since the 1960s, he has remained an astute and outspoken social critic. Compositionists familiar with Chomsky's work only through his transformational grammar and its compositional application, sentence combining, may not be aware of how profoundly Chomsky has influenced modern thought on language. It would be fair to say that Chomsky's scholarship over the last three decades has forever altered our notions of the integral relationship between language and the human mind.

Especially noteworthy about Chomsky's positions as recorded in the interview below is that in this age of social construction, meaning relativity, and Derridean indeterminacy, Chomsky tenaciously contends that at the heart of most human cognitive operations is a fixed, structured, biological directiveness. In an age in which the preferred target of many intellectuals is Plato, Chomsky serenely declares that "the reasoning in the Platonic dialogues ... is valid if not decisive," and he holds up "Plato's problem" as the key strategy for studying most phenomena in the human sciences. Dismissing poststructuralist thought as "uninteresting," Chomsky notes that the question of indeterminacy is not new, that "people have come at the question of indeterminacy from many points of view," and that it's just part of the age-old philosophic debate over the analytic/synthetic distinction. Yes, to a certain extent "elements of fluidity and indeterminacy do enter," he concedes, but also "there is a highly determinate, very definite structure of concepts and of meaning that is intrinsic to our nature and as we acquire language or other cognitive systems these things just kind of grow in our minds, the same way we grow arms and legs."

In fact, Chomsky complains of a "pernicious epistemological dualism," in that "questions of mind are just studied differently than questions of body." Certainly, there is "an element of truth" to theories such as the social construction of knowledge, but we seem, he argues, to ignore the powerful evidence that "systems of knowledge in particular [are] substantially directed by our biological nature." For example, if we want to study a physical phenomenon such as puberty, "we allow our conception of rational inquiry to guide us, and it guides us right to the study of innate structure"; if we want to study meaning, "people don't follow the same line of inquiry" even though "the logic is the same." Thus, Chomsky expresses frustration with the current trend to dismiss out-of-hand all explanations of cognitive or epistemological operations that rely on theories of innateness. "That's a very pernicious dualism," he insists, "an extremely dangerous version of traditional dualism."

Chomsky also disputes Kuhn's notion that scientific knowledge is the product of community consensus and periodically changes in "paradigm shifts." To Chomsky, there has been only one true scientific revolution: "the Galilean revolution, the seventeenth-century revolution stretching over a period including Galileo." Even the so-called cognitive revolution of the mid-1950s, of which generative grammar was a major part, was only a recapitulation of changes that first occurred in the seventeenth century, according to Chomsky. What's more, he argues, in many ways this second cognitive revolution was a *regression* from advances made during the time of Descartes. Thus, Chomsky is uncomfortable with talk of paradigm shifts. About his own so-called Chomskyan revolution, he says, "It seems to me like just normal progress."

Chomsky also comments on a range of other issues relevant to composition scholarship. While he supports the feminist movement, he claims that there is nothing inherent in language that works to reproduce patriarchal ideology; he agrees, though, that actual language use tends to maintain structures of authority and domination. He believes without question that "there's a big degree of illiteracy and functional illiteracy" in the nation and that the media, through their insistence on "concision," help to foster illiteracy, impose conventional thinking, and block "searching inquiry and critical analysis." Chomsky applauds Paulo Freire's liberatory learning pedagogy and believes that "composition courses are perfectly appropriate places" for helping students develop "systems of intellectual self-defense" and "the capacity for inquiry."

Throughout the interview, Chomsky has much to say about teaching. He feels that teaching is "mostly common sense" and contends that "ninety-nine percent of good teaching is getting people interested." Paraphrasing nuclear physicist Victor Weisskopf's teaching philosophy, Chomsky says, "It doesn't matter what you cover; it matters how much you develop the capacity to discover." However, he does believe that a "sensible prescriptivism ought to be part of any education." That is, all students should master "standard English" even though "much of it is a violation of natural law." Although "a good deal of what's taught in the standard language is just a history of artificialities," students should learn it nonetheless because it's part of our "rich cultural heritage." In keeping with his past statements denying the relevance of linguistics to other disciplines, he doubts that linguistics has anything to contribute to teaching reading and writing.

Chomsky's views on ideology, propaganda, and indoctrination are also of interest to compositionists. He claims that intellectuals are "ideological managers," complicit in controlling "the organized flow of information" because intellectuals are by definition those who have "passed through various gates and filters" in order to become "cultural managers." In effect, "the whole educational system involves a good deal of filtering towards submissiveness and obedience." By definition, those who are subversive or independent minded are not called intellectuals but "wackos." In fact, Chomsky is quite critical of the distinction established between intellectuals—those in the universities—and non-intellectuals. Arguing that often non-intellectuals have a richer cultural life, he speaks disparagingly of the principal activity that sets academics apart from others: "From an intellectual point of view, a lot of scholarship is just very low-level clerical work."

In examining the media's role in indoctrination, Chomsky says that "the media's institutional structure gives them the same kind of purpose that the educational system has: to turn people into submissive, atomized individuals who don't interfere with the structures of power and authority." Similarly, democratic governments use propaganda and "the manufacture of consent" in place of violence and force to control the masses. "Indoctrination is to democracy," he philosophizes, "what a bludgeon is to totalitarianism." This atomization of individuals, this breakdown of independent thought, and this general depoliticizing of society together create the perfect environment, in Chomsky's view, for a charismatic, fascist dictator to seize power. "I think that's one of the reasons why I'm very much in favor of corruption.... A corrupt leader is going to rob people but not cause that much trouble.... Power hunger is much more dangerous than money hunger," he argues.

Chomsky sees no contradiction between his somewhat radical political views and his conservative, essentialist views on language. In fact, he insists on separating his two (as he calls them) full-time professional careers. He bristles at the criticism that he does not apply his expertise as a linguist to the very same inequities that he denounces as a social critic—exploring how language helps maintain power hierarchies, for example. Such questions, he claims, have no intellectual depth and are of "marginal human significance." Infinitely more significant is helping Salvadoran peasants or attending a demonstration in Washington.

Still, Chomsky's political progressivism and philosophical foundationalism seem oddly incongruous at first glance. He confidently and steadfastly champions an eighteenth-century, rationalist view of the world, while railing against state capitalism and private ownership of the means of production. On second glance, however, Chomsky's world view is perhaps not so schizophrenic after all. Just as his essentialist philosophy of innateness and biological directiveness derives from eighteenth-century notions, especially Humboldt's concept of "infinite use of finite means" (from which grew Chomsky's generative grammar), so too does his political ideology derive directly, as he puts it, from "classical liberalism—as developed, for example, by

Humboldt." In the face of Marxists, poststructuralists, and social constructionists, Noam Chomsky remains unshaken—a devoted eighteenth-century rationalist.

Q. You have published an overwhelming number of works. Do you think of yourself as a writer?

A. No, I've never particularly thought of myself as a writer. In fact, most of what I've published is written-up versions of lectures. For example, *Syntactic Structures*, the first book that actually appeared, was essentially lecture notes for an undergraduate course at MIT, revised slightly to turn them into publishable form. I would say probably eighty or ninety percent of the work I do on political issues is sort of working out notes from talks. Much of the material that ends up as professional books is based on class lectures or lectures elsewhere, so I tend to think out loud.

Q. So you see yourself first as a *speaker*, a lecturer.

A. The fact is that most of the writing I do is probably letters. I spend about twenty hours a week, I guess, just answering letters. Many of the letters are on questions that are in response to the hundreds of letters that I receive which are thoughtful and interesting and raise important questions (here's today's batch). Hundreds go out every week, and that requires thought; some of them are rather long. Those are actually written without being spoken. Sometimes I do sit down and write a book, too, but most of the time I don't think of myself as a writer particularly.

Q. You *have* had a few words to say about your writing process. In fact, you commented once, "I'm able to work in twenty-minute spurts. I can turn my attention from one topic to another without start-up time. I almost never work from an outline or follow a plan. The books simply grow by accretion." Would you tell us more about your writing process?

A. The reason for the twenty-minute spurts—which is a bit of an exaggeration; maybe hour spurts would be more accurate—is just the nature of my life, which happens to be very intense. I have two full-time professional careers, each of them quite demanding, plus lots of other things. I just mentioned one—lots and lots of correspondence—and other things as well, and that doesn't leave much time. In fact, my time tends to be very chopped up. I discovered over the years that probably my only talent is this odd talent that I seem to have that other colleagues don't, and that is that I've got sort of buffers in the brain that allow me to shift back and forth from one project to the other and store one.

Q. So you can't when writing a book, for example, concentrate for ten hours at a time.

A. No, I know that a lot of people don't seem to be able to do that, and it's certainly an advantage to be able to do it. I can pick up after a long stretch and be more or less where I left off. In fact, I've sometimes had to. I have friends like this. I had, in particular, one friend who just died a couple of years ago who was an Israeli logician and who'd been an old friend since I was twenty or so. We would meet every five or six years and usually pick up the conversation we had been having as if we had just had it five minutes ago and go on from there. As far as my books just sort of writing themselves, that's pretty much what happens. I don't recall ever having sat down and planned a book—except maybe for saying, "Well, I'm going to talk about X, Y, and Z, and I'll have Chapter One on X, Chapter Two on Y, and Chapter Three on Z." Then it's just a matter of getting the first paragraph, and it just goes on from there.

Q. That's quite a talent.

A. Well, it's probably because I've thought about most of it before, or lectured on it before, or written a letter to someone about it, or done it twenty times in the past. Then it becomes mainly a problem of trying to fit it all in. I *have* discovered, if it's of any interest to you, that I write somewhat differently now that I have a computer—quite a bit differently. I don't know if it shows up any different, but I know I write differently. I was very resistant to the computer. I didn't want to use it, and finally the head of the department just stuck it in my room. My teenage son who was—like every teenager, I guess—a super hacker carried me gently through the early stages, which I never would have had the patience to do. Once I was able to use the computer, I discovered that there were a lot of things that I could do that I'd never done before. For example, I'd never done much editing, simply because it was too much trouble; I didn't want to retype everything. And I never did much in the way of inserting and rearranging and so on. Now I do a fair amount of that because it's so easy. Whether that shows up differently for the reader, I don't know. But I know I'm writing quite differently.

Q. As someone who is profoundly interested in the structure of language as well as the use and abuse of rhetoric in political contexts, you must have some thoughts about the nature of rhetoric. For you, what are the most important elements of rhetoric?

A. I don't have any theory of rhetoric, but what I have in the back of my mind is that one should not try to persuade; rather, you should try to lay out the territory as best you can so that other people can use their own intellectual powers to work out for themselves what they think is right or wrong. For example, I try, particularly in political writing, to make it extremely clear in advance exactly where I stand. In my view, the idea of neutral objectivity is largely fraudulent. It's not that I take the realistic view with regard to fact, but the fact is that everyone approaches complex and controversial questions—especially those of human significance—with an ax to grind, and I like that ax to be apparent right up front so that people can compensate for it. But to the extent that I can monitor my own rhetorical activities, which is probably not a lot, I try to refrain from efforts to bring people to reach my conclusions.

Q. Is that because you might lose credibility or lose the audience?

A. Not at all. In fact, you'd probably lose the audience by not doing it. It's just kind of an authoritarian practice one should keep away from. The same is true for teaching. It seems to me that the best teacher would be the one who allows students to find their way through complex material as you lay out the terrain. Of course, you can't avoid guiding because you're doing it a particular way and not some other way. But it seems to me that a cautionary flag should go up if you're doing it too much because the purpose is to enable students to be able to figure out things for themselves, not to know this thing or to understand that thing but to understand the next thing that's going to come along; that means you've got to develop the skills to be able to critically analyze and inquire and be creative. This doesn't come from persuasion or forcing things on people. There's sort of a classical version of this—that teaching is not a matter of pouring water into a vessel but of helping a flower to grow in its own way—and I think that's right. It seems to me that that's the model we ought to approach as best possible. So I think the best rhetoric is the least rhetoric.

Q. In his critique of Western metaphysics, Jacques Derrida exposed the indeterminacy of language, showing how meaning is never fixed, always fluid, never certain. What are your thoughts on this issue?

A. I don't know this literature very well, and to tell you the truth, the reason I don't know it is that I don't find it interesting. I try to read it now and then but just don't find it very interesting. People have come at the question of indeterminacy from many points of view, and I think there's an element of truth to it, but there's also a respect in which it's not true. These are questions of fact, not of ideology; therefore, there's no grounds for dogmatism concerning them, and they're not a matter of pronouncements but of discovery. To the extent that we understand things about language, the facts point rather clearly, *rather* clearly, to a specific conclusion which is halfway like that, but only halfway. What we find is that there is a highly determinate, very definite structure of concepts and of meaning that is intrinsic to our nature and that as we acquire language or other cognitive systems these things just kind of grow in our minds, the same way we grow arms and legs. To that extent, meaning is determinate. However, there's a sense in which it's not fully determinate, and that is the way we use these conceptual and, in particular, these rich semantic structures in our interactions with one another and our interactions with the world. In that domain, there's a high degree of interest-relativity, intrusion of value, relativity to purposes and intentions, modifiability often in a somewhat rather creative fashion, and so on. At that level it's true that elements of fluidity and indeterminacy do enter; however, they have their own structure. It's just that we don't understand very much about it. So I think there's an element of truth to that but it can be carried much too far.

In the philosophical literature—those parts of it that I feel more comfortable with and where I think I understand what people are talking about—similar ideas arise in the study of what's called "meaning holism." Take Hilary Putnam as an example, someone who's extended views originally due to Quine towards a general theory of semantics which would express a viewpoint related to this—namely, that the meaning of a word is never determinate (it's certainly not something in the mind), and if it's not determinate then it depends on the place of the concept within the whole intellectual structure, and it can change, your beliefs change, the meanings change, and so forth; that is, the intentions change, the meaning may be modified, and so on. Well, I think that this thesis is half true. In the same respect, there is a *fixed* structure of meaning and it's an interesting one, a very intriguing one. In fact, contrary to what is believed by many people—for example, Richard Rorty—there are strong empirical grounds for believing that there is quite a sharp analytic/synthetic distinction that derives from intrinsic semantic structures and is just a reflection of the fact that there are probably biologically determined and quite rich and intriguing semantic structures that are basically fixed. But there's a sense in which meaning holism is correct; that is, what we describe as meaning in common-sense discourse, and in philosophical discourse, is never fixed entirely by the structures that are present in the mind and we've gotten that way because that's the kind of creature we are. So in that sense there's some truth to meaning holism.

Q. So you probably wouldn't agree with Bakhtin. Are you familiar with his work?

A. No, I'm not.

Q. His ideas sound very similar to this concept of meaning holism.

A. Yes, but that's the standard view. That's the view of Derrida to the extent that I understand him, but also of a large sector of analytic philosophy and, again, Richard Rorty. Donald Davidson, for example, whom Rorty quotes, argued—actually, I should say "asserted"—that Quine's demolition of the analytic/synthetic distinction, his demonstration that this distinction doesn't hold, created the modern philosophy of language as a serious discipline. Well, the analytic/synthetic question is a technical one, but the point is the same. If there were determinate meanings, there would be an analytic/synthetic distinction. So the domain in which this issue is fought out in philosophical terrain is over the analytic/synthetic issue, but the real question is whether there are fixed, determinate meanings. Does the word *house* have a determinate meaning or can it vary arbitrarily, depending on the way our belief systems vary? I think the answer is right in between. There's a fixed and quite rich structure of understanding associated with the concept "house" and that's going to be cross-linguistic and it's going to arise independently of any evidence because it's just part of our nature. But there's also going to be a lot of variety in how we use that term in particular circumstances, or against the background of particular kinds of theoretical understanding, and so on.

Q. Some thinkers draw on Rorty's work to posit that knowledge itself is a socially constructed artifact. That is, knowledge is not absolute; rather, it is the *product* of consensus within any given discourse community. This concept is related to Kuhn's notion of how knowledge is formed within the scientific community. What are your thoughts about this theory?

A. There is an element of truth to it, obviously. There is no doubt that the pursuit of knowledge is often, not always, but is often—in fact, typically—a kind of communal activity. In particular, that's true of organized knowledge, say research in the natural sciences, say what we do in this corridor; that's obviously a social activity. For example, a graduate student will come in and inform me I was wrong about what I said in a lecture yesterday for this or that reason, and we'll discuss it, and we'll agree or disagree, and maybe another set of problems will come out. Well, that's normal inquiry, and whatever results is some form of knowledge or understanding; obviously, that's socially determined by the nature of these interactions. On the other hand, most domains we don't understand much about—like how scientific knowledge develops, something we basically understand nothing about—but if we look more deeply at the domains where we do understand something, we discover that the development of cognitive systems, including systems of knowledge in particular, is substantially directed by our biological nature. In the case of knowledge of language, we have the clearest evidence about this. Part of my own personal interest in the study of language is that it's a domain in which these questions can be studied much more clearly, much more easily than in many others. Also, it's one intrinsic to human nature and human functions, so it's not a marginal case. There, I think, we have very powerful evidence of the directive effect of biological nature on the form of the system of knowledge that arises.

In other domains like, for example, the internalization of our moral code, or our style of dress, we just know less. But I think the qualitative nature of the problem faced strongly suggests a very similar conclusion: a highly directive effect of biological nature. When you turn to scientific inquiry, again, so little is known that everything that one says is virtually pure speculation. But I think the qualitative nature of the process of acquiring scientific knowledge again suggests a highly directive effect of biological nature. The reasoning behind this is basically Plato's, which I think is quite valid. That's why it's sometimes called "Plato's problem." The reasoning in the Platonic dialogues, which is valid if not decisive, is that the richness and specificity and commonality of the knowledge we attain is far beyond anything that can be accounted for by the experience available, which includes interpersonal interactions. And, besides being acts of God, that leaves only the possibility that it's inner-determined. That's the same logic that's constantly used by every natural scientist studying organic systems. So, for example, when we study, metaphorically speaking, physical growth below the neck, everything but the mind, we just take this reasoning for granted. For example, let's say I were to suggest to you that undergoing puberty is a matter of social interaction and people do it because they see other people do it, that it's peer pressure. Well, you laugh, just as you're laughing now. Why do you laugh? Everyone assumes that it's biologically determined, that you're somehow programmed to undergo puberty at a certain point. Is it that something is known about that biological program? Is that why you laugh? No, nothing's known about it. In fact, we know a lot more about the acquisition of meaning and the fixed factors in that than we do about the factors that determine puberty. Is it that social factors are irrelevant to puberty? No, not at all. Social interaction is certainly going to be relevant. Under certain conditions of social isolation, it might not even take place. Why do people laugh? That's the question.

Q. What about knowledge in a particular field, say linguistics? You came along with *Syntactic Structures* and changed the way we think of linguistics. If your colleagues and followers had not accepted and then helped champion that cause, you would simply be a kook out in the wilderness with some crazy idea. But what happened is that a large part of your discourse community accepted the ideas and worked with them and perhaps refined them, and that became the "knowledge" of the time. Well, perhaps in the future there will be some revolution within the field that turns it completely in another direction; your discourse community will have *constructed* new "knowledge."

A. That has happened several times in the last thirty years, but that's a totally different question. In fields that have a rational nature, where the conditions of rational inquiry are observed and there's a sort of a common understanding of what it means to move towards truth (or at least a better grasp of truth), and where there's a sort of common and rational understanding of the nature of argument and evidence—and I think those things are essentially fixed—in such fields, there's a course of development. It's not perfect; all sorts of erratic things happen. Sure, changes take place and some things are accepted while others are not accepted, sometimes rightly, sometimes wrongly, and there are ways of correcting error. But I don't understand what that has to do with the social determination of knowledge. That's a matter of how, through social interaction, each person contributing tries to advance a common enterprise. Now this is somewhat idealized because there are all sorts of personal conflicts and somebody's trying to undercut someone else, but let's abstract away from that; let's abstract away from the vile nature of human beings and talk about it as if we're living up to the ideals that at least theoretically we hold. To that extent there's a common enterprise, and understanding will grow as people participate in this common enterprise. And it will change, and sometimes change radically.

Q. Has your colleague down the hall, Thomas Kuhn, ever discussed the Chomskyan revolution in terms of a "paradigm shift"?

A. He hasn't, but other people have; I don't. My own view is that while there have been several significant changes (Tom and I kind of differ on this), there's been basically *one* scientific revolution: the Galilean revolution, the seventeenth-century revolution stretching over a period including Galileo. That was a real revolution, a different way of looking at things in many respects. For example, there was a very sharp shift at that point from a kind of natural history perspective to a natural science perspective. A different attitude toward fact developed, a different attitude toward idealization, a different concept of explanation. There was a complete breakdown, especially with Newton, of the common sense notion of mechanical explanation which led in new directions. Put all these things together and I think that's a radical shift in perspective. Now there are very few fields of human endeavor where that shift of perspective has taken place. In the study of language, I think that shift did take place to an extent in the 1950s. You could call that a "paradigm shift" if you want to use the term, but it seems to me to be adapting the methods of the natural sciences to another domain; in that respect, it's not really a dramatic shift.

Furthermore, even if you look at the basic intellectual developments and changes in points of view associated with what's called "the cognitive revolution" in the mid-1950s—of which the development of generative grammar was a part and, in fact, a major contributing part—I think they're quite real; but in a number of respects, rather critical respects, they recapitulate and revise changes that took place during what I prefer to call "the first cognitive revolution," namely in the seventeenth century. For example, a major shift in the 1950s was a shift of perspective *away* from concern for behavior and the products of behavior *towards* the inner processes that determine behavior and determine the processes of behavior. Now that's a shift towards the natural sciences because the inner processes are real. They're part of psychology, part of biology. So that's a shift towards the natural sciences, away from behavior towards inner mechanisms and inner processes that underlie behavior. It's also a shift towards explanation rather than description. Now that's a big shift. But a shift like that took place in what we might call the "Cartesian revolution" in the cognitive sciences. Associated with this was a revival—it wasn't a new interest—of interest in what are sometimes called computational models of the mind, that is, theories of rules and representations, roughly. Now that's part of the same thing because the inner mechanisms and inner processes appear to be computational systems, mentally representative and, in some unknown manner, physically instantiated. But that again is highly reminiscent of something that took place in the seventeenth century—in particular, Descartes' theory of vision, which was a crucial breakthrough and developed a kind of a representational, computational theory of mind. It was a major shift.

Another change that took place in the 1950s, part of the cognitive revolution, had to do with things like, say, the Turing test for general intelligence. But that's just a watered-down version of a much richer and more interesting seventeenth-century notion: the Cartesian tests for the existence of other minds, which crucially used aspects of linguistic performance, the fact that normal human linguistic behavior has what I sometimes call—they didn't call it this—a creative aspect, meaning it's appropriate to situations but not caused by situations (which is a fundamental difference); it's innovative, unbounded, and not determined by internal stimuli or external causes; it's coherent, whatever that means (we recognize that but we can't characterize it); it evokes thoughts in others that they may express themselves, and so on. There's a collection of properties and one can turn those properties into an experimental program, as in fact was suggested in the seventeenth century, to determine whether another organism has a mind like yours. Now in that context there's real scientific inquiry being carried out in which one tries to determine whether a machine, let's say, is a person with a mind. That's a real scientific question embedded in that rich framework of scientific inquiry dealing with real questions, noting crucial facts about human beings, which, in fact, are true facts. That all makes a lot of sense. In contrast, the twentieth-century version of this, sometimes called the Turing test, is almost totally pointless. It's just an operational test to determine whether, say, a computer program manifests intelligence, and like most operational tests it doesn't matter how it comes out because operational tests are of no interest or significance except in some theoretical context. The reason I mention that is to indicate that in this respect the second cognitive revolution was a regression, in my view, from the first cognitive revolution.

Another question has to do with the body/mind relation. In the seventeenth century, in the Cartesian system, the body/mind relation was absolutely central. Descartes and the Cartesians had a plausible, though we now know an incorrect, argument for the existence of mind. The argument basically was that they had a conception of body based on a kind of intuitive mechanics, a sort of contact mechanics—you know, things pushing and pulling each other. Our normal intuitive, common-sense notion of mechanics was what they meant by body. They argued correctly that that concept had certain limits, and they therefore postulated a second substance, a thinking substance, to deal with things that plainly go beyond those limits, like the creative aspects of language use. Well, then a body/mind problem arises. That's a real problem, but it didn't survive Newton because Newton blew the theory of mechanics out of the water. The concept of body disappeared, and, since then, there is no concept of body and no classical body/mind problem—at least there shouldn't be, in my view. In the new version, what we really just have is different levels of understanding and they're all natural and we try to relate them as much as we can. In the twentieth-century cognitive revolution, something like the body/mind problem reemerged but in a pernicious way, a way that's again a regression from the earlier version. The earlier version was a metaphysical problem, hence a problem of reality, and a serious one. The modern version is a kind of an epistemological dualism; that is, questions of mind are just studied differently than questions of body. The example I just mentioned is one. In the case of studying puberty, we allow our conception of rational inquiry to guide us, and it guides us right to the study of innate structure. In the case of the study of, say, meaning, people don't follow the same line of inquiry, though they should because the logic is the same. That's one of numerous examples showing that the way we study the traditional phenomena of mind departs from the way we study other aspects of physical reality. That's a very pernicious dualism, an extremely dangerous version of traditional dualism which ought to be abandoned. So that's another respect in which I think there's regression from the first cognitive revolution.

The point I'm trying to make is that there was a very substantial change in general psychology, including linguistics, in the mid-1950s and in some ways it was a regression. There are some ways in which it was real progress. The traditional view about language, which is correct, is that, as Humboldt put it, language makes "infinite use of finite means," and that's correct. But nobody knew what to make of that notion because they had no concept of infinite use of finite means. By the mid-twentieth century, we had a concept of what that means. It came out of mathematics, really. Out of parts of mathematics and logic there came a sharp understanding of the notion, infinite use of finite means, and it was therefore possible to apply that to the traditional questions. That led to a huge move forward in understanding; in fact, that's generative grammar. It's looking at a lot of the classical questions in the light of the modern understanding of what it means to make infinite use of finite means. That confluence did make possible a substantial change. If one wants to call this a revolution, okay; if not, okay; I don't. It seems to me like just normal progress when new understanding arises and you can apply it to old problems.

Q. You're talking about biological directiveness, and in your work over the last three decades you have emphasized that there is this strong element of innateness in language. What about writing, which is a learned phenomenon—something, unlike language, that not every healthy human has? Would you pursue this same line in talking about written language?

A. I'm sure if we look at written language we're going to find the conditions of Plato's problem arising once again. Namely, we just know too much. The basic problem that you always face when you look at human competence, or for that matter at any biological system, is that the state it has attained is so rich and specific that you cannot account for it on the basis of interactions, such as learning, for example. That's something that's found almost universally. The case of puberty that I gave you is only one example, but it's true from the level of the cell on up. When you look at any form of human activity, whether it's speech or moral judgment or ability to read, I think you'll find exactly the same thing. When you understand the actual phenomenon, what you discover typically is that there's some kind of triggering effect from the outside—often what we call "teaching" or "learning"—that sets in motion inner directive processes. That's how you can gain such rich competence on the basis of such limited experience. It's not unlike the fact that when a child eats, it grows. The food makes it grow, if you like, but it's not the food that's determining the way it grows; the way it grows is determined by its inner nature. It won't do it without food; if you keep the food away, the child won't grow. But when you give the child the food, it's going to grow into what it's going to be, a human and not a bird, and the reason for that is the inner nature. That's basically Plato's argument.

Q. Many feminists have argued that because language controls thought and because ours is a male-inscribed, male-dominated language, language works to reproduce patriarchal ideology and thus the oppression of women. Do you agree with these assumptions and the conclusion?

A. I understand the point, but I wouldn't call it a property of language. There are many properties of language use which reflect structures of authority and domination in the society in which this language is used, and that's true. However, I don't think there's anything *in the language* that requires that. You could use the same language without those aspects of use in it. For example, there are ways of using language which are deeply racist, but the very same language can be used without the need to be racist.

Q. But given how language is actually used . . .

A. Well, given language use, it's undoubtedly correct, and it's true of all sorts of systems of authority and domination, one being the gender issue.

Q. Here's one brief example: some feminists have argued that the term *motherhood* is something like a semantic universal and that that oppresses women. Do you see any justification for that argument?

A. Well, you have to ask what you mean by "semantic universal." First of all, there's the question of whether it's true, but let's say for the sake of argument that every language known has a concept like "motherhood," and let's say that every one of those languages and every one of those concepts has something that oppresses women in it. Suppose, for the sake of argument, that this were discovered to be true. We still would not have finished because it may simply be that every culture you sample is a culture that oppresses women. That doesn't yet show that it's inherent in our nature that women be oppressed. That just shows that the cultures that exist oppress women. And therefore it'll turn out that in every language that's developed in those cultures there will be a concept which reflects this relation of authority and control. But that doesn't tell you it's a semantic universal. In fact, there's ambiguity in the notion "semantic universal" which ought to be clarified. Some things are semantic universals in the sense that you find them in every language. Other things are semantic universals in the sense that they're part of our nature and therefore *must* be in every language. That's a fundamental difference. For example, it's a fact that every human society we know—I suppose this is probably close to true if not totally true—places women in a subordinate role in some fashion. But it doesn't follow from that that it's part of our nature. That just shows that it's part of the society. If that were true, it would be a "weak universal." That is, it would be a descriptive universal but not a deep universal, something that's necessarily true. Now, there *are* things that are necessarily true. For example, there are properties of our language which are just as much part of our nature as the fact that we have arms and not wings. But just sampling the language of the world is not enough to establish it.

Q. In a recent article in *Mother Jones,* one of your former students was quoted as saying, "Chomsky thinks he's a feminist, but—at heart—he's an old-fashioned patriarch. . . . He just has never really understood what the feminist movement is about." Do you support the goals and aspirations of the feminist movement?

A. I don't think there's such a thing as *the* aspirations and goals of the feminist movement, and I don't think there's such a thing as *the* feminist movement. There are many aspirations and goals of the feminist movement—or the feminist movements, I should say—which I think are timely and proper and important and have had an enormous effect in liberating consciousness and thought and making people aware of forms of oppression that they had internalized and not noticed. I think that's all for the good. In fact, my own view, and I've said this many times, is that of all the movements that developed in what's called the sixties—which really is not the sixties, because the feminist movement is basically later, but what is metaphorically called the sixties—the one that's had the most profound influence and impact is probably the feminist movement, and I think it's very important. As to the student's comment, that could very well be correct, but I'm not the person to judge.

Q. For the last few years, the media and the political establishment have asserted that the U.S. is experiencing a literacy crisis. Do you agree?

A. Sure. It's just a fact. I don't think it's even questioned. There's a big degree of illiteracy and functional illiteracy. It's remarkably high. What's more, the interest in reading is declining, or it certainly looks as if it's declining. People do seem to read less and to want to read less and be able to read less. I know of colleagues, for example, academic people whose world is reading, who won't subscribe to some journals that they are sympathetic to and find important because the articles are too long. They want things to be short. That just boggles my mind. In fact, let me report to you a personal case. I once had an interview at a radio station in which the interviewer was interested in why I don't appear on *MacNeil/Lehrer*, *Nightline*, and that sort of program. He began the interview by playing a short tape of an earlier interview he'd had with a producer of *Nightline*. The interviewer asked him this question: "It's been claimed that the people on your program are all biased in one direction and that you cut out critical, dissident thought. How come, for example, you never have Chomsky on your program?" The producer first went into sort of a tantrum, saying I was from Neptune, and "wacko" and so on; but after he'd calmed down he said something which, in fact, has an element of truth to it: "Chomsky lacks concision." *Concision* means you have to be able to say things between two commercials. Now that's a structural property of our media—a very important structural property which imposes conformism in a very deep way, because if you have to meet the condition of concision, you can only either repeat conventional platitudes or else sound like you *are* from Neptune. That is, if you say anything that's not conventional, it's going to sound very strange. For example, if I get up on television and say, "The Soviet invasion of Afghanistan is a horror," that meets the condition of concision. I don't have to back it up with any evidence; everyone believes it already so therefore it's straightforward and now comes the commercial. Suppose I get up in the same two minutes and say, "The U.S. invasion of South Vietnam is a horror." Well, people are very surprised. They never knew there was a U.S. invasion of South Vietnam, so how could it be a horror? They heard of something called the U.S. "defense" of South Vietnam, and maybe that it was wrong, but they never heard anybody talk about the U.S. "invasion" of South Vietnam. So, therefore, they have a right to ask what I'm talking about. Copy editors will ask me when I try to sneak something like this into an article what I mean. They'll say, "I don't remember any such event." They have a right to ask what I mean. This structural requirement of concision that's imposed by our media disallows the possibility of explanation; in fact, that's its propaganda function. It means that you can repeat conventional platitudes, but you can't say anything out of the ordinary without sounding as if you're from Neptune, a wacko, because to explain what you meant—and people have a right to ask if it's an unconventional thought—would take a little bit of time. Here in the United States, to my knowledge, it's quite different from virtually every other society, maybe with the exception of Japan, which is more or less in our model. But at least in my experience, when you appear on radio and television in Europe and the Third World—first of all you *can* appear on radio and television if you have dissident opinions, which is virtually impossible here—you have enough time to explain what you mean. You don't have to have three sentences between two commercials, and if it takes a few minutes to explain or, more often, an hour, you have that time. Here, our media are constructed so you don't have time; you have to meet the condition of concision. And whether anybody in the public relations industry thought this up or not, the fact is that it's highly functional to impose thought control. Pretty much the same is true in writing, like when you've got to say something in seven-hundred words. That's another way of imposing the condition of conventional thinking and of blocking searching inquiry and critical analysis. I think one effect of this is a kind of illiteracy.

Q. Speaking of critical analysis and literacy, Paulo Freire and others argue that writing, because it can lead to "critical consciousness," is an avenue to social and political empowerment of the disenfranchised. Do you agree?

A. Absolutely. In fact, writing is an indispensable method for interpersonal communication in a complicated society. Not in a hunter-gatherer tribe of fifteen people; then you can all talk to one another. But in a world that's more complicated than that, intellectual progress and cultural progress and moral progress for that matter require forms of interaction and communicative interchange that go well beyond that of speaking situations. So, sure, people who can participate in that have ways of enriching their own thought, of enlightening others, of entering into constructive discourse with others which they all gain by. That's a form of empowerment. It's not the case if a teacher tells the kid, "Write five-hundred words saying this." That's just a form of reducing; that's a form of de-education, not education.

Q. There's a movement within composition studies to make a kind of critical/ cultural studies based on a Freirean model the subject matter for the first-year English course. Do you think that's a good idea?

A. Doing things that will stimulate critical analysis, self-analysis, and analysis of culture and society is very crucial. In fact, it seems to me that part of the core of all education ought to be the development of systems of intellectual self-defense and also stimulation of the capacity for inquiry, which means also collective inquiry. And this is one of the domains in which it can be done. It is done, say, in the natural sciences, but localized in those problems. It ought to be done in a way so that people understand that this is a general need and a general capacity; English composition courses are perfectly appropriate places for that.

Q. In 1973 you had an extended discussion on Dutch television with Michel Foucault, one of the most important of the French poststructuralist philosophers. In a subsequent interview, you said that you and Foucault found some areas of agreement, but you commented that he was much more skeptical than you were about the possibility of developing a concept of human nature that is independent of social and historical conditions.

How would you ground a concept of human nature beyond human capacity to acquire language?

A. I would study it the same way. I would apply the logic of Plato's problem. Take any domain—the domain of moral judgment, let's say. I don't think we're in a position to study it yet, but the *way* you would study it is clear. You'd take people and ask what is the nature of the system of moral judgment that they have. We certainly have such systems. We make moral judgments all the time, and we make them in coherent ways and with a high degree of consistency; we make them in new cases that we've not faced before. So we have some sort of a theory, or a system, or a structure that underlies probably an unbounded range of moral judgments. That's a system that can be discovered; you can find out what it is. We can then ask questions about the extent to which different systems that arise in different places are different and the extent to which they're the same. We can ask the harder, deeper question: "What was the nature of the external input, the external stimulation or evidence on the basis of which the system of moral judgment arose?" To the extent that you can answer that, you can determine what the inner nature was from which it began. The logic is exactly like the problem of why children undergo puberty. You first find out what happens to them at that age; you ask what factors, what external events took place; and then you'd say what must have been the internal directive capacity that led to this phenomenon given those external events. That's a question of science, a hard question of science. In these domains it's usually not hard because you usually find that the external events are so impoverished and so unstructured and so brief, in fact, that they couldn't have had much of an effect. So qualitatively speaking, most of it is going to be internal. That's a way of finding out our entire moral nature.

You can also study other things, like moral argument, for example. Take a real case; take, say, the debate about slavery. A lot of the debate about slavery took place, or as we reconstruct it could have taken place, on shared moral grounds. In fact, one can understand the slave owner's arguments on *our* moral grounds, and one can even see that those arguments are not insignificant. Take one case just to illustrate. Suppose I'm a slave owner, and you're opposed to slavery, and I give you the following argument for slavery: "*Suppose you rent a car and I buy a car. Who's going to take better care of it? Well, the answer is that I'm going to take better care of it because I have a capital investment in it. You're not going to take care of it at all. If you hear a rattle, you're just going to give it back to Hertz and let somebody else worry about it. If I hear a rattle, I'm going to take it to the garage because I don't want to get in trouble later on. In general, I'm going to take better care of the car I own than you're going to take of the car you rent. Suppose I own a person and you rent a person. Who's going to take better care of that person? Well, parity of argument, I'm going to take better care of that person than you are. Consequently, it follows that slavery is much more moral* than capitalism. *Slavery is a system in which you own people and therefore you take care of them. Capitalism, which has a free labor market, is a system in which you rent people. If you own capital, you rent people and then you don't care about them at all. You use them up, throw them away, get new people. So the free market in labor is totally immoral, whereas slavery is quite moral.*" Now that's a moral argument, and we can understand it. We may decide that it's grotesque. In fact, we *will* decide that it's grotesque, but we have to ask ourselves why. It's not that we lack a shared moral ground with the slave owner; we *have* a shared moral ground, and we would then want to argue that ownership of a person is such an infringement on the person's fundamental human rights that the question of better or worse doesn't even arise. That's already a complex argument, but it's an argument based on shared moral understanding. Now where's that shared moral understanding coming from? I have a strong suspicion that if we understood the nature of the problem better we might discover that that shared moral understanding comes from our inner nature. Let's return to the feminist question. The respect in which the feminists are exactly right, I think, is that when they bring forth and make you face the facts of domination, you see that such domination is wrong. Why do you see that it's wrong? Well, because something about your understanding of human beings and their rights is being brought out and made public. You didn't see it before but that's because you're now exploring your own moral nature and finding something there that you didn't notice before. To the extent that there's any progress in human history—and there's some, after all—it seems to me that it's partly a matter of exploring your own moral nature and discovering things that we didn't recognize before. It wasn't very far back when slavery *was* considered moral, in fact, even obligatory. Now it's considered grotesque. I think there are social and historical reasons for that—like the rise of industrial capitalism, and so on—but that's not the whole story. That may be something that stimulated something internal, but what it stimulated was a deeper understanding of our own moral nature. It seems to me that these are various ways in which one might hope to discover the innate basis of moral judgment. But I think anywhere you look, if there's any system that's even complex enough to deserve being studied, you're going to get roughly the same result and basically for Plato's reasons.

Q. In Asian societies, especially Chinese society, there's a strong patriarchal assumption. While in Singapore, one of us had this very debate on innate human moral authority, and they said, "No, the innate human moral authority is that men should be superior to women." So there's a strong cultural impasse that we seem to bring out. Do you have any insights on that? Is it that we're more advanced than Asians or Chinese society?

A. Well, I think we are. For example, I admit that this is a value judgment and I can't prove it, but I would suspect that there's going to be an evolution (assuming that the human race doesn't self-destruct, which it's likely to do) from rigid patriarchal societies to more egalitarian societies and not the other way around. I would suspect an asymmetry in development because, as circumstances allow, people do become more capable of exploring their own moral nature. Now "circumstances allow" means that the conditions of freedom generally expand, either partially for economic reasons or partly for other cultural reasons. As there's an expansion of the capacity to inquire into our own cultural practices instead of just accepting them rigidly, the assumptions about the need for domination or the justice of domination are challenged and typically overthrown—like peeling away layers of an onion. If that's correct, then yes, for cultural reasons, the move away from patriarchy is a step upwards, not just a change. It's a step toward understanding our true nature.

Q. You have suggested that "intellectuals are the most indoctrinated part of the population ... the ones most susceptible to propaganda." You have explained that the educated classes are "ideological managers," complicit in "controlling all the organized flow of information." How and why is this so? What can be done to change this situation?

A. Well, there's something almost tautological about that; that is, the people we call intellectuals are those who have passed through various gates and filters and have made it into positions in which they can serve as cultural managers. There are plenty of other people just as smart, smarter, more independent, more thoughtful, who didn't pass through those gates and we just don't call them intellectuals. In fact, this is a process that starts in elementary school. Let's be concrete about it. You and I went to good graduate schools and teach in fancy universities, and the reason we did this is because we're obedient. That is, you and I, and typically people like us, got to the positions we're in because from childhood we were willing to follow orders. If the teacher in third grade told us to do some stupid thing, we didn't say, "Look, that's ridiculous. I'm not going to do it." We did it because we wanted to get on to fourth grade. We came from the kind of background where we'd say, "Look, do it, forget about it, so the teacher's a fool, do it, you'll get ahead, don't worry about it." That goes on all through school, and it goes on through your professional career. You're told in graduate school, "Look, don't work on that; it's a wrong idea. Why not work on this? You'll get ahead." However it's put, and there are subtle ways of putting it, you allow yourself to be shaped by the system of authority that exists out there and is trying to shape you. Well, some people do this. They're submissive and obedient, and they accept it and make it through; they end up being people in the high places—economic managers, cultural managers, political managers. There are other people who were in your class and in my class who didn't do it. When the teacher told them in the third grade to do x, they said, "That's stupid, and I'm not going to do it." Those are people who are more independent minded, for example, and there's a name for them: they're called "behavior problems."

You've got to deal with them somehow, so you send them to a shrink, or you put them in a special program, or maybe you just kick them out and they end up selling drugs or something. In fact, the whole educational system involves a good deal of filtering of this sort, and it's a kind of filtering towards submissiveness and obedience.

This goes on through professional careers, as well. You're a journalist, let's say, and you want to write a story that's going to expose people in high places, and somebody else is going to write a story that serves the needs of people in high places; you know which one is going to end up being the bureau chief. That's the way it works. So in a way there's something almost tautological about your question. Sure, the people who make it into positions in which they're respected and recognized as intellectuals are the people who are not subversive of structures of power. They're the people who in one way or another serve those structures, or at least are neutral with respect to them. The ones who would be more subversive aren't called intellectuals; they're called wackos, or crazies, or "wild men in the wings," as McGeorge Bundy put it when he said, "There are people who understand that we have to be in Indochina and just differ on the tactics, and then there are the wild men in the wings who think there's something wrong with carrying out aggression against another country." (He said that in *Foreign Affairs*—a mainstream journal.) But that's the idea. There are wild men in the wings who don't accept authority, and they remain wild men in the wings and not intellectuals, not respected intellectuals. Of course, this isn't one-hundred percent. These are tendencies, actually very strong tendencies, and they're reinforced by other strong tendencies.

Another strong tendency has to do with the role of intellectuals. Why are you and I called intellectuals but some guy working in an automobile plant isn't an intellectual? I don't think it's necessarily because we read more or go to better concerts or anything like that. Maybe he does; in fact, I've known such cases. I grew up in such an environment. I grew up in an environment where my aunts and uncles were New York Jewish working class, and this was still the 1930s when there was a rich working-class culture. Lots of them had barely gone to school. I had one uncle who never got past fourth grade and an aunt who never graduated from school. But that was the richest intellectual environment I've ever seen. And I mean high culture, not comic book culture: Freud, Steckel, the Budapest String Quartet, and debates about anything you can imagine. But those people were never called intellectuals. They were called "unemployed workers" or something like that. Now why are they *not* intellectuals whereas a lot of people in the universities who are basically doing clerical work (from an intellectual point of view, a lot of scholarship is just very low-level clerical work) *are* respected intellectuals? First of all, it's a matter of subordination and power, and secondly it's a matter of which role you choose for yourself. The ones we call intellectuals, especially the public intellectuals—you know, the ones who make a splash or who are called upon to be the experts—are people who have *chosen* for themselves the role of manager. In earlier societies they would have been priests; in our societies they form a kind of secular priesthood.

In fact, in the nineteenth and twentieth centuries, intellectuals have rather typically taken one or another of two very similar paths. One is basically the Marxist/Leninist path, and that's very appealing for intellectuals because it provides them with the moral authority to control people. The essence of Marxism/Leninism is that there's a vanguard role and that's played by the radical intellectuals who whip the stupid masses forward into a future they're too dumb to understand for themselves. That's a very appealing idea for intellectuals. There's even a method: you achieve this position on the backs of people who are carrying out a popular struggle. So there's a popular struggle, you identify yourself as a leader, you take power, and then you lead the stupid masses forward. That basically captures the essence of Marxism/Leninism—a tremendous appeal to the intellectuals for obvious reasons, and that's why that's one major direction in which they've gone all over the world. There's another direction which is not all that different: a recognition that there's not going to be any popular revolution; there's a given system of power that's more or less going to stay, I'm going to serve it, I'm going to be the expert who helps the people with real power achieve their ends. That's the Henry Kissinger phenomenon or the state capitalist intellectual. Well, that's another role for the intellectuals. Actually, Kissinger put it rather nicely in one of his academic essays. He described an expert as "a person who knows how to articulate the consensus of his constituency." He didn't add the next point: "Your constituency is people with power." But that's tacit. Knowing how to articulate the consensus of unemployed workers or the homeless doesn't make you an expert. The point is that an expert is a person who knows how to articulate the consensus of the people of power, who can serve the role of manager.

Those two conceptions of the intellectual are very similar. In fact, I think it's a striking fact that people find it very easy to shift from one to the other. That's called "the god that failed phenomenon." You see there isn't going to be a popular revolution and you're not going to make it as the vanguard driving the masses forward, so you undergo this conversion and you become a servant of "state capitalism." Now, I won't say that everybody who underwent that was immoral. Some people really saw things they hadn't seen. But by now it's become a farce. You can see it happening: people perfectly consciously recognizing, "Well, there isn't going to be a revolution. If I want the power and prestige I'd better serve these guys. So I suddenly undergo this conversion, and I denounce my old comrades as unregenerate Stalinists." It's a farcical move which we should laugh at at this point. I think the ease of that transition in part reflects the fact that there isn't very much difference. There's a difference in the assessment of where power lies, but there's a kind of commonality of the conception of the intellectual's role. Now, my point is that the people we call intellectuals are people who have passed the filters, gone through the gates, picked up these roles for themselves, and decided to play them. Those are the people we call intellectuals. If you ask why intellectuals are submissive, the answer is they wouldn't be intellectuals otherwise. Again, this is not one-hundred percent, but it's a large part.

Q. You alluded to the media a minute ago. You have written repeatedly that the state and the media collaborate to support and sustain the interests and values of the establishment. Yet, we in the U.S. boast proudly of our "free press." Are our media victims of ideological indoctrination, or are they willing conspirators in suppressing truth?

A. I wouldn't exactly put it either way. They're not victims and they're not conspirators. Suppose, for example, you were to ask a similar question about, say, General Motors. General Motors tries to maximize profit on market share; are they victims of our system or are they conspirators in our system? Neither. They are *components of the system* which act in certain ways for well-understood institutional reasons. If they didn't act that way, they would not be in the game any longer. Let's take the media. The media have a particular institutional role. We have a free press, meaning it's not state controlled but corporate controlled; that's what we call freedom. What we call freedom is corporate control. We have a free press because it's corporate monopoly, or oligopoly, and that's called freedom. We have a free political system because there's one party run by business; there's a business party with two factions, so that's a free political system. The terms *freedom* and *democracy*, as used in our Orwellian political discourse, are based on the assumption that a particular form of domination—namely, by owners, by business elements—is freedom. If *they* run things, it's free, and the playing field's level. If they don't run things, the playing field isn't level and you've got to do something about it. So if popular organizations form or if labor unions are too important, you've got to level the playing field. If it's El Salvador, you send out the death squads; if it's at home you do something else, but you've got to level the playing field.

Coming back to the free press: yes, our press is free. It's fundamentally a narrow corporate structure, deeply interconnected with big conglomerates. Like other corporations, it has a product which it sells to the market, and the market is advertisers, other businesses. The product, especially for the elite press, the press that sets the agenda for others that follow, is privileged audiences. That's the way to sell things to advertisers. So you have an institutional structure of major corporations selling privileged elite audiences to other corporations; now it plays a certain institutional role: it presents the version of the world which reflects the interests and needs of the sellers and buyers. That's not terribly surprising, and there are a lot of other factors that push it in the same direction. Well, that's not a conspiracy, any more than G.M.'s making profit is a conspiracy. It's not that they're victims; they're part of the system. In fact, if any segment of the media, say the *New York Times*, began to deviate from that role, they'd simply go out of business. Why should the stockholders or the advertisers want to allow them to continue if they're not serving that role? Similarly, if some journalist from the *New York Times* decided to expose the truth, let's say started writing accurate and honest articles about the way power is being exercised, the editors would be crazy to allow that journalist to continue. That journalist is undermining authority and domination and getting people to think for themselves, and that's exactly a function you don't want the media to pursue. It's not that it's a conspiracy; it's just that the media's institutional structure gives them the same kind of purpose that the educational system has: to turn people into submissive, atomized individuals who don't interfere with the structures of power and authority but rather serve those structures. That's the way the system is set up and if you started deviating from that, those with real power, the institutions with real power, would interfere to prevent that deviation. Now that's the way institutions work, so it seems to me almost predictable that the media will serve the role of a kind of indoctrination.

Q. You have said that "propaganda is to democracy what violence is to the totalitarian state," which, of course, relates to what you are saying here.

A. And, in fact, there's a very intriguing line of thought in democratic theory that goes back certainly to the seventeenth-century English revolutions—sort of the first major modern democratic revolutions. There's been a recognition which becomes very explicit in the twentieth century, especially in the United States, that as the capacity to control people by force declines, you have to discover other means of control. Harold Lasswell, one of the founders of the modern area of communications in the political sciences, put it this way in the 1930s in an article on propaganda in the *International Encyclopedia of Social Sciences*: "We should not succumb to democratic dogmatism about men being the best judges of their own interests. They're not. We're the best judges." In a military state or what we would now call a totalitarian state, you can control people by force; in a democratic state you can't control them by force, so you'd better control them with propaganda—for their own good. Now this is a standard view; in fact, I suspect this is the dominant view among intellectuals.

Q. This, of course, relates to Walter Lippmann's concept of "the manufacture of consent," the idea that government distrusts the public's ability to make wise decisions and so it reserves real power for a "smart" elite who will make the "right decisions" and then create the illusion of public consensus.

A. Yes, but you really have to think considerably about the framework of thinking that that came from. Lippmann designed this notion of "manufacture of consent" as progress in the art of democracy, and he believed it was a good thing—and that's important. It's a good thing because, as he put it, "We have to protect ourselves from the rage and trampling of the bewildered herd." So there's this mass of people out there who are the bewildered herd, and if we just let them go free—if we allow things like democracy, for example—there's just going to be rage and trampling because they're all totally incapable. The only people who are capable of running anything are we smart guys—what he called "the specialized class." He didn't add—something, again, which is tacitly understood—that we make it to the specialized class if we serve people with real power. So it's not that we're smarter; it's that we're more submissive. And we, the specialized class, the servants of power, have to save ourselves and our prestige and power from the rage and trampling of the bewildered herd. For that you need manufacture of consent because you can't shoot people down in the streets; you can't control them by force. In that respect, indoctrination is to democracy what a bludgeon is to totalitarianism.

Q. In fact, it's even better, much more effective.

A. It's certainly much more important. In a totalitarian state, let's say the Soviet Union under Stalin's direction (that's about as close as you can come), it didn't matter too much what people believed. They could more or less believe what they liked. What mattered was what they *did*, and what they did you control by force or by threat. In fact, rather commonly fascist and totalitarian states have been reasonably open. In Franco's Spain, for example, a lot of people were reading more widely than they were here in many respects and debating much more, and it didn't matter that much because you've got them under control: you have a bludgeon over their heads; there's not much they can do. In the Soviet Union, for example, *samizdat* were very widely read. I read some studies of this which had astonishingly high figures of distribution of *samizdat*. The authorities could have stopped it, but they probably just didn't care that much: "So people have crazy ideas. Who cares? They're not going to do anything about it because we control them." Now, in a more free and more democratic society, it becomes very dangerous if people start thinking because if they start thinking they might start *doing*, and you don't have the police to control them. If they're blacks in downtown Boston, it's not a big problem: you *do* have the police to control them. But if they're relatively privileged, middle-class white folk like us, then you don't have the police to control them because they're too powerful to allow that to happen. They share in the privilege of the wealthy and therefore you can't control them by force so you've got to control what they think. Indoctrination is, therefore, a crucial element of preventing democracy in the form of democracy.

Q. Recently, you told Bill Moyers that you'd "like to see a society moving toward voluntary organization and eliminating as much as possible the structures of hierarchy and domination, and the basis for them in ownership and control." How can this be achieved? The system that you've been describing is quite entrenched.

A. Different societies have different forms of domination. Patriarchy is one, and in principle we know how to overcome that—it's not too easy to do, but we know in principle. But in our kinds of society, the major forms of domination, at least the core ones, are basically ownership. Private ownership of the means of production grants owners the ultimate authority over what's produced, what's distributed, what takes place in political life, what the range of cultural freedom is, and so on. They have decisive power because they control capital, and there's no reason why that should be vested in private hands. In my view, if you take the ideals of the eighteenth century seriously, you become very anti-capitalist. If you take the ideals of classical liberalism seriously, I think it leads to opposition to corporate capitalism. Classical liberalism—as developed, for example, by Humboldt—or much of Enlightenment thought was opposed to the church and the state and the feudal system, but for a reason: because those were the striking examples of centralized power. What it was really opposed to was centralized power that's not under popular control. Nineteenth-century corporations are another form of centralized power completely out of public control, and by the same reasoning we should be opposed to them. If you take classical liberal thought and apply it rationally to more recent conditions, you become a libertarian socialist and a kind of a left-wing anarchist. I don't mean *anarchist* in the American sense where it means right-wing capitalist, but *anarchist* in the traditional sense, meaning a socialist who's opposed to state power and in favor of voluntary association to the extent that social conditions permit and who regards the role of an honest person as one of constant struggle forever, as long as human history goes on, against any forms of authority and domination, maybe many that we don't even see now and will only discover later.

Q. What society do you think comes closest to achieving anything like this kind of voluntary association? Do you think any society even comes close?

A. Well, sure, every society has aspects of it and they differ. Sometimes you find things in very poor, backward, undeveloped societies that you don't find in advanced societies. In many ways the United States is like this. There are very positive things in the United States. In many respects, the United States is the freest country in the world. I don't just mean in terms of limits on state coercion, though that's true too, but also just in terms of individual relations. The United States comes closer to classlessness in terms of interpersonal relations than virtually any society. I'm always struck by the fact when traveling elsewhere, let's say to England, that the forms of deference and authority that people assume automatically are generally unknown here. For example, here there's no problem with a university professor and a garage mechanic talking together informally as complete equals. But that is not true in England. That's a very positive thing about the United States. Intellectuals in the United States are always deploring the fact that intellectuals here aren't taken seriously the way they're taken seriously in Europe. That's one of the *good* things about the United States. There's absolutely no reason to take them seriously for the most part. I remember in the 1960s, sometimes I would sign an international statement against the war in Vietnam—signed by me here, Sartre and some other person in Europe, and so on. Well, in Paris there'd be big front-page headlines; here nobody paid any attention at all, which was the only healthy reaction. Okay, so three guys signed a statement; who cares? The statement signed by 120 intellectuals in the time of the Algerian War was a major event in Paris. If a similar thing happened here, it wouldn't even make the newspapers—correctly.

All that reflects a kind of internalized democratic understanding and freedom that's extremely important. One shouldn't underestimate it. I think that it's one of the reasons why we have the Pentagon system. Compare the United States, say, with Japan. How come we had to turn to the Pentagon system as a way to force the public to subsidize high-technology industry, whereas Japan didn't? They just get the public to subsidize high-technology industry directly, through reduction of consumption, fiscal measures, and so on. That makes them a lot more efficient than we are. If you want to build the next generation of, say, computers, the Japanese just say, "Okay, we're going to lower consumption levels, put this much into investment, and build computers." If you want to do it in the United States, you say, "Well, we're going to build some lunatic system to stop Soviet missiles, and for that you're going to have to lower your consumption level and maybe, somehow, we'll get computers out of that." Obviously, the Japanese system is more much efficient. So why don't *we* adopt the more efficient system? The reason is that we're a freer society; we can't do it here. In a society that's more fascist than state capitalist, and I mean that culturally as well as in terms of economic institutions, you can just tell people what they're going to do and they do it. Here you can't do that. No politician in the United States can get up and say, "You guys are going to lower your standard of living next year so that IBM can make more profit, and that's the way it's going to work." That's not going to sell. Here you have to fool people into it by fear and so on. We need all kinds of complicated mechanisms of propaganda and coercion which in a well-run, more fascistic society are quite unnecessary. You just give orders. That's one of the reasons fascism is so efficient.

Q. You've even expressed fear that the U.S. is ripe for a fascist leader. You write, "In a depoliticized society with few mechanisms for people to express their fears and needs and to participate constructively in managing the affairs of life, someone could come along who was interested not in personal gain, but power. That could be very dangerous." Is this statement rhetorical, or cautionary, or do you have serious fears that the U.S. can fall victim to a charismatic, fascist dictator?

A. It's real. I mentioned something very good about the United States, but there are also a number of things that are very bad. One is the breakdown of independent social organization and independent thought, the atomization of people. As we move towards a society which is optimal from the point of view of the business classes—namely, that each individual is an atom, lacking means to communicate with others so that he or she can't develop independent thought or action and is just a consumer, not a producer—people become deeply alienated, and they may hate what's going on but have no way to express that hatred constructively. And if a charismatic leader comes along, they may very well follow. I think the United States is very lucky that that hasn't happened. I think that's one of the reasons why I'm very much in favor of corruption. I think that's one of the best things there is. You'll notice that in my books I never criticize corruption. I think it's a wonderful thing. I'd much rather have a corrupt leader than a power-hungry leader. A corrupt leader is going to rob people but not cause that much trouble. For example, as long as the fundamentalist preachers—like Jim Bakker, or whatever his name is—are interested in Cadillacs, sex, and that kind of thing, they're not a big problem. But suppose one of them comes along who's a Hitler and who doesn't care much about sex and Cadillacs, who just wants power. Then we're going to be in real trouble. The more corrupt these guys are, the better off we are. I think we all ought to applaud corruption. In fact, that's true in authoritarian societies too. The more corrupt they are, the better off the people usually are because power hunger is much more dangerous than money hunger. But I think the United States *is* ripe for a fascist leader. It's a very good thing that everyone who's come along so far is impossible: Joe McCarthy, for example, was too much of a thug; Richard Nixon was too much of a crook; Ronald Reagan was too much of a clown; the fundamentalist preachers are ultimately too corrupt. In fact, we've escaped, but it's by luck. If a Hitler comes along, I think we might be in serious trouble.

Q. Your political views have been called "radical," while your notions of language have been termed "conservative." Jay Parini writes, "Some colleagues take Chomsky to task for ignoring the social realities of language and, therefore, defining it too narrowly. Chomsky's work, for example, isn't concerned with showing how language is used in everyday situations to sustain inequities between men and women." Is this a fair assessment? How do you reconcile these two seemingly contradictory perspectives?

A. There's something to that, but let me tell you what my own choices and priorities are. Like any human being, I'm interested in a lot of things. There are things I find intellectually interesting and there are other things

I find humanly significant, and those two sets have very little overlap. Maybe the world could be different, but the fact is that that's the way the world actually is. The intellectually interesting, challenging, and exciting topics, in general, are close to disjoint from the humanly significant topics. If I have x hours a day, I, like any other person, am going to distribute them somehow. I'm not saying I spend every waking moment trying to help other people: I eat, take a walk, read a book, work on problems that excite me, and so on. I do these things just for myself because I like them. I also spend a part of my time, and in fact quite a large part, doing things that I think are humanly significant. Now, I'm going to make this much too mechanical to make a point, but suppose I say, "Okay, now it's my hour for doing something humanly significant and I have two choices: one is to study the way in which language is used to facilitate authority, and the other is to do something to help Salvadoran peasants who are getting slaughtered." Well, I'm going to do the second because that's overwhelmingly more significant than the first, by huge orders of magnitude. That's why I don't spend time on things like the use of language to impose authority. Doubtless it's true, but it's a topic that's not intellectually interesting; it has no intellectual depth to it at all, like most things in the social sciences. Also, it's of marginal human significance as compared with other problems. Therefore, I don't think it's a reasonable distribution of my own priorities.

There are people who think differently, and I think they are making a very poor moral judgment. If people want to study, say, social use of language because they find it interesting, fine; that's on a par with my reading a book. There's no moral issue involved. Similarly, I find technical problems about language structure or Plato's problem interesting, so I study them. On the other hand, if people claim they are doing that out of some moral imperative, they're making a severe error because in terms of moral imperatives that's a much lower order than others. People often argue, and I think this is a real fallacy, "Look, I'm a linguist; therefore, in my time as a linguist I have to be socially useful." That doesn't make sense at all. You're a *human being*, and your time as a *human being* should be socially useful. It doesn't mean that your choices about helping other people have to be within the context of your professional training as a linguist. Maybe that training just doesn't help you to be useful to other people. In fact, it doesn't.

I have a feeling there's a lot of careerism in this. For example, if I spend all my time working as a linguist and some fraction of it is on things of marginal social utility, I can say, "Look how moral I am," and at the same time be advancing my career. On the other hand, if I take that segment of my life and use it for going to last week's demonstration in Washington about the Romero assassination, I'm not advancing my career at all, though I may be helping people more. You have to be careful not to fall into that trap. So if people want to work on these problems—and I think they're perfectly valid problems—they simply have to ask themselves why they're doing it. Are they doing it because that's the way to help other human beings? If so, I think they're making a poor judgment. If they're doing it because that's what they're interested in, well fine, I've no objection. People have a right to do things they're interested in.

Q. Your discussions of creativity were influential, even inspirational, to those who developed sentence combining as a way of teaching writing. We know one teacher who began each writing course by asking students to combine four or five short sentences into one. Of course, the number of possible solutions is large, and students were always impressed that nearly all of their sentences were different. Nonetheless, anyone who has taught writing at any level can attest that many students fall into predictable patterns of language use. Do you think creativity in language can be fostered so that more of a student's innate potential is used?

A. I'm sure it can be fostered. Creative reading, for example, surely is a way of fostering it; getting people to wrestle with complex ideas and to find ways of expressing them ought to be at the heart of the writing program. Frankly, I doubt very much that linguistics has anything to contribute to this. Perhaps it can suggest some things, but I don't suspect it can really be applied. My own feeling is that teaching is mostly common sense. I taught children when I was a college student. I worked my way through college in part by teaching Hebrew school. I've taught graduate students across the range, and just from my own experience or anything I've read, it seems to me that ninety-nine percent of good teaching is getting people interested in the task or problem and providing them with a rich enough environment in which they can begin to pursue what they find interesting in a constructive way. I don't know of any methods for doing that other than being interested in it yourself, being interested in the people you are teaching, and learning from the experience yourself. In that kind of environment, something good happens, and I suppose that's true with writing as much as auto mechanics. I often quote a famous statement from one of MIT's great physicists, Victor Weisskopf, but it's a standard comment. He was often asked by students, "What are we going to cover this semester?" His standard answer was supposed to have been, "It doesn't matter what we cover; it matters what we *dis*cover." That's basically it: that's good teaching. It doesn't matter what you cover; it matters how much you develop the capacity to discover. You do *that* and you're in good shape.

Q. In *College English* in 1967, you wrote that "a concern for the literary standard language—prescriptivism in its more sensible manifestations—is as legitimate as an interest in colloquial speech." Do you still believe that a sensible prescriptivism is preferable to linguistic permissiveness? If so, how would you define a sensible prescriptivism?

A. I think sensible prescriptivism ought to be part of any education. I would certainly think that students ought to know the standard literary language with all its conventions, its absurdities, its artificial conventions, and so on because that's a real cultural system, and an important cultural system. They should certainly know it and be inside it and be able to use it freely. I don't think people should give them any illusions about what it is. It's not *better*, or more sensible. Much of it is a violation of natural law. In fact, a good deal of what's taught is taught because it's *wrong*. You don't have to teach people their native language because it grows in their minds, but if you want people to say, "He and I were here" and not "Him and me were here," then you have to teach them because it's probably wrong. The nature of English probably is the other way, "Him and me were here," because the so-called nominative form is typically used only as the subject of the tense sentence; grammarians who misunderstood this fact then assumed that it ought to be, "He and I were here," but they're wrong. It should be "Him and me were here," by that rule. So they teach it because it's not natural. Or if you want to teach the so-called proper use of *shall* and *will*—and I think it's totally wild—you have to *teach* it because it doesn't make any sense. On the other hand, if you want to teach people how to make passives you just confuse them because they already know, because they already follow these rules. So a good deal of what's taught in the standard language is just a history of artificialities, and they have to be taught because they're artificial. But that doesn't mean that people shouldn't know them. They should know them because they're part of the cultural community in which they play a role and in which they are part of a repository of a very rich cultural heritage. So, of course, you've got to know them.

Q. The standard literary language, what's called "standard English," is an object of great controversy in some parts of the Third World now. For example, there's a debate in India over whether people should still be taught the colonial language to give them greater access to technology or whether there should be just a few people who are very active translators into the local languages. What's your sense of the desirability of the spread of world English? First of all, do you think that it is continuing to spread now that American economic hegemony has been broken? Also, is it desirable that it spread?

A. I've never seen a real study, but my strong impression is that it's continuing to spread and that U.S. cultural hegemony is growing even while U.S. economic hegemony is declining. Take the relations between the United States and Europe. Europe is becoming relatively more powerful economically and will soon be absolutely more powerful. On the other hand, my strong impression is that it's much more culturally colonized by the United States in terms of ways of thinking, the sources of news, and so on. This is not an unusual phenomenon. Look at the relations between

England and the United States, say, around 1950. England was declining as a power sharply relative to the United States, but that was combined with a high degree of Anglophilia and often a rather childish imitation of British cultural styles and modes on the part of the intellectual classes here. These things aren't necessarily parallel, but my strong impression is that the hegemony of U.S. English and U.S. culture in general is extending in everything from the sciences to pop music.

Now, what should they do in places like India? Well, that's a hard problem. It's like what should you do with Black English? I don't think there are simple answers to that. There are good reasons to preserve and develop national languages and national cultures because they enrich human life for the participants and for others. On the other hand, the people who are in them may suffer. For example, if people in Wales learn Welsh, the way the world is they're going to be worse off in many respects than if they had learned English. You might want the world to be some other way, but this is the way it is. The same kinds of questions arise in the case of Black English and in the case of teaching English as a second language in India. How you balance those values is tricky, and I don't think there's any general answer to it. I think there are particular answers in particular places. In the case of India, the answer being pursued is that people ought to learn English, and I think that's probably reasonable.

Q. In 1979, you gave a series of lectures in Pisa which were later published and which many linguists think introduced the most important development of the 1980s: the principles and parameters approach. Yet, unlike your earlier work in the aspects phase, it's not known outside of linguistics, and it hasn't had the same impact. Do you think people outside of linguistics should know about the principles and parameters approach?

A. I think it's more important than the aspects-type approach. In fact, if anything deserves to be called a revolution, that's probably it. It leads to a conception of language which is, in fact, radically different from anything in the historical tradition. Early transformational grammar, early generative grammar, say in the 1950s and 1960s, had a kind of a traditional feel to it. In many ways, it was more acceptable to traditional grammarians than to structural linguists because in a lot of ways it had a traditional look. It was more like Jespersen than it was like Bloomfield, for example, and traditional grammarians recognized that. They may not have understood the details or liked the way it was being done, but they could kind of see the point. For example, there were particular rules for particular constructions, and just as a traditional grammar had a chapter on the passive or on the imperative and so on, the early generative grammars were like that in structure: there was a passive rule and a question rule and a chapter on what verb phrases look like, and so on. The post-1980s theories are radically different. There are no constructions; there are no rules. Things like traditional constructions, say relative clauses, are just taxonomic artifacts. They're like "large mammal." A large mammal is a real thing, but it has no meaning in the sciences. It's just something that results from a lot of different things interacting. The same seems to be true of the passive: it's not a real thing; it's just a taxonomic phenomenon. So there's no meaning to the question, "Is Japanese passive the same as English passive?" Furthermore, there don't seem to be any rules—that is, language-specific rules. In fact, you can speculate without being thought absurd that there may be only one computational system and in that sense only one language. The variety of languages may be a matter of a number of lexical options, where those lexical options probably leave out a large part of the substantive vocabulary, meaning nouns and verbs and so on. So it looks as if the variety of languages is very narrowly circumscribed and the apparent radical difference among languages derives from the fact that in quite complicated systems, if you make small changes here and there, the output may look very different at the end, even though they're basically the same. That's all work of the 1980s, and I think if it's right it's very rich in its implications. I don't think it's going to be so easily assimilated elsewhere because you have to understand it. In the work of the 1960s, you could have a rough feel for what it was like and misunderstand it but apply it nonetheless. And a lot of the apparent impact of this linguistics was kind of casual misunderstanding of things that look more or less familiar; this new work is quite different. You have to understand what it's about and that means some work.

Q. What would you suggest people read—people who are out of the field who want to understand this new approach?

A. Well, there are some pretty good relatively introductory books. It depends on what level they want to understand it. I've tried myself. I have a book called *Language and Problems of Knowledge* which is a collection of lectures given in Managua to a public audience of non-linguists. This was just a general audience and they seemed to find it intelligible, and other people have told me they find it intelligible. At a somewhat more technical level, there's a book by Howard Lasnik and a student of his, Juan Uriagereka, called *A Course in GB Syntax: Lectures on Binding and Empty Categories*, which is actually first-year graduate lectures from the University of Connecticut. Now those are very lucid and carry it much further into the technical intricacies. But for the general points, at least as I understand them, I'd recommend the first book.

Q. What readership did you target in your 1986 book, *Knowledge of Language*?

A. That's a funny sort of book. One chapter is pretty technical linguistics; one chapter is about thought control; the rest is sort of philosophy of language. I had an original idea for that book, but it just turned out to be too encyclopedic to carry off; it's sort of described in the Preface. It was going to be about two problems in the theory of knowledge: Plato's problem, or how we know so much given so little evidence; and Orwell's problem, or how we know so little given so much evidence. I still think that would be a nice book to write. It went too far.

Q. Well, you did sketch out Orwell's problem in the last chapter. What's your sense of the treatment of your work in popularizations such as Neil Smith's *The Twitter Machine*?

A. That's a very good book. I think he knows what he's doing; he's very sophisticated. I don't agree with him on everything, but I think it's an intelligent presentation not just on my work but on lots of things in the field, including lots of interesting work done on relevance theory and pragmatics and so on.

Q. Well, he does deal quite extensively with your work.

A. That's a mistake people make: they call it "mine" because I sometimes write about it. Take the Pisa lectures. They weren't "mine." They were the result of years of very interesting work. There's a reason why they were given in Pisa: a lot of the best work was being done by Italian and European linguists. So I happened to give some summer lectures there. These things don't have individual names attached to them.

Q. Earlier in the interview you raised the issue of semantics and your interest in it, but you've also consistently reiterated over your career, most recently in *The Generative Enterprise*, that linguists' chief concern should not be semantics. We were surprised to hear that you're now teaching a course in semantics.

A. It's not surprising. Part of this is terminological. In my view, most of what's called semantics is syntax. I just *call* it syntax; other people call the same thing semantics. *Syntactic Structures*, in my view, is pure syntax, but the questions dealt with there are what other people call semantics. I was interested in the question, "Why does 'John is easy to please' have a different meaning from 'John is eager to please'?" I wanted to find a theory of language structure that would explain that fact. Most people call that semantics; I call it syntax because I think it has to do with mental representations. Take a point we discussed earlier: the word *house*, the concept "house," and the use of the word *house* in real situations to refer to things. There are two relations there, and I don't think you can turn them into one as is commonly done. The common idea is that there's one relation, the relation of reference, and I don't believe that. I think there's a relation that holds between the word *house* and a very rich concept that doesn't only hold of *house* but of all sorts of other things. That relation most people would call semantics. I call it syntax because it has to do with mental representations and the structure of mental representations. Then there's the relationship between that rich semantic representation and things in the world, like some place I'm going tonight after class. Now *that* relationship is what is *real* semantics, and about that there is almost nothing to say. That's the part that's subject to holism and interest relativity and values and so on; and you can sort of assemble Wittgensteinian particulars about it, but there doesn't seem to be anything general to say. Where I depart from Wittgenstein is that I think there is something very general and definite to say about the relation between words and concepts. I call that syntax because it has to do with mental representations, things inside the skin, rules and computations and representations and so on, going all the way into intrinsic semantic properties, analytic/synthetic distinctions, and most problems of the theory of meaning that can be dealt with.

Now, there are plenty of people who call their work semantics who in my view are not dealing with semantics at all. Take "all possible world semantics." In my view, that's just straight syntax. It's either right or wrong (and I think it's right), but if it's right, it's right in the sense in which some other theory of phonology is right. It's a form of syntax. Problems of semantics will arise when you begin to tell me how a possible world relates to things, and the people who work with this topic don't deal with it. When you start dealing with the relation of mental constructions to the world, you discover that there's very little to say other than Wittgensteinian-type questions about ways of life. At that level, I think he's basically right; you can discuss ways of life. So this is largely illusion. I do think that syntax and semantics should deal with what I call syntax, mostly, because that's where the richness in the field is.

Q. In your famous review in 1959 of Skinner's verbal behaviorist psychology, you argued convincingly that terms such as *reinforcement*, which have well-defined meanings in experiments using rats, become meaningless when extended to the complexity of human behavior. Many of *your* terms have also been metaphorically extended. Can you think of any instances in which metaphorical extensions of a concept like "deep structure" might be justified, or should such extensions always be avoided?

A. I think you've got to be careful. In the case of "deep structure," I simply stopped using the term because it was being so widely misunderstood. "Deep structure" was a technical term. It didn't have any sense of "profundity," but it was understood to mean "profound," or "far-reaching," or something like that. It might turn out that what I call "surface structure" is much more profound in its implications. Most invariably in the secondary literature, "deep structure" has been confused with what I would call "universal grammar." So "deep structure" is identified as kind of the innate structure, and that's not correct. The term was so widely misunderstood that I decided—I think it was in *Knowledge of Language*—to drop the word and just make it an obvious technical term so nobody would be confused; nowadays I just refer to it as "D" structure. I figure that's not going to confuse anybody. It looks technical and it is technical.

It's very rare that you ever get a free ride from some other field. People who think they're talking about "free will" because they mention Heisenberg usually don't know what's going on. Or people who say, "Well, people aren't computers. Remember Gödel." That's too easy. Life isn't that easy. You'd better understand it before you start drawing conclusions from it. Sometimes people who do understand what they're talking about can make plausible suggestions or even inferences or guesses from outside the field. That's not impossible, but first you've got to understand what you're talking about. These topics are not like political science. I mean they're not just there on the surface; there's some intellectual structure and some degree of intellectual depth. It's not quantum physics either, so I think any person who's interested can figure it out without too much trouble. But you've *got* to take the trouble. I've been appalled by what I've read on how "deep structure" is used.

Q. Some of your work both in linguistics and in political analysis has generated considerable controversy. Are you aware of any specific misunderstanding or criticism of your work that you'd like to take issue with at this time?

A. We could go on forever. On the linguistics side, there's plenty of misunderstanding but I think it's resolvable. I'm enough of a believer in the rational side of human beings to think that if you sit down and talk these questions through and you think them through you can reach a resolution. On the political side, I don't think it's resolvable because I think there's a deep functional need *not* to understand. The problem is that if what I'm saying is correct, then it's also subversive and, therefore, it'd better not be understood. Let me put it this way: if I found that I did have easy access to systems of power like journals and television, then I'd begin to be worried. I'd think I'm doing something wrong because I ought to be trying to subvert those systems of power, and if I am doing it and I'm doing it honestly, they shouldn't want to have me around. In those areas, misunderstanding (if you want to call it that) is almost an indication that you may well be on the right track. It's not proof that you're on the right track, but it's an indication you may be. If you're understood and appreciated, it's almost proof that you're not on the right track.

Response to "Language, Politics, and Composition: A Conversation with Noam Chomsky"

JAMES SLEDD

It's with considerable trepidation that an inveterate doer of low-level clerical work responds to the conversation of two eminent compositionists with Professor Noam Chomsky, especially because this lowly clerk is tempted to pick a bone or two with both Chomsky and the compositionists; but perhaps the fear-of-giving-oneself-away disease is even less creditable than ambition beyond one's station.

There's not much point in bothering with the smaller bones. The compositionists did ask some enormous, conversation-stopping questions ("For you, what are the most important elements of rhetoric?"), and sometimes they were imperceptive, as when they asked whether "our media" are victims or conspirators. Generally, though, they prompted good talk without getting in Chomsky's way. Once or twice, however, they asked questions which invited, and got, inadequate answers.

Who can say, for example, whether or not the United States is experiencing a "literacy crisis"? The term *crisis* suggests a dangerous deterioration from an earlier, better state; but data and definitions adequate to establish such deterioration are simply lacking. Chomsky says what anyone might have said at any time for some centuries past—namely, that "there's a big degree of illiteracy and functional illiteracy"; however, he then launches into "looks as if" and "seems" and goes anecdotal about colleagues (disgruntled readers of *Z Magazine*?) who complain that "the articles are too long." Though his remarks on the media's demand for "concision" are enlightening, the discussion would have been more useful if it had examined the way in which corporate executives have used the cry of crisis to extend their control of the educational system.

An even unhappier question appears to have been deliberately loaded: "Do you still believe that a sensible prescriptivism is preferable to linguistic permissiveness?" *Permissiveness* is about as useful a term in argument as *you son of a bitch*, for everybody tolerates some things that others don't. Real questions are what time is available for any subject in a crowded curriculum, and what prescriptions can and should be applied in the allotted time, for what reasons, by what methods, and with what policies toward non-learners. To those questions, as Chomsky said of the use of English in India, there are no simple answers; yet the foolish antithesis of "sensible prescriptivism" to "permissiveness" prompted a reply which is simplicity itself—and devastating simplicity at that. Students, Chomsky replied, "ought to know the standard literary language with all its conventions [and] absurdities"—should "know it and be inside it and be able to use it freely," because the standard language is "a real cultural system," an important part of "a very rich cultural heritage."

Citing that answer, resolute grammaticasters will feel justified in continuing to teach *They thought him to be me* but *He was thought to be I*—and with what results on the shores of Roxbury Pond? As Chomsky himself says in response to another question, much teaching ends in real or feigned submissiveness (far worse than imagined permissiveness) and in unfeigned contempt for foolish teachers. Independent-minded students, however, don't learn absurd and unnatural conventions just to keep teachers off their backs, especially not if they understand that the absurdities are essential to the functioning of the standard language as a class-marking barrier; and the appeal to a "rich cultural heritage" won't persuade them. Slavery was once a part of a genuinely rich inherited culture in the southern states, and patriarchy is not dead even in the enlightened north. Some parts of one's cultural heritage must be critically considered.

Two of Chomsky's answers will leave some readers wishing that the interviewers and the interview-situation had prompted and allowed a fuller development of oppositions which he invokes. In one instance, Chomsky opposes police control to thought-control. Of "middle-class white folk" he says, "If they start thinking they might start *doing*.... They share in the privileges of the wealthy and therefore you can't control them by force so you've got to control what they think." That conclusion is too optimistic, and it's too flattering to a stodgy middle class. As one can gather from Chomsky's remarks elsewhere in the interview, the powerful have many ways of preventing action besides police power. One notable way has very recently been exemplified: since one party under two names controls elections, voters can't act on the common conviction that both the Democratic and the Republican candidates are unworthy (otherwise, NOTA would be governor of both Texas and Massachusetts). Again, control of capital means control of jobs, and the fear of joblessness is a great preventive of subversive activity, just as administrative control of raises, promotions, and other goodies keeps radical academics from doing anything much except endlessly talking. Though force may be the last resort of threatened rulers, they are stupid if they let themselves be driven to use it. Control of other institutions than the police can keep the most convinced rebel from actively rebelling until the time comes when rebellion hurts less than continued submission.

The second opposition that some readers may wish to hear more of is that between the "intellectually interesting" and the "humanly significant," which Chomsky says have little overlap: "The intellectually interesting, challenging, and exciting topics, in general, are close to disjoint from the humanly significant topics." That opposition would seem to make single-minded intellectuals humanly insignificant, no matter how great their genius. Few readers will suspect Chomsky of holding so strange an opinion, but fuller exposition is needed to prevent another of the misunderstandings of which he justly complains.

Still, when all bones, real or imagined, have been picked, it must be acknowledged that Chomsky gave his usual distinguished performance. Even imperceptive questions produced powerful answers. For example, when Chomsky denied that he had any theory of rhetoric and alleged that he tried "to refrain from efforts to bring people to reach [his] conclusions," the question came back, "Is that because you might lose credibility or lose the audience?" Chomsky's answer, "Not at all," led him through a characterization of good teaching to the assertion that "the best rhetoric is the least rhetoric." Repeatedly, the interviewers peppered him in this way with ideas popular (or faddish) among compositionists, and the result was an exhilarating kind of demolition derby. Thus, an interviewer risked the challenging assertion, "If your colleagues and followers had not accepted and then helped champion [your] cause [in *Syntactic Structures*], you would simply be a kook out in the wilderness with some crazy idea." That defense of servile conformity, akin to the common stupidity that knowledge is constructed when successful rhetoric breeds consensus, prompted a salutary disquisition on "rational inquiry" and "rational understanding of the nature of argument and evidence." Chomsky added, "I think these things are essentially fixed."

For compositionists in particular and the English professoriate in general, the interview may be read as having two special values: in it, a man of huge intelligence and undeniable nobility of character offers a reasoned alternative to some current fashions in the composition industry and suggests limitations on the powers which intellectuals, and especially teachers, sometimes too eagerly claim. A reader's sensitivity in these matters may be heightened by perusing the 1990 *Program* of the MLA, where a great pomp of buzzwords betrays a foolishness that appears even in minute details (of the first 200 titles of papers, 108 included a medial colon, too often separating an unintelligibility from its supposed explanation).

No fashion among compositionists is more irritating than loose talk about the "new paradigm" and the "revolution" in the teaching of writing. What some compositionists call their new paradigm is only an ill-defined conglomerate of practice and belief, not a coherent set of interdependent propositions susceptible of precise statement, and certainly not remotely comparable to "the seventeenth-century revolution" which Chomsky briefly characterizes as "a very sharp shift . . . from a kind of natural history perspective to a natural science perspective." No such fundamental change has taken place among compositionists, who in fact are engaged in a practical activity where the wisdom of long and sensitive experience ("lore") is more valuable than wildly over-ambitious attempts to state "laws" that explain and even predict "the ways in which people do, teach, and learn writing" (Stephen North).

We comp teachers, in fact, because we have petty authority over a captive audience of younger victims, are constantly tempted to inflated estimates of our own importance. We like to think of ourselves as modern intellectuals, superior to benighted predecessors; we pick up odds and ends from other fields (too often, as Chomsky says, without real understanding) and toss them about to show that our work is "interdisciplinary"; and we claim to do far more than in fact we can for students, who commonly are brighter than we are. For these weaknesses, however painful they may be to confess, Chomsky's remarks on the making of intellectuals and on the nature of good teaching are excellent correctives.

Most of all, we may thank the *JAC* interviewers for mediating the most important of all educational experiences: the acquaintance with greatness. Optimists may dream that that acquaintance might inspire the boss compositionists to undertake a *real* revolution in the teaching of their subject: an end to the systemic exploitation of graduate students and contingent workers, the principal teachers of writing in U.S. colleges and universities.

University of Texas
Austin, Texas

Language and the Facilitation of Authority: The Discourse of Noam Chomsky

ROBERT DE BEAUGRANDE

In his revealing interview with *JAC*, Noam Chomsky declares it a "real fallacy" if a linguist tries to be "socially useful"; there's "a lot of careerism in this," and it shows "very poor moral judgment." Moreover, "studying the way in which language is used to facilitate authority" is not "intellectually interesting" and is of "marginal human significance." These standards make him and his followers the most "moral" linguists we've had and their work the most "intellectual" and "significant," but they do not explain their skyrocketing careers.

Still, Chomsky's own discourse in the interview is such a striking use of language to facilitate authority that it cries out for study. I propose to apply discourse analysis to Chomsky's interview—a method he might call immoral and insignificant but whose results, I hope to show, can be fairly interesting. Rather than assigning structural descriptions to invented John-and-Mary sentences (as proper language scientists ought to do), the analyst works to uncover the key moves in actual discourse and to relate them to the fabric of legitimizing ideologies and interests and to their inherent tensions, conflicts, and contradictions, often designed to disguise privileges and inequalities as the "natural order" or "the way the world is."

Idealism and Radical Dualism

The two dominant and conflicting ideologies here are idealism and scientism. From Plato down to Chomsky, idealism has professed to exalt knowledge (under such labels as "ideas" and "truth") for its abstractness, generality, and permanence, and to devalue experience for its concreteness, specificity, and mutability. The high-minded and disinterested qualities of this campaign have at times disguised more expedient motives: to market as genuine insights wishful thinking about the human mind, to legitimize the construction of theses by magisterial speculation, to save the labors of empirical demonstration, and to disqualify opponents as small-minded theorizers about the accidental, the trivial, and the idiosyncratic. These motives constitute the authoritarian and partisan underside of idealism, the implicit rhetoric of its explicit logic, and the pressure points where its discourse shows stress and fissures. Rationalism and rationalization are not just etymologically related.

By setting such contrary values, idealism encourages a radical dualism between knowledge and experience. The seventeenth-century rationalists hoped to submerge the dualism and annex scientism to its framework of authority by using empiricism itself to justify their anti-empiricist position. In his "Notes against a Certain Programme" of 1647, which Chomsky invokes in *Aspects of the Theory of Syntax*, Descartes says, "Nothing reaches our mind from external objects through the organs of sense beyond certain corporeal movements, but even these" are not "conceived by us in the shape they assume in those organs of sense; hence, it follows that the ideas" are "innate in us" (*Aspects* 48). This argument, which Chomsky accepted without reservation,[1] is echoed in the "Port-Royal *Logic*" of 1662: no idea "in our minds has taken its rise from sense," because *ideas* have "rarely any resemblance to what takes place in the sense and in the brain," and "some have no connection with any bodily image" (*Aspects* 49). In modern terms, by denying that sensory impressions give rise to abstractions unconnected to mental imagery, the argument hinged crucially on an unduly strict empiricist thesis—namely, that left to itself the brain could only process sensory information in analog terms, for example, by making a mental replica of the object being perceived (hence "resemblance" through "shape"). Thus, the rationalist refutation would hold only if the very empiricism it attacked were true in the most literal sense. The claim that ideas are innate was made plausible by denying the capacity of the mind to process sensory information abstractly; yet, that very capacity is what the "innate ideas" were supposed to explain. Empiricism was further raided by endowing these "ideas" with a quasi-biological status: "Ideas are innate in the sense that in some families," says Descartes, "diseases like gout or gravel" are innate (qtd. in *Aspects* 49).

A favorite domain of these "ideas" has naturally been mathematics. Chomsky calls on Leibniz to testify: the senses give us only "examples, i.e. particular or individual truths," whereas "the truths of numbers," that is, "all arithmetic and geometry, are in us virtually" to "set in order what we already have in the mind" (*Aspects* 50). Leibniz too made the leap to biology: "Necessary truths must have principles whose proof does not depend on examples nor consequently" on the senses and which "form the soul" of our thoughts, "as necessary thereto as the muscles and sinews are for walking" (50).

These moves, whereby idealism explicitly claimed to refute empiricism while implicitly presupposing its validity, return in Chomsky's own proceedings. His most intricate and controversial theorizing is often devoted to papering over the rationalist dualism between knowledge and experience with the tried but not very true argument: (1) the world reaches the mind through sensory analogs of stimulating movements and objects; (2) human knowledge is too organized and complex to have been generated this way; (3) ergo, the organization of knowledge is run by innate ideas and biological determinism.

Chomsky's ancestry is complicated because he wants to sever rationalism altogether from its seventeenth-century ties to theology, theodicy, and theocracy and to found it solely on natural science. His theorizing is thus more acutely entrained in the contradiction of invoking natural science to support rationalist idealizations about language and mind while shielding them against real or potential scientific counterevidence. Since such evidence is highly likely to come from the social sciences, he makes them the object of his most categorical attacks and dismissals. Like his ancestors, he appeals instead to less threatening sciences: mathematics, which is relatively free of empirical content, and biology, whose empirical findings are reassuringly remote from his own mentalism. The indirectness of biological evidence allows him optimal latitude for deciding which linguistic theses it can be claimed to support.

Change and the Role of the Intellectual

Chomsky's theorizing puts him in a peculiar position regarding the traditional role of the intellectual. In the seventeenth and eighteenth centuries, the role required two steps: discovering the "natural order" and then measuring up the prevailing order against it. The means and arguments for discovering the natural order were relatively rich and diverse: mathematics, logic, natural science (especially physics and astronomy, which were in the process of merging), and theology—plus a palette of philosophies grouped mainly around rationalism, empiricism, and enlightenment. And the principles were comfortably abstract, general, and flattering: human virtue, true moral nature, divine providence, and so on. The means for discovering the prevailing order, however, were relatively sparse and undifferentiated, since even empiricism relied at that time on speculation when human phenomena rather than, say, physics or astronomy were involved. And the human phenomena were uncomfortably concrete, specific, and unflattering: violent conflicts, unjust rulers, and all manner of inequalities.

The second step opened out onto two asymmetrical options. If the prevailing order compared favorably, the intellectual's task was complete, and in Chomsky's pessimistic portrayal this result is precisely the one "intellectuals" are enlisted and paid to attain. If the prevailing order compared unfavorably, the intellectual's task was incomplete and much harder: to discover and state how the prevailing order might be brought closer to the natural order. The latitude for performing this task depended on the rigidity of the institutions wherein the intellectuals worked. Rationalism and idealism, which flourished in absolute monarchies like France and Prussia, proposed to strive for ideal states that best accord with innate ideas, a solution with little force for social change. Empiricism and pragmatism—which fared better in more egalitarian societies like Switzerland, England, and America—advocated improving human nature through education by experience, and the need for general public education was soon widely recognized.

Though the twentieth-century intellectuals have retained their role, the options are more checkered and the prospects of achieving change more perplexing. In Czechoslovakia in the fall of 1989, intellectuals actually took the lead in transforming the prevailing order, after having been severely persecuted over the years for their criticisms of it. But such triumphs are rare, and the fate of too many intellectuals has been either to be co-opted into the prevailing order or else to be cut off from any effective means for acting upon it. Ironically, Chomsky's dualism has enabled him to suffer both these fates, the first as a scientist and the second as an activist, and now he is an old Angry Young Man anxious to blame anybody but himself.

His ostensible hope for change rests on "our moral nature," another entity compounded from idealism and determinism (does it develop like *puberty*?). For him, the way you would study moral judgment is "clear," because it's a carbon copy of the way he thinks you should study language: "You take people and ask what is the nature of the moral system they have," though he doesn't say if you ask yourself (as he would) or the people (as social science would). Without having examined such studies, which he thinks we're "not in a position" to undertake, he asserts that people make moral judgments "in coherent ways and with a high degree of consistency." He attributes this to "a theory or a system or a structure" underlying "an unbounded range of moral judgment," rather like a grammar for generating (assigning ethical descriptions to) an infinite set of moral sentences. True to philosophies of past centuries, he suggests that "shared moral understanding comes from our inner nature"; and "progress" in human history is "stimulated" by "a deeper understanding of our own moral nature" (18).

Recent empirical research in sociology, social psychology, and discourse analysis,[2] disciplines he misprizes one and all, have conclusively shown that moral judgments and their justifications in modern societies reveal not coherence and consistency but a startling lack of them. Such findings undermine his recipe for "progress in human history." And if the 1980s have brought people closer to an "underlying system," its most consistent values include selfishness and greed.

Chomsky's Dualism

Chomsky's personal response to the inherited dualism between knowledge and experience is a fresh dualism—namely, two contrary solutions to the same problem. As a linguist, he accentuates and legitimizes the dualism in various guises—for example, in *competence* versus *performance* or *deep structure* versus *surface structure*—and moves away from objectivity. Whereas his first book *Syntactic Structures* had espoused the "aim" of "replacing obscure intuition with a rigorous and objective approach" (56), *Aspects* championed "intuition" and decried "objective methods" as unfit for "the actual situation in which the linguist must, for the present, proceed" (19). He then cudgeled the social and behavioral sciences for demonstrating that "objectivity can be pursued with little consequent gain in insight and understanding" (*Aspects* 20). Now in the *JAC* interview, he bluntly says, "The idea of neutral objectivity is largely fraudulent" (5).

As a political activist, he adopts the contrary solution by assuming that the only knowledge one needs is what one gets directly and objectively from ordinary experience: "In the analysis of social and political issues it is sufficient to face the facts"; only "Cartesian common sense, which is quite evenly distributed, is needed," the "willingness to look at the facts with an open mind, to put simple assumptions to the test" (*Language* 5). This faculty presumably empowers him to tell us "that's the way the world is" or "you might want the world to be some other way but that's the way it is," which he just happens to say when he needs to justify himself for taking morally questionable positions on linguistic issues: here, for refusing to "study the way in which language is used to facilitate authority" and for championing the languages of the rich and powerful over indigenous and minority languages whose speakers are going to be "worse off" than if they had learned English. Such appeals to "the way the world is" provide alibis both for the social irrelevance of his linguistics and for the moral inconsistencies in his political activism.

The well-known discrepancy between the linguistic and the political sides of his career is thus necessary because he insists on two separated levels of understanding, depending on whether or not he holds credentials. If he does, the domain is complicated and technical; if he doesn't, it's simple and accessible. So if his credentials for "discussing or debating social issues" are "repeatedly challenged," he doesn't obtain credentials in social science but avows that the "alleged complexity" and "depth" of the social sciences is an "illusion created by the system of ideological control" to "make the issues seem remote from the general population" and to "persuade them of their incapacity to organize their own affairs or understand the social world in which they live" (*Language* 4). This additional alibi not merely exonerates his lack of credentials, but advertises it as his political weapon to clarify the issues by simplifying them properly for the "general population." Credentials Chomsky doesn't have are therefore unnecessary and tainted. In Orwellian paradox, a contradiction whose social and political grounding Chomsky does recognize, ignorance is knowledge.

In this sense, his linguistic and political stances are more similar than has been widely supposed: they are both opportunistic projections of his own views and limitations, the one onto the natural order and the other onto the prevailing order. The conflict lies in the incompatible means he uses for the projection: abstraction and idealization on the one side versus immediacy and cynicism on the other. He compensated for the idealizations which rendered his linguistic theory sparse and largely limited it to abstract sentence structures by devising correspondingly rarified notations and complex constraints. Ironically, the outcome was a brand of linguistics that perfectly fits his own conspiracy theory by "making the issues seem remote from the general population." The technicality and complexity helped conceal the fundamental dualism between his theoretical theses and the actual data and experience of language.

"Chomsky's Problem"

Chomsky's self-projection is further complicated by his unswerving determination to uncover and denounce serious flaws in everyone's theories and models except his own. Like the negative campaigners dominant in current politics, he sets forth complicated arguments to undercut all opposing views. Instead of justifying his view with extensive corpuses of realistic language data, he presents it as the only alternative to a carefully constructed straw man and, for good measure, questions the intellectual and moral character of the linguists whose view his straw man purports to embody.

"Chomsky's problem" (of which his "Plato's problem" is a major corollary) is his self-centered resolve to equate the world as it is with the world as he sees it by situating his personal interests and limitations in the things themselves.[3] If his approach prevents him from grasping an issue, then the issue itself is at fault: it isn't "interesting," it "lacks depth," and "there is nothing to say about it," or "nothing's known about it," because "we don't understand much about it," since "everything is pure speculation," and so on. The narrowness and dualism of his approach oblige him to assign this status to a wide range of issues whose importance and relevance has long since been established by other approaches, notably in discourse analysis and social psychology, two disciplines whose legitimacy he must therefore deny. This denial peaks in the charge that people studying such issues are making a "very poor moral judgment" for the sake of careerism—the same charge we might well raise against him.

To link the conflicting frameworks of authority he invokes, he oscillates between idealist philosophy and natural science by jumping over social science and much of cognitive and educational psychology, including pedagogy and, of course, rhetoric and composition. Like his ancestors, he makes interpretive short circuits to connect up his idealizing theses about language and mind with biological principles and necessities. In *Aspects*, he presents the odd thesis that information regarding situational context need not "play any role in determining how language is acquired" once the "acquisition device" has been "set in operation" (33)—convenient because his theorizing about both language and acquisition disregards contexts. As evidence for the thesis, he makes a conjecture about "animal learning": the lamb's "theory of visual space" does not "depend on" "mother-neonate contact," which merely "facilitates" it (34). What the biologists in fact "observed" (his term), however, was the "facilitation," not its irrelevance to some theory of visual space. Thus, the scientific, biological finding does not support his thesis except through his own non-biological interpretation, although it may well impress, distract, or intimidate potential disbelievers.

"Plato's problem" is a corollary of "Chomsky's problem" and was prefigured by the rationalists: if you cannot understand how a given human accomplishment is attained, such as the acquisition of knowledge or of language, you literally—that is, organically—build it into the mind. And Chomsky sees Plato's problem "always" and "universally," "anywhere you look," in "any domain," in "any form of human activity" because his radical dualism between knowledge and experience leaves him no other way to explain the acquisition of anything.

His Cartesian ancestors still had the theological recourse of arguing that the mind was made so rich and complex by "an act of God," whereas Chomsky proffers the alternative (the "*only*" alternative he allows for this straw man) of "inner determinism," which he opportunistically attributes to "every natural scientist studying organic systems," though as we have seen it came from rationalist philosophy. Since even Chomsky admits that empiricist doctrine had "much appeal in the context of eighteenth-century struggles for scientific naturalism," he turns that doctrine into a straw man as well (*Aspects* 59). Like his ancestors, he reduces and misrepresents the empiricist approach as a crude atomistic behaviorism that "limits" all "acquisition" of knowledge to "peripheral processing mechanisms" and "primitive unconditioned reflexes" (*Aspects* 47). The "approach" is then said to assume the "taxonomic principles of segmentation and classification" developed by his adversaries in modern linguistics. This last link in the chain of argument is the weakest, since taxonomic linguists never (though Chomsky did) offered their methods as a model of language acquisition, nor did these methods in any way operate though "peripheral processing" or "unconditioned reflexes."

Chomsky's straw-man version of empiricism is accused of being not "scientific" but "dogmatic and aprioristic" in saying that "arbitrarily selected data-processing mechanisms" are the "only ones available," and in "attributing a complex human achievement to months or at most years of experience rather than to millions of years of evolution or to principles of neural organization" that are "even more deeply grounded in physical law" (*Aspects* 207, 59). This accusation helps snatch biological determinism away from empiricism and reserve it for the rationalist approach, to which Chomsky finds it "difficult to see an alternative" because the obvious alternative has been craftily designed to seem unacceptable (207). And he actually praises rationalism for entailing no "dogmatic assumptions as to the nature of mental processes" and "no preconceptions" about "the internal structure" of the "language acquisition device," although it does precisely that, and to a conspicuous extreme (*Aspects* 48).

Chomsky's Method

To the degree that Chomsky does perceive his own dualism between knowledge and experience, he apparently hopes to transcend it simply by blurring it and then dismissing its consequences. His treatment of the mind/body dualism is a good illustration. He begins again by reducing and misrepresenting the contrary position, in this case by equating body with the "intuitive mechanics" prevailing before Newton—"you know, things pushing and pulling each other." Next, he says the theory of mechanics "was blown out of the water" by Newton, who in fact created a far more powerful but less intuitive theory of mechanics by uniting celestial and terrestrial motion—a step which genuinely moved toward replacing theology with natural science. But Chomsky admits only his own straw-man "theory of mechanics," after whose refutation by Newton "there is no classical mind/body problem" because "there shouldn't be" and "the logic is the same." He contradicts himself at once by invoking "numerous examples showing that the way we study the traditional phenomena of mind departs from the way we study other aspects of physical reality." Three characteristic moves should be noted here: equating "should be" with "is," passing over obvious contradictions that ensue, and including "phenomena of mind" under "aspects of physical reality."

This inclusion is vital for Chomsky's standard tactic of constructing idealizations and justifying them as biological necessities, thereby solving both "Plato's problem" and his own while fending off counterarguments. Hence, "a rich structure of understanding" is claimed to "arise independently of any evidence because it's just part of our nature"; and "the development of cognitive systems, including systems of knowledge," is "substantially directed by our biological nature." Put in a more simplistic metaphor, the acquisition of "rich competence" from "limited experience" is attributed to "inner determinism" just as "when a child eats, it grows." Or, "deep universals" in language are "just as much a part of our nature as the fact that we have arms and not wings." Or again, the "facts" of language are said to point to "a highly determinate very definite structure of concepts and of meaning that is intrinsic to our nature" and "just kind of grows in our minds, the same way we grow arms and legs."

This "structure" in turn constitutes the tidy preserve of "meanings" Chomsky judged admissible for linguistics and semantics, to be expressed in "descriptive feature matrices" in his "lexicon." The features determined by *context*, on the other hand, being "unspecified in underlying structures," can make "no contribution to sentence interpretation"—a truly astonishing conclusion (*Aspects* 182). Evidently, the idealization of meanings requires that they be fixed and determinate, and that interpretation consist of putting together their lexical features like so many building blocks. So Chomsky has to follow Katz and Fodor in saying that "the meaning of a sentence is based on the meaning of its elementary parts and manner of their combination" (*Aspects* 162). And since those parts are specified in "underlying" or "deep" structure, he has to conclude that "the manner of combination provided by the surface structure is in general almost totally irrelevant to semantic interpretation" (162). This conclusion too is astonishing, especially for a syntax-centered approach, but Chomsky is forced into it by the idealizing and unimaginative design of his theory. Besides, the more outrageous the conclusion, the more likely it is to give him opportunities to use his greatest talent: public debating.

Moreover, such conclusions allow his genuinely seventeenth-century belief in a timeless "basically fixed structure of meaning" to act as a deflector of unwelcome complications. Only when we use these "rich semantic structures in our interactions with one another and our interactions with the world" are they subjected to "interest-relativity, intrusion of value, relativity to purposes and intentions, modifiability," and so on. So disregarding the use of language and meaning with its untidy "fluidity and indeterminacy" that "we don't understand very much about" is the proper scientific choice, and, as a recent stipulation, the "moral" one as well.

Appeals to determinism and fixity are awkward because they imply that when Chomsky changes his mind the "mind" of humanity changes as well. In *Aspects*, he invoked "the best information now available" (without saying what it was) as proof that "a child cannot help constructing" a transformational grammar "any more than he can control his perception of solid objects or his attention to line and angle" (59). When Chomsky later dispensed with transformations, he must have determined that "the best information available" was all wrong and the child was doing no such thing. But he avoids such issues by overlooking his own inconsistencies and assuming we will too—for example, when in the interview he includes "rules" among the "things" people have "inside the skin" only two pages after averring that, according to the work of the 1980s, "there don't seem to be any rules." Or when he announces that "kernel sentences" play "no distinctive role" in the "interpretation of sentences" (*Aspects* 18) without recalling his earlier labor-saving announcement that "to understand a sentence it is necessary to know the kernel sentences from which it originates," so that "the general problem of analyzing the process of 'understanding' is thus reduced" to "explaining how kernel sentences are understood" (*Syntactic* 92). Each new thesis and each new version of his theory is asserted with the same aggressive confidence as the very mirror of nature and with the same cheerful expectation he will be believed as fervently as ever; and his grammar is still "transformational" in the practical sense that he can't stop transforming it. Even today, after changing his mind time and again to gain some momentary advantage in an argument, he has no qualms about telling us where "the truth" lies (9 times in the interview) and what is "true" (19 times), and he doth protest too much by adducing "crucial facts which are in fact true facts."

If he sees an advantage, not even the most basic concepts of linguistics are secure. The very first sentence of *Syntactic Structures* (the book begins on page 11 so it will have over 100 pages of text) reads: "Syntax is the study of the principles and procedures by which sentences are constructed." Toward the book's end, he insists his own theory is "completely formal and non-semantic," "meaning" being no more relevant for "constructing a grammar" than "the hair color of speakers" (93). He exempts himself from "the burden of proof" for his thesis by placing it "completely on linguists who claim" to "develop some grammatical notion in semantic terms" (94). In a footnote, Chomsky shares Nelson Goodman's hope that "the meaning of words can be at least in part reduced" to "reference of expressions" (102). Predictably, "semantic reference" was later said to "facilitate syntax-learning but not affect the manner" and, therefore, like "information about situational context," should not be relevant for theories of "acquisition" (*Aspects* 33).

In the interview, however, the term *syntax* is redefined as whatever "has to do with mental representations and the structure of mental representations" and with "the relation between words and concepts." The majority of researchers in cognitive science, artificial intelligence, and linguistics itself, who assign these issues to *semantics*, are summarily brushed aside and their results annexed. "Most of what is called semantics is syntax," and "plenty of people who call their work semantics" are "not dealing with semantics at all."[4] As in the footnote to *Syntactic Structures*, Chomsky allows "real semantics" to keep only "the relation between representation and things in the world," and "about that there is almost nothing to say." Besides, says Chomsky in the interview, "that's the part that's subject to holism and interest relativity and values and so on," about which, again, "there doesn't seem to be anything general to say." So, like Saddam Hussein seizing Kuwait and saying it's an Iraqi province, Chomsky seizes semantics and renames it "syntax," his own territory, leaving behind only an issue he has nothing to say about and dumping there the factors that disturb his tidy view of "fixed determinate meaning."

Juggling terminology has long been a commodious way for Chomsky to secure his authority. In *Aspects*, he advanced a strong argument that a "theory of language" can be regarded as a hypothesis about the "language-forming capacity of humans." He therefore proposed to formulate problems of linguistic theory as "questions about the construction of a hypothetical language acquisition device" (30, 47). But what he "formulated" was terms and ideals, not testable hypotheses. Just as he had proceeded in *Syntactic Structures* by "never considering the question of how one might have arrived at the grammar," he now adopted an "idealized 'instantaneous' model" wherein "successful language acquisition" happens in one "moment" (*Syntactic* 56; *Aspects* 36). This leap (like Athena from the head of Zeus) authorized him to postpone "considering" the "order and manner" that "linguistic data" are presented and "the continual accretion of linguistic skill and knowledge" (*Aspects* 36, 202). And since he could not "imagine how in detail" his model might be tested (neither can I), he stipulated that "in this case, no evaluation procedure will be necessary as a part linguistic theory" (*Aspects* 36).

The missing model of child learning a language was unimaginatively but strategically supplied by a model of the Chomskyan linguist constructing a grammar—strategic in his campaign to dismiss all competing theories (especially those of the descriptive structuralists) that did not purport to be a model of the child. The child's achievement was thus circumscribed as "having developed and internally represented a generative grammar," that is, "a theory" and "a system of rules that determine how sentences are to be formed, used, and understood" (*Aspects* 25). Just as the rationalists had suggested that experience reaches the mind as atomistic sensations so that "innate ideas" must be at work, Chomsky portrayed data in "actual speech" as "finite," "scattered," and "restrictive in scope"—indeed, "degenerate in quality," rife with "non-sentences," "fragments, and deviant expressions" so that a generative grammar must be at work (*Aspects* 43, 311, 58, 201, 25). And the terminology was deployed to clinch the argument, replace empirical testing, and hide the Chomskyan dualism behind two "systematic ambiguities": "using the term 'grammar' both for 'the native speaker's internally represented theory of his language'" and for "the linguist's account of this"; plus using "theory of language" "both for the child's innate predisposition" and for "the linguist's account" (*Aspects* 25). This correspondence is precisely what any linguistic theory must be required to demonstrate.

How the linguist can obtain an account is itself unclear if "any interesting generative grammar will be dealing, for the most part, with mental processes" that are "far beyond the level of actual or even potential consciousness" (note the key word *interesting*, whose role we'll examine later), and if "the speaker's reports and viewpoints about his behavior and competence may be in error" (*Aspects* 8). But, like many other problems, this one became a virtue, since it saved the labor of gathering data or interviewing informants: Chomsky went on to assert that "sharpening the data by objective test" is of "small importance" for "new and deeper understanding of linguistic structure" (20).

Chomsky's evasions about how grammars get constructed by children or linguists are all the more problematic in view of his famous "unanswerable" attack upon structuralist grammars for "natural languages," whose "inadequacy" he purported to have "established beyond any reasonable doubt" (*Aspects* 54, 67). As we've seen, his main thrust was to blur the distinction between atomistic behaviorism and linguistic fieldwork and to disqualify the structuralists for a claim they never even made. Intransigently ignoring the grammars produced for over 350 languages by the Summer Institute of Linguistics alone, mainly through tagmemics (1964 estimate by Kenneth Pike),[5] Chomsky said flatly that "knowledge of grammatical structure cannot arise" from the "operations" of structural linguistics, and he claimed that the methods of "taxonomic linguistics are intrinsically incapable of yielding systems of grammatical knowledge that must be attributed to the speaker of a language" (*Aspects* 54, 67). The irony is indigestibly rich: Chomsky baldly asserted that a theory of language is a hypothesis about language learning, dismissed out of hand rival theories which never pretended to be such a hypothesis, transformed his own theory into one with a mere "systematic ambiguity," and then skipped over the whole learning process by adopting an "ideal instantaneous model"! Thus, he flailed the structuralists for failing to address the very issue his own theory addressed only in the emptiest and most abstract way.

Few who were targeted in that memorable onslaught can be anything but dumbfounded by Chomsky's remarks in the interview that "one should not try to persuade" and that he "tries to refrain from efforts to bring people to reach his conclusions." He grants that "you'd probably lose the audience by not doing it," but warns it is "an authoritarian practice one should keep away from." Such warnings come distinctly late in his own case. If trying to "undercut" someone else is indeed a mark of the "vile nature of human beings," he would rank among the vilest linguists, along with his cohorts Lees, Katz, Fodor, Klima and the rest of the jargonizing MIT elite he unleashed, armed with slippery theoretical arguments about "adequacy" and "evaluation," on practical-minded American linguists. But he prefers to think of himself merely "laying out the territory" so "other people can use their own intellectual powers to work out for themselves what they think is right or wrong."

Chomsky, Creativity, and Composition

Among the disciplines which have suffered from Chomsky's opportunistic theorizing and defensive evasions have been not merely sociolinguistics and applied linguistics, but composition. Searching for theoretical expertise on language, we were offered only unhelpful idealizations and overcomplicated notations, both of which left behind the impression that transformations of sentence structure are the essence of language competence and that communication by language consists chiefly of assigning structural descriptions to sentences.

If we ask him for advice, "Chomsky's problem" reappears: since he lacks credentials on the teaching of language and composition, the issues must, like social problems, be simple and hence unrelated to the complicated ones he reserves for what he likes to call "technical linguistics." He justly doubts that linguistics (meaning, as always, his approach) has "anything to contribute." It certainly offers nothing to help students "wrestle with complex ideas and find ways of expressing them," the activities Chomsky, like most of us in composition, would place "at the heart of the writing program." Nor are any means offered to enlist *writing* in "intellectual," "cultural," and "moral progress."

We should recall here his spurious justification for the claim that his theory could "attempt an explicit formulation of creative processes" in terms of "technical devices for expressing a system of recursive processes," as developed in mathematics (*Aspects* 8). Again, he was seeking support by appealing to an impressive but irrelevant technicality. Recursion is anything but creative; it can only crank out the same thing at fixed increments. Language is "creative" not merely because we can make sentences steadily longer and more complex, but because we can modify and adapt the conventional patterns and meanings Chomsky takes as the sole concern of linguistics. And the means, motives, and effects of doing so are among the factors he has already idealized out of language—witness his inclusion of creative modifiability among the issues (like "interest" and "value") he separates from the "determinate, very definite structure of meaning" and thus by implication among the issues he dumped into what was left of "semantics" after his summary annexation of the rest.[6]

But Chomsky expressly made "the syntactic component" the "sole 'creative' part" of the grammar. Taking him at his word, composition researchers hit upon *sentence combining*, which cannot count as a pedagogical application of Chomsky's theory, however, for at least two reasons, one practical and one theoretical. From a practical standpoint, sentence combining neither adhered to the detailed design of transformational grammar (for example, to the "derivational history" of each sentence) nor was intended to test that design (for example, to adjudicate whether the "passive transformation" should be "obligatory").[7] From a theoretical standpoint, sentence combining ignored Chomsky's expedient thesis that the child "discovers" a "deep and abstract theory" (a generative grammar) "only remotely related to experience by long and intricate chains of unconscious quasi-inferential steps" and makes no "conscious formulation and expression" of "rules" (*Aspects* 58). This thesis leads him in the interview to the astonishing sophistry that guidelines for usage which must be "taught" are "probably wrong" or "don't make any sense."[8] In fact, they are in "violation of natural law," doubtless meaning: contrary to the biological necessities which create "fixed deterministic meaning," compel "the child to construct a transformational grammar," and generally make happen whatever Chomsky's theorizing calls for but can't account for any other way.

Since Chomsky "doesn't know of any methods" in educational theory either, it too must be just as simple as social science. His declaration that "teaching is mostly common sense" not merely ignores decades of reputable and innovative research in educational psychology and language teaching and implies that specialized teacher training is pointless, but it also clashes dramatically with his own portrayal of the educational system as a means for enforcing subservience. He tells us that "ninety-nine percent of good teaching is getting people interested in the task or problem and providing a rich environment to pursue what they find interesting," befitting his earlier advice, from the context of his Platonic rejection of "rhetoric," for the teacher to "enable students to figure out things for themselves" rather than getting them to "reach his conclusions." But this advice could hardly be followed if the purpose of the educational system is indeed "to turn people into submissive atomized individuals who don't interfere with the structures of power and authority but rather serve those structures." The logical contradiction here could be avoided only through the tortuous assumption (which he doesn't advance) that ninety-nine percent of good teaching constitutes an insignificant exception (say one percent?) among the activities in the educational system.

The goals of *writing* are included under "forms of empowerment," but Chomsky's statement of these goals again contradicts his dark assessment of power in education: to "enrich one's own thought," to "enlighten others," and to "enter into constructive discourse with others which they all gain by." Predictably, he extols the natural sciences as a model for English composition courses, striving to "stimulate critical analysis, self-analysis, and analysis of culture and society" as well as to "develop systems of intellectual self-defense." He forgets that his notion of natural science is diametrically opposed to social science, which really does analyze culture and society. And his advice is again not helpful if the educational system "interferes to prevent deviations" because "that's the way institutions work"—that is, "that's the way the world is."

Activism and the Intellectual

Seeing education and social science as instruments of conformism is directly related to Chomsky's vision of the *intellectual*—one as opportunistic and self-contradictory as his vision of linguistics: "The dominant view among intellectuals" is that "you'd better control people with propaganda for their own good." They constitute a "specialized class" of "smart guys" who are "capable of running things" and who judge "the mass of people" totally incapable. They pass through "gates and filters" by being "submissive and obedient" all through school and their professional careers, until they attain positions in "high places" as "cultural managers." There, they enjoy respect and recognition because they refrain from "subverting structures of power"—for example, by doing scholarship in the universities, which is basically "low-level clerical work" (*trahison de clericals*?).

Chomsky plainly considers himself an intellectual and sometimes uses the first person ("we smart guys," "we're obedient"). So two contradictory theses about *intellectualism* arise, and the interview provides support for both: either he also serves power structures (for instance, by handling linguistics as "clerical work") or else his work is such a distinguished and influential exception that the controls cannot be as tight as he maintains. The contradiction disappears if we adopt a third, less evident thesis Chomsky would not accept: that both his politics and his linguistics constitute conspicuous deviations but have been accepted and encouraged because they ultimately reinforce prevailing power structures. His politics are applauded because they provide reverse evidence for the claim that the United States is the "freest country in the world." The domination, repression, and concealment he denounces are necessary in the first place because in the U.S. you "can't tell people what they're going to do," so "you have to fool people into it by fear and so on." His linguistics has been generously funded, for example, by the military,[9] whom he now requites by citing "the Pentagon system" as a indicator of America's "internalized democratic understanding and freedom," so that the military must "force the public to subsidize high-technology industry." In an efficient fascist society, in contrast, "you just give orders"; and if popular organizations dispute them "you send out the death squads."

And his generously funded linguistics has repaid its dues by blocking research on "the use of language to impose authority"—not just indirectly, in that such use can hardly be treated in terms of assigning structural descriptions to sentences, but directly in that Chomsky roundly declares it "a topic that's not intellectually interesting and has no intellectual depth to it at all, like most things in the social sciences." This declaration hinges on Chomsky's bizarre but convenient tenet that there is "very little overlap" between what is "intellectually interesting" and what is "humanly significant." This notion of "intellectually interesting" has nothing to do either with his vision of the intellectual as a servant of power or with the "interest" that intrudes on "fixed determinate meaning"—on the contrary. In *Language and Responsibility*, he distinguishes "things that are interesting in themselves like human action" versus those which are interesting because they "have some bearing" on "theoretical" and "explanatory principles" or on "hidden structures that have some intellectual interest" (58). The second kind of interest, the only one surviving in the interview, calls for "abstraction" and "idealization." And opposition to "idealization" amounts to the "insistence that we shall not have meaningful intellectual work" (*Language* 57). The ratio seems clear: the more abstract and idealized the approach, the more interesting and meaningful it must be—flattering for Chomsky's theory and derogatory for sociolinguistics, which Chomsky was in this very context booting out from "the rational study of language" (*Language* 56). Once more, the remoteness of his theory from human actions and other experiential and empirical data is advertised as an asset. His conspiracy theory helps out by supplying the perverse alibi that "if you're understood and appreciated, it's almost proof that you're not on the right track," so let's all be as incomprehensible and outrageous as he is.

Chomsky's views on society and politics fall on the other side, among the "humanly significant," and now his values are suddenly just the reverse: the more specific and immediate, the better. Thus, "doing something to help

Salvadoran peasants who are getting slaughtered" is "overwhelmingly more significant" than "studying the way in which language is used to facilitate authority." This comparison leads to the already cited charge that choosing the latter issue is to make a "very poor moral judgment." Chomsky remarks that professional training as a linguist "doesn't help you to be useful to others"—correct if you're trained in his method.

On the face of it, Chomsky seems to be advocating the most direct activism. But he contradicts this semblance in the context of another argument attempting to rationalize his political role. First, he hails the American "classlessness" that makes "complete equals" of "a university professor and garage mechanic talking together." This salute may be a gesture of Chomsky's nostalgia for his own childhood in a "1930s working class environment" among "unemployed workers" who relished the Budapest String Quartet—the "richest intellectual environment he's ever seen." Also, it may be a residual solidarity with the masses, a vestige of the Marxist-Leninist thought whose "essence" he purports to "capture" with a crude parody. (I, on the other hand, was once hounded out of a garage mechanic's job when the shop owner learned I held two master's degrees, and his daughter was so unintellectual she'd never heard of the city of Berlin where I got them. And having lived and worked in the German Democratic Republic, I know that Marxism-Leninism never named "radical intellectuals" for the "vanguard role" but assigned it to the socialist or communist party whose membership should be mainly working-class, and who should help the masses not because they are "dumb" and "stupid" but because they are excluded from control over production.)

Second, he hails this classlessness as rich compensation for the fact that intellectuals aren't "taken seriously" in the United States. Here, he rationalizes away, indeed glorifies, "one of the *good* things about the United States," and accounts for the fact that he is very rarely "asked to comment on international affairs by press, radio, or television"; but how this can be a compensation is not clear if he cites the same neglect as more proof of "ideological control" and "conformist attitudes."

Third, he undercuts his own political activism by actually justifying the American government and the media for "paying no attention" when "intellectuals" do such things as "sign an international statement against the war in Vietnam." "Intellectuals aren't taken seriously," he contends, because "there's absolutely no reason to," and the failure of their "statements" to make the newspapers is quite "correct." So Chomsky must know how little he is achieving for the victims of power like Salvadoran peasants by doing things like "demonstrating in Washington about the Romero assassination." If death squads make fascist societies more "efficient" from the top down, demonstrations make democratic societies more efficient from the bottom up—but only if the moral and intellectual integrity of the demonstrators is taken very seriously on a wide scale, as for example with that of Czechoslovakian intellectuals such as Vaclav Havel, who paid for their oppositional views by going to prison or doing menial jobs, while Chomsky was on an "enemies list" and "nothing happened" to him (*Language* 21). And despite his suggestion to the contrary, "the demonstration" does "advance his career," namely as a public speaker who is paid more these days for political than for linguistic addresses.

His admission and defense of the public disinterest in intellectual opposition to human crimes like warfare helps explain why he might be "very much in favor of corruption" and call on all of us to "applaud" it as "one of the best things there is." His rationale is the most cynical sophistry in the whole interview: "money-hunger" is less "dangerous" than "power hunger"; a corrupt leader is going to "rob people but not cause much trouble." A political activist who fails to see that money is power and who says mass robbery isn't "much trouble" can only be described as shallow and corrupt himself. In much of the Third World, the corruption of the rich and powerful is simply the other side of the same coin from the starvation and slaughter of "peasants" Chomsky professes to be helping by protesting after an archbishop (a true and moral intellectual) who has already been assassinated.

The Future of Intellectualism

Let us hope both linguistics and intellectualism will survive Professor Chomsky's self-centered renditions of them by turning to more relevant and worthwhile issues and examining them from unified scientific and social perspectives. The pressure is mounting, both on linguists who treat their relevance too casually, and on intellectuals who take their relevance too readily for granted out of narcissistic rather than democratic motives.

Few would deny that science and intellectualism are in crisis in the United States, and the fate of being either co-opted or excluded by real power structures is relentlessly becoming more imminent. But the model for linguists and intellectuals of the future must not be Chomsky: careerist, opportunist, vociferous debater, marketeer of labor-saving idealizations, creator of dubious justifications for astonishing conclusions, juggler of terminologies, brandisher of irrelevant technicalities, fabricator of alibis, reducer and misrepresenter of counterarguments, defamer of his adversaries' intelligence and morality, disdainer of socially useful science, applauder of corruption, and apologist for governmental indifference to protests against war and colonialism.

The future of the science of language lies in its potential to contribute to critical awareness and analysis, both in the sciences and in daily life. The future of intellectualism lies in seeking a comprehensive and empirically sound conception of both the natural order and the prevailing order, and in transcending personal overconfidence, opportunism, dilettantism, sophistry, and cynicism. The human race is "likely to self-destruct" less through nuclear holocaust than through the uncritical thought and discourse (including "the breakdown of independent thought" into "consumerism") that justify complacency, self-interest, and inequality. We must focus on real discourse and seek out its hidden assumptions and contradictions by every available means. Here, I have tried to provide a taste by taking Chomsky at his word, by probing how his own discourse is constructed to "facilitate authority."

University of Florida
Gainesville, Florida

Notes

[1] Chomsky remarks in the interview that Descartes had a "plausible" but "incorrect argument for the existence of mind," but Chomsky doesn't admit how heavily his own arguments, particularly in *Aspects*, have borrowed upon it.

[2] See, for example, Potter and Wetherell, and the special issue of *Text* (8.1, 1988) on discourse, racism, and ideology.

[3] Paul Robinson states "the Chomsky problem" as the dualism between "technical linguistic scholarship" and "maddeningly simple-minded politics," but he fails to see its enormous expedience, obsequiously suggesting that "Chomsky is arguably the most important intellectual alive"—a terrifying prospect indeed.

[4] Chomsky can't even maintain the new terminology himself, saying at one point "semantic representation" instead of "mental representation."

[5] And in reply to Robert Longacre's protest at the 1962 Congress of Linguists that "tagmemics is not narrowly taxonomic," Chomsky made it clear he included tagmemics in his charge (*Proceedings of the Ninth International Congress* 998ff.).

[6] We might recall here his suggestion that "selectional rules," which "impose a hierarchy of deviation from grammaticalness" on sentences "generated by relaxing" "constraints," might be "dropped from the syntax" and put in "the semantic component" (*Aspects* 153, 158).

[7] This is an issue raised in *Syntactic Structures* 71f.

[8] As usual, his illustration misses the point: what would seem to be "natural" is "me and him were here," not "him and me were here."

[9] This is announced in the Acknowledgements to *Aspects*.

Works Cited

Chomsky, Noam. *Aspects of the Theory of Syntax*. Cambridge: MIT P, 1965.

———. *Language and Responsibility*. New York: Pantheon, 1979.

———. *Syntactic Structures*. The Hague: Mouton, 1957.

Potter, Jonathan, and Margaret Wetherell. *Discourse and Social Psychology*. London: Sage, 1987.

Robinson, Paul. "The Chomsky Problem." Rev. of *Language and Responsibility*, by Noam Chomsky. *New York Times Review of Books* 25 Feb. 1979: 3,37.

Jacques

Derrida

Jacques Derrida on Rhetoric and Composition: A Conversation

Gary A. Olson

Jacques Derrida's work has forever altered how we perceive the relationships among writers, readers, and texts and has transformed our very notions of "rhetoric" and "writing." Not only have composition theorists drawn on his work, but recently some have attempted to apply it to the classroom. The publication of Gregory Ulmer's *Applied Grammatology*, G. Douglas Atkins and Michael Johnson's *Writing and Reading Differently*, Jasper Neel's *Plato, Derrida, and Writing*, and Sharon Crowley's *A Teacher's Introduction to Deconstruction* indicates just how influential his ideas have become in our field.

While Derrida has, of course, had much to say about writing and rhetoric, this interview is his first extended discussion of rhetoric and composition *per se*. He describes his own growth as a writer, proposes a model of composition instruction, discusses problems compositionists should avoid, and comments on a range of other related topics, including liberatory learning, social constructionism, logocentrism, and feminism.

The theme that perhaps will most surprise at least some readers is that Derrida vigorously asserts the importance of the "canon," the "tradition," and rigorous academic discipline. He concludes that many critics have seriously misrepresented his ideas. Pointing to his own rigorous academic training, Derrida maintains that even as he seeks to deconstruct pedagogies and ways of thinking, he is "at some level true" to the "classical" training he received in the French educational system. He stresses that deconstruction "doesn't mean simply destroying the norms or pushing these norms to utter chaos." In fact, if what passes as deconstruction produces "neglect of the classical authors, the canonical texts, and so on, we should fight it."

This theme recurred throughout the session, indicating how strongly he feels that deconstruction has been misrepresented and maligned. He is convinced that "if deconstruction is only a pretense to ignore minimal requirements or knowledge of the tradition, it could be a bad thing." Apparently, it is often supporters of deconstruction themselves who feed this misunderstanding: "Sometimes the most ferocious critics who react vehemently and passionately and sometimes with hatred understand more than supporters do." Those who "play at deconstruction, try to behave deconstructively" before reading "the great texts in our tradition" give deconstruction a bad name. Certainly, we need to open the canon, to broaden it, to question it, but we can't do so before acquiring at least a "minimal knowledge of the basic foundations of the canon." Only then can we develop "a deconstructive practice." As if to warn supporters as well as to answer critics, Derrida insists, "If you're not trained in the tradition, then deconstruction means nothing. It's simply nothing."

Derrida also has firm convictions about how composition should be taught. Although there is no formal composition instruction in the French system, he believes there should be. He speaks of "much anxiety" in France over the level of students' writing competency. While he hesitates to call this situation a "literacy crisis," he says that many of his generation feel that the young no longer "respect the same norms," the same values—that they "don't read and write the way they should." Derrida perceives this problem as a "restructuring of the norms." He suggests that it is not that students are less intelligent but that "their intelligence is applied differently." However, he contends that instruction in composition would be beneficial, that there should be "parallel teaching of composition everywhere: in the teaching of French literature, of history, and so on."

It's no mistake that this sounds like a writing-across-the-disciplines model of writing instruction; Derrida fully endorses such a model. While he is not sure how such a model would work, he is certain that writing instruction centralized in a single academic department will lead to the "hegemony of some kind of norm in writing." Aside from "minimal requirements in grammar, clarity of exposition, and so on," writing competence is inextricably linked to the discourse conventions of specific disciplines. He questions whether it is possible to teach writing without being "competent in the content of a discipline." After all, he argues, "you can't teach writing simply as a formal technique." Of course, he is quick to point out that he does not advocate establishing "boundaries"; yet, he is concerned that writing instruction detached from specific discourse communities will be artificial and, therefore, ineffective—a mere matter of mechanical, formal "technique."

On the other hand, he does not propose that compositionists be "scattered" helter-skelter throughout the university. While he does think it important that writing instruction take place within particular disciplines and therefore that writing specialists be associated with and competent in those disciplines, he feels just as strongly that compositionists must have "something in common"; that is, they must have shared training and expertise in the teaching of composition—in effect, a common discipline of their own. Thus, fully aware of the complexity of the subject and the contradictory nature of his response, Derrida says, "I would not rely on a model in which composition instructors are confined simply within one discipline; nor would I rely on a model in which they are simply dispersed, scattered among a variety of disciplines."

Nor does he recommend that compositionists form their own academic departments apart from English departments. While he acknowledges that "it's important that a large number of composition teachers belong to the English department," he reiterates that it would be counterproductive to "confine" compositionists to any single department.

Clearly, Derrida has a keen grasp of the complexity of the very issues we ourselves are struggling with, and his reluctance to seek security in a "unilateral solution" may well be an example we should follow in shaping the future of writing instruction and our own professional relationships within the structure of the university.

Moreover, we would do well, Derrida advises, to "deconstruct" not only written texts but the institution of composition and the very notion of "composition" itself. He cautions against imposing rigid schemes of writing on students and suggests that we continually question and destabilize the authority of models of composition and that we seek to "invent each time new forms according to the situation." Echoing the recent concerns of many composition theorists, Derrida reminds us that writing is always contingent upon context—the "situation, the audience, your own purpose"—not on pre-established, formulaic models. So we should "analyze these models" and determine "where their authority comes from" and "what interests they serve."

Compositionists should be especially wary of what Derrida calls "rhetoricism": "thinking that everything depends on rhetoric." Certainly, rhetoric is central to almost every facet of life, but we must not attribute to rhetoric more power than it has—an "inherent danger" in the teaching of rhetoric and composition. This is not to say that "rhetoric is simply subordinate," but that "rhetoric is not the last word." Derrida believes that "a self-conscious and trained teacher, attentive to the complexity, should at the same time underline the importance of rhetoric and the limits of rhetoric." We need to help students understand the full complexity of language use—its power *and* its limitations.

It is evident from the conversation recorded here that Derrida takes writing instruction quite seriously and shares with compositionists many of the same concerns, both theoretical and pedagogical. He supports our attempts to improve composition pedagogy and applauds our efforts to deconstruct ourselves—our self-reflexive examination of the notion of "composition," the field, and our institutional relationships. Such continual analysis and self-examination will lead to productive change and growth. Not only is his support somewhat comforting, but his insights, I believe, contribute productively to the ongoing dialogue in rhetoric and composition about who we are and who we should be.

Q. Do you think of yourself as a writer?
A. It's difficult to answer this question without some preliminary precautions. I don't think of myself as a writer if by "writer" you mean merely a literary writer, an author of poems and fiction in the traditional sense. From that point of view, I'm not a writer. But neither am I a philosopher who writes or a theoretician who writes without being attentive to writing—to the form, techniques, and so on. So, I think of myself neither as a writer (in the sense of working within literary genres) nor as a scientist or philosopher who wouldn't be interested in questions of writing. I'm interested in the way I write, in the form, the language, the idiom, the composition. When I write a text—and I write different kinds of texts—I'm as attentive to, let's say, the content as to the formal style and also to the performative shape, the genre, all the aspects that belong to a given genre. All those problems which are traditionally called "formal" are what interest me most. To that extent, I think of myself as a sort of writer. But I'm unhappy with the boundaries between, let's say, literary writing and philosophical writing. I'm not a writer, but writing to me is the essential performance or act. I am unable to dissociate thinking, teaching, and writing. That's why I had to try to transform and to extend the concept of writing, which is not simply "writing down" something. So, "yes and no" would be the answer to the first question.
Q. Who were key "writing teachers" for you? By that I mean not necessarily people who held official faculty positions, but people who advised you well about your writing or whose writing inspired your own composition processes.
A. There are a number of possible answers to this. Paradoxically, I learned a lot from my teachers both in high school and in what we call the *khâgne*—a grade between high school and the *Ecole Normale Supérieure*—the university. We had to prepare a composition we call the *concours d'entrée*. This instruction was very hard and heavy, very demanding according to classical norms. I was trained in those very classical norms. And probably people who read me and think I'm playing with or transgressing norms—which I do, of course—usually don't know what I know: that all of this has not only been made possible by but is constantly in contact with very classical, rigorous, demanding discipline in writing, in "demonstrating," in rhetoric. Even if I feel, or some of my readers think, that I am free or provocative toward those norms, the fact that I've been trained in and that I am at some level true to this classical teaching is essential. I think that perhaps my American readers—when they read me in English, for example—don't or can't pay attention to the fact that this classical superego is very strong in terms of rhetoric, whether it's a question of rhetoric in the sense of the art of persuasion or in the sense of logical demonstration. When I take liberties, it's always by measuring the distance from the standards I know or that I've been rigorously trained in. So, my classical training in France

has been a great influence—all those competitions that I suffered from. The French system was and still is terrible from that point of view; you have to go through a number of selective competitions which make you suffer to make you better. I'm politically against this system and I fight it; nevertheless, I had to go through it. Yet, however negative it may be from some point of view, it's good discipline and I learned a lot from it. The way I write is probably marked by this experience. So, first, there are those teachers at school. But then, you learn from everything you read; every writer or philosopher you admire is a kind of writing teacher. So I learned from many, many writers.

Q. Anyone in particular?

A. No, because it depends on the type of text I write. I write different types of texts. I won't say I imitate—that's certainly not true—but I try to match in my own idiom the style or the way of writing of the writers I write on. When I write on Mallarmé, I don't write the same as when I write on Blanchot or Ponge. It's not a mimetic behavior, but I try to produce my own signature in relation to the signature of the other, so I don't learn a model way of writing. It's not learning; it's listening to the other and trying to produce your own style in proportion to the other. It's not a lesson you learn; it's something else.

Q. Would you describe this as being "influenced" by these authors?

A. It's not an "influence." Even though I write differently when I write on Mallarmé or Blanchot or Ponge, this difference doesn't mean that I'm under their influence. But I adjust. I don't write like Blanchot, but my tone changes; everything is differently staged, but I wouldn't speak of "influence."

Q. So it's a matter of "responding."

A. Yes, responding; that's it. Responding is responding to the other. Blanchot remains other, and I don't write the way he writes so my writing is other, too. But this otherness is responding or co-responding, so to speak.

Q. Most European universities do not offer courses in writing. Is composition taught in French universities? If not, do you think that formal courses in writing should be taught there?

A. No, there is no such instruction in France. We don't teach composition, as such. Of course, through the teaching of French and literature, there has been, or there should be, the concurrent teaching of composition. The teacher of French literature, for example, requires students to write correctly, elegantly, and so forth. There are grammatical and stylistic norms. But this is a very mobile situation. Now we are seeing problems which look or sound like yours. I wouldn't call it "illiteracy," but there has been a massive change during the last two decades. The level of what is required seems to have dropped, and this is something that everyone in my generation complains about. But it's not that simple, and I don't share these complaints. It is true that our norms are not respected, and we cannot recognize in children and young people now the same respect we had for spelling, and so on. In France the pedagogy which was built through the ideology of the Third Republic was very rigorous, and the social authority of the teacher was enormous. This meant that there was an ethics of spelling, of *orthographe*, and every transgression, every misspelling, was a crime. This was the case in my generation and before me. Now, of course, this is no longer the case, and respect for these values has disappeared, for the students and for the young teachers, too. But this doesn't mean that these people have given up any respect for anything; it's that the norms have changed. They're not less intelligent but their intelligence is applied differently, and it's very difficult for people from my generation to understand this shifting, this restructuring of the norms. So there is no teaching of composition, as such. There should be parallel teaching of composition everywhere: in the teaching of French literature, of history, and so on. Now, everyone believes that French young people, however intelligent they may be, don't read and write the way they should. This is the cause of much current anxiety in France.

Q. What university department do you think should teach writing? Would it be the French department? Would it be a separate department?

A. I wouldn't think that one single department should be in charge, because if you concentrate the teaching of composition in a single department—for instance, the literature department—then you'll have the hegemony of some kind of norm in writing. The people in mathematics and history and law don't have to write the same way. Of course, the minimal requirements in grammar, clarity of exposition, and so on can be addressed everywhere. But then you have to adjust the transformations of the way you write according to each discipline, the discourse of the discipline. There is writing competence for a lawyer, for a historian, and there are also changes in those competencies. So if you concentrate composition teaching in one single place, you won't be able, first, to differentiate between the different requirements, and then to take into account the necessary transformations in style. And, of course, I'm in favor of transformations in rhetoric and in the mode of argument. Such changes have to be specific to each discipline. And, if possible, crossing the boundaries would be good, too. I have no model for this, but I would not rely on a model in which composition instructors are confined simply within one discipline; nor would I rely on a model in which they are simply dispersed, scattered among a variety of disciplines. There should be a specificity and also a crossing of the boundaries. So, it's a very difficult question.

Q. In fact, there's a model here that we call "writing across the disciplines" in which all or many of the academic departments are involved in the teaching of writing.

A. I don't know what your feeling is, but is it possible to teach writing without being competent in the content of a discipline? You can't teach writing simply as a formal technique. Each technique is determined by the specific content of the field. So the one who teaches writing in law school should, I think, be informed about the laws and not simply a rhetorician.

Q. You say that the ideal situation would be to teach within the discourse of each particular discipline and not isolate rhetoric in a particular department. However, the political situation in American universities is such that rhetoric and composition specialists typically hold faculty positions in English departments, along with specialists in traditional literary areas and critical theory. Composition programs (and their faculty) are beginning to emerge as powerful components of many English departments because of the increasing political, economic, and curricular importance of writing instruction. Understandably, the co-existence in many institutions of traditional literature professors and these newer composition professors has created a certain amount of tension and professional rivalry. Given this political situation, do you believe that writing/rhetoric programs should be housed in English—that is, *literature*—departments? Or should they, as in a few American institutions, exist as independent departments devoted exclusively to the study of and instruction in language, writing, and rhetoric?

A. Both, I would say. I'm not attempting to avoid your question, but I would say that any unilateral solution would be bad. First, there's the question of English in this country. And this is a political question: why should composition and the teaching of rhetoric be linked not to English as English literature but to English as the English language, the American language? There are linguistic minorities in this country, so, to some extent, you have to teach English, including composition. Of course, English is and will remain the predominant language in this country, but if it's not the only spoken and written language in this country, if there are also the languages of minorities and also people who know other foreign languages—French or Spanish or Chinese or Japanese—then you have to respect this diversity. How to do so I don't know, but if English remains the only vehicle for the teaching of rhetoric and composition, that would be limiting, especially in this country. That's one level of this question. Another level is exactly the one you mentioned: whether it's a good thing that writing teachers be in English departments because the English departments are the most powerful and the largest, even though differences among colleagues may occur. Many of my best students in this country are in English departments; their fields are more differentiated, and there are more struggles. So, I think it's important that a large number of composition teachers belong to the English department. But it would be a bad thing that they be confined in them because there are other perspectives and, of course, other disciplines which are not literary disciplines. So, it's important, too, that to some extent, in some ways, teachers of rhetoric and composition not remain confined in the English department. My answer is apparently contradictory, but that's politics. You have to be contradictory in a sense; you have to do both.

Q. You wouldn't, then, put them in their own department by themselves—a department of rhetoric and composition?

A. No, but there must be some specificity, something in the training of teachers in rhetoric, something in common. They should have something in common, as well as a specialization in a field or discipline. So my answer is what we call in French *une réponse de Normand*, which is "yes and no; on the one hand and on the other hand." Any unilateral solution would be bad.

Q. A few other questions about the teaching of writing. One connection between deconstruction and composition may be a recognition of the incredibly complex nature of communication processes and a recognition of the "fleeting uncertainty" of knowledge. Do you see any specific implications for composition studies in the recognition that we are trapped in a logocentric world? If so, what are they?

A. Of course there is a connection between deconstruction and composition. Of course composition should recognize the complexity of communication processes and the uncertainty of knowledge. But before reaching the level of these concerns—the university level, where we should really face these questions—I think deconstruction should go through a reflection on the institution of composition. As you know, deconstruction is not simply a critical questioning about, let's say, language or what is called "communication processing." It's not only a way of reading texts in the trivial sense; it's also a way of dealing with institutions. Not only with content and concepts, but with the authority of institutions, with the models of institutions, with the hard structures of institutions. And we know that "the complex nature of communication processes, and so on" depends on many institutions, and, to begin with, on schools. So, the connection between deconstruction and composition should be problematized—first, I would say, in political and institutional terms. The word *composition*, as you know, is an old word, implying that you can distinguish between the meaning, the contents of the meaning, and the way you put these together. As you know, *deconstruction* means, among other things, the questioning of what synthesis is, what thesis is, what a position is, what composition is, not only in terms of rhetoric, but what *position* is, what *positing* means. Deconstruction questions the *thesis*, the theme, the positionality of everything, including, among other things, *com*position. Writing is not simply a "composition." So once you realize that writing is not simply a way of positing or posing things together, a number of consequences follow.

Without remaining at this level, which is radical—but we have to mention this radicality—I would say that in the university, or in high school, or in any academic field, deconstruction should provoke not only a questioning of the authority of some models in composition, but also a new way of writing, of composing—composing oral speeches and composing written papers. Now, this new way is not simply a new model; deconstruction doesn't provide a new model. But once you have analyzed and questioned and destabilized the authority of the old models, you have to invent each time new forms according to the situation, the pragmatic conditions of the situation, the audience, your own purpose, your own motivation to invent new forms. And these depend on what I was just calling the "pragmatic" in the sense of speech act theory. In each situation you have to write and speak differently. Teachers should not impose a rigid scheme in any situation. A moment ago, I was speaking of my training in France; the rigidity of those forms, those norms for rhetoric and composition, was terrible. It had some good aspects too, but it was terrible. You had to write what we called a *dissertation* according to a certain pattern: in the introduction you should ask a question after having played naive; that is, you should act as if you do not know what the question is, then you *invent* the question, you justify the question, and at the end of the introduction you ask the question. Then in three parts you.... Well, there's no need to describe the formula, but it was terribly rigid. So I think through deconstruction you should study and analyze these models and where they come from, where their authority comes from, what the finality of these models is, what interests they serve—personal, political, ideological, and so on. So we have to study the models and the history of the models and then try not to subvert them for the sake of destroying them but to change the models and invent new ways of writing—not as a formal challenge, but for ethical, political reasons.

Q. As a matter of fact, there have been at least three new books published in the 1980s in America that attempt to apply your work in the classroom: Gregory Ulmer's *Applied Grammatology*, G. Douglas Atkins and Michael Johnson's *Writing and Reading Differently*, and Sharon Crowley's *A Teacher's Introduction to Deconstruction*. Are you familiar with any of these texts and, if so, what is your response to them? Generally, are you satisfied with how your work has been applied pedagogically?

A. I must confess that the only one you mentioned that I know is Greg Ulmer's *Applied Grammatology*. I greatly admire Gregory Ulmer's book—not only this book but everything he writes. It's very important for me and very rigorous. I think what he did in *Applied Grammatology* is, first, very original, which means that it's not simply an "application." It moves very far from, let's say, the premises, what he would call "the premises"; it's not simply an applied grammatology. It goes much further. This means to me that he opens a new field; he's not only applying something relating to the field, but he has discovered a field of new possibilities. I agree with him that in *Of Grammatology* pedagogical problematics were not applied but *implied*. This doesn't mean I would apply these implications the way he does. I don't know; I haven't done such work. But I'm sure he's right in trying to propose a new pedagogy that takes into account new technologies, the new space opened by those questions, and that is not frightened by the modernity of telecommunications, video, etc. I'm not sure I would agree or disagree with his approach; I don't have anything very specific to say about the methodology he would practice. But I'm sure that an awareness of the problematics is absolutely necessary, and it's what is expected from all of us. [Note: A week after this interview, Derrida wrote in a personal correspondence, "I'm currently reading another book, as new and as important, by Greg Ulmer: *Teletheory: Grammatology in the Age of Video* (Routledge, 1989). I find it illuminating for the questions we were discussing in New York."]

Q. So you're encouraged by such attempts.

A. Of course, absolutely.

Q. For close to two decades, Roland Barthes has been refining a classroom practice of deconstruction aimed at throwing literary texts into disorder and deconstructing academic, professional discourse. He lets classroom discourse "float," "fragment," and "digress." Do you believe these techniques would be appropriate not only in the literature classroom but in the *writing* classroom? If so, in what way?

A. I wouldn't approve of simply throwing literary texts into disorder. First, deconstructing academic, professional discourse doesn't mean simply destroying the norms or pushing these norms to utter chaos. I'm not in favor simply of disorder. In fact, there are many ways of practicing order and disorder. I'm sure that there are very conservative ways of throwing texts into disorder, or very conservative ways of disorganizing the classroom. On the contrary, there are very disturbing ways of teaching quietly and, apparently, according to the most traditional forms. I'm not presenting myself as a model for pedagogy, far from it, but people who have a certain image of deconstruction and associate it with me would be very surprised by the way I teach, the way I read papers, the way I give advice to students; it's apparently a very traditional way. The scenario is very classical. In my case, in order to convey what I want to say or to provoke what I want to provoke, I need a very quiet and classical staging of the teaching. But this is not a model; my situation is very specific. When I started teaching, I arrived in the classroom (as everyone does) with a few notes, spoke according to these notes, asked questions, and so on. Now, I just lecture. I arrive with a written paper. I don't change a word for two hours. Everybody is quiet (which is usually the case in France). In some ways it's a liberal way of teaching, in that everyone can cooperate and interrupt me—though, in fact, no one does except when I stop and say, "Well, now we'll start the discussion." Nevertheless, I think that through these very academic, very quiet and conservative ways of teaching, something nonconservative and disturbing arises. But it depends on the situation. At CUNY, for instance, I don't teach the same way. I've only a few notes, and I improvise. So, I don't think there is a model for teaching and an alternative between, let's say, a conservative and a progressive teaching.

What we have to do, perhaps, once the minimal requirements are fulfilled in terms of language, grammar, comprehension, and so on, is to let each teacher have maximum freedom for his or her idiom in teaching, according, again, to the situation. And the situation depends on the audience and the teacher, and the situation is different in New York and Florida, even in some sections in New York and other sections. You have to adjust your teaching according to the situation. I call my students in France back to the most traditional ways of reading before trying to deconstruct texts; you have to understand according to the most traditional norms what an author meant to say, and so on. So I don't start with disorder; I start with the tradition. If you're not trained in the tradition, then deconstruction means nothing. It's simply nothing.

Q. What about those teachers who are afraid of what deconstruction might bring to the classroom, afraid, perhaps, of confusing students, afraid that it may just undermine some of the goals they thought they had? Is there anything we can tell them?

A. First, I would say, when they say this in good faith, I understand them and I approve. I think that if what is called "deconstruction" produces neglect of the classical authors, the canonical texts, and so on, we should fight it. I wouldn't be in favor of such a deconstruction. I'm in favor of the canon, but I won't stop there. I think that students should *read* what are considered the great texts in our tradition—even if that's not enough, even if we have to change the canon, even if we have to open the field and to bring into the canonical tradition other texts from other cultures. If deconstruction is only a pretense to ignore minimal requirements or knowledge of the tradition, it could be a bad thing. So when those colleagues complain about the fact that some students, without knowing the tradition, play at deconstruction, try to behave deconstructively, I agree that's a mistake, a bad thing, and we shouldn't encourage it. However, sometimes some colleagues refer to these situations simply in order to *oppose* deconstruction: "Well, the effect of deconstruction is this, so we must exclude deconstruction." That's what I would call bad faith in the service of conservative politics. So, I would say that we should require, according to the situation—which may be very different from one country to the other, one city to the other—a minimal (the definition of *minimal* is problematic, I know) culture and minimal knowledge of the basic foundations of the canon. On this ground, of course, students could develop, let's say, a deconstructive practice—but only to the extent that they "know" what they are "deconstructing": an enormous network of other questions.

Q. Vincent Leitch says that deconstructive pedagogy moves "beyond" traditional liberalism in that it could serve conservative or liberal agendas. Such "heterogeneity," says Leitch, is the "hallmark of deconstructive productions." Peter Shaw, on the other hand, says that deconstruction is the child of French radical, leftist politics; it is by nature already political and "leftist." Which perspective is more in line with your own?

A. I understand why Vincent Leitch says what he says. In fact, according to the privilege you give to one or another aspect, deconstruction may look conservative. I'm in favor of tradition. I'm respectful of and a lover of the tradition. There's no deconstruction without the memory of the tradition. I couldn't imagine what the university could be without reference to the tradition, but a tradition that is as rich as possible and that is open to other traditions, and so on. That's conservative; tradition is conservative to that extent. But at the same time deconstruction is not conservative. Out of respect for the tradition, deconstruction asks questions; it puts into question the tradition and even the concept of "question" (which I did in *Of Spirit: Heidegger and the Question* [Chicago UP, 1989])—and this, clearly, is a nonconservative stand. So this oscillation is not pertinent here. Deconstruction is, at the same time, conservative and nonconservative. This political translation is not pertinent here either. If you use these political criteria, these old criteria, to describe the effects of deconstruction in the academy, you say, "Well, sometimes, of course, some professors are comforted by deconstruction because it helps them to reinforce the tradition and to exclude other politically subversive questions." That may happen, of course; or it may happen the other way around. That's why there is not one deconstruction, and deconstruction is not a single theory or a single method. I often repeat this: deconstruction is not a method or a theory; it's something that happens—it happens. And it happens not only in the academy; it happens everywhere in the world. It happens in society, in history, in the army, in the economy, and so on. What is called deconstruction in the academy is only a small part of a more general and, I would say, older process. There are a number of deconstructions occurring everywhere.

Now, if we refer to deconstruction as an organized discourse which appeared under that name some twenty-five years ago, of course, this phenomenon, as such, appeared in France. Nevertheless, it was not originally French; it appeared in France as already the heritage of a number of old things—German things, for instance. It was a new hybrid or graft, the French graft, of something older which implies Marxism, Heideggereanism, psychoanalysis, structuralism, and so on. So if it's a child, it's a bastard, I would say. As a child of French leftist politics, it was already a bastard, a hybrid. Now, I should say, since deconstruction is always associated with me, that I consider myself a leftist. I won't say it's visceral, but I never thought of myself as anything other than a leftist. But this doesn't mean that deconstruction, as such, is leftist. Depending on the situation, it can be a weapon to resist, let's say, liberal capitalism; in other situations, a way of resisting leftist totalitarianism. So it's not intrinsically one or the other. This doesn't mean that I have a relativistic view of deconstruction. I would say it's not a theory that can be abstracted from a given field of forces—political, economical, etc. You see, even in France it's not always considered radical and leftist. It's considered such by some and the other way around by others. If it were really only the child of French radicalism, how could you account for its success in the United States, which is more widespread than in France? For me, deconstruction is rather an American child. The fact that apparently it came from France and landed in the States but received in the States a welcome and extension which is out of proportion with what it has been in Europe, and the fact that now it is beginning to come back to Europe through the United States means that the real birthplace, if we follow this metaphor—which I would not want to follow very far—the richer, most fecund birthplace is the United States, and probably for very serious reasons. I apologize for quoting myself, but in *Mémoires for Paul de Man*, the three lectures I gave at Irvine a few years ago about deconstruction in America, I ventured to say at some point that "deconstruction *is* America." It's for essential reasons that deconstruction has had such a development in this country. And we have to understand why—for what historical, political, and theological reasons in the tradition of the United States—deconstruction is such a phenomenon. So if it's a child, it's as well a child of the United States.

Q. Many compositionists draw on the work of Paulo Freire and his notions of "critical literacy" and "liberatory learning." Are you familiar with Freire's work? If so, do you believe that deconstruction and liberatory learning share similar goals?

A. This is the first time I've seen his name.

Q. He's a Marxist educator in Brazil, and he's got quite a following in America and internationally. He is interested in subverting the traditional kinds of teaching which help to reinforce and reproduce the ideology of the ruling class and that keep people illiterate in the name of literacy. Freire wants to subvert such hierarchies.

A. Well, I'm not familiar with his work, but, referring to your description, I would say that in some situations—and we have to take such situations into account—deconstruction would help liberatory learning. I think that you couldn't compare, for instance, the situation in industrial, rich societies and the situation in oppressed, Third World countries. But in the situation of a repressive teaching institution, in the situation in which learning and culture are used in order to confirm the given hegemony, I think that deconstruction could help, could have some emancipatory effect. However, I can imagine some perverse use of deconstruction in the hands of the authorities, who might, for instance, maintain the given order by using apparently deconstructive arguments. So you have to suspect the strategy of self-appointed deconstructionists. To act in a liberatory or emancipatory way, it's not enough to *claim* to be a deconstructionist or to apply deconstruction. In each situation you have to watch, and I can imagine (of course, I try not to do so) someone using deconstruction with reactionary and repressive effects or goals. That's why you can't stop watching and analyzing. You can't simply rely on names, titles, or claims.

Q. Hélène Cixous and other French feminists advocate that women create a "women's language"—a language that inscribes femininity, a "new insurgent" language that liberates, ruptures, and transforms "phallogocentric" discourse. Such a language aims "to break up, to destroy," to "wreck partitions, classes, rhetorics, regulations and codes." Do you see these strategies as identical to those of deconstruction? Can deconstruction serve to help bring about the goals and aspirations of feminism? Or do you believe that such attempts are merely replacing one hierarchy with another?

A. Sometimes it does; it depends on the way women and sometimes men practice this writing, teaching, speaking, and so on. Sometimes feminism replaces phallogocentrism with another kind of hegemony. I wouldn't say that all women do that, but it's a structural temptation. It's perhaps inevitable at some point that they try to reverse the given hierarchy, but if they do only that—reverse the hierarchy—they would reinscribe the same scheme. Sometimes feminism, as such, does that, and I know that some women are not happy about that. You are quoting Hélène Cixous, a very old friend of mine whom I admire deeply, and she is, I would say, one of the greatest writers in France today. She, at some point, of course, spoke of "feminine writing," but I don't think she would still do that, if by "feminine writing" you refer to a specific essentially feminine way of writing. At some points in history, women have had to claim that there is some irreducible feminine way of writing—themes, style, position in the field of literature—not in order to essentialize this, but as a phase in the ongoing war or process or struggle. But if some of them—and I don't think this is the case with Hélène Cixous—would try to say it's the eternal essential feminine which is manifested in this feminine writing, then they would repeat the scheme they claim they are fighting.

Q. Several composition theorists are especially interested in social constructionism because if you posit that all "facts" and knowledge, even *reality* itself, are community created and maintained, then rhetoric becomes the central, paradigmatic epistemic activity. That is, if all of our knowledge and facts and reality are created by social groups, by discourse communities, then rhetoric is the key to it all. What are your thoughts about social constructionism?

A. I must confess, I'm not familiar with the term "social constructionism."
Q. It's a movement drawing in part from the work of Thomas Kuhn and others that posits that all knowledge, all facts, even the ways we think are not "essential" but rather depend on the social group. So, for example, if the community of, let's say, philosophers believes such and such, then that becomes the current "knowledge" until the community of philosophers decides to change this knowledge.
A. I wouldn't be inclined to think that the beliefs, the values, the norms in the community depend on, let's say, thinkers or philosophers, as such. This doesn't mean that philosophy or thinking is simply a symptom, but it's not a *cause* of the shared values. The social structure doesn't obey this kind of causality. I would say that philosophy is neither just an epiphenomenon, nor the cause of or the place where everything is decided on or constructed. Although I'm unfamiliar with social constructionism, I'd like to make a point about rhetoric becoming the central paradigmatic, epistemic activity. On the one hand, I would think that we should not neglect the importance of rhetoric, as if it were simply a formal superstructure or technique exterior to the essential activity. Rhetoric is something decisive in society. On the other hand, I would be very suspicious of what I would call "rhetoricism"—a way of giving rhetoric all the power, thinking that everything depends on rhetoric as simply a technique of speech. Certainly, there are no politics, there is no society without rhetoric, without the force of rhetoric. Not only in economics but also in literary strategy, rhetoric is essential. Even among diplomats, rhetoric is very important; in the nuclear age much depends on some kind of rhetoric. (I tried to show this in an article called "No Apocalypse, Not Now" in *Diacritics*.) Now, this doesn't mean that everything depends on verbal statements or formal technique of speech acts. There are speech acts everywhere, but the possibility of speech acts, or performative speech acts, depends on conditions and conventions which are not simply verbal. What I call "writing" or "text" is not simply verbal. That's why I'm very interested in rhetoric but very suspicious of rhetoricism.
Q. How might composition teachers and theorists avoid falling into this rhetoricism? How can they be cautious; what steps can they take?
A. There is an inherent danger of rhetoricism in the teaching of rhetoric. You can't avoid that. It's intrinsic. When you teach rhetoric you are inclined to imply that so much depends on rhetoric. But I think that a self-conscious and trained teacher, attentive to the complexity, should at the same time underline the importance of rhetoric and the limits of rhetoric—the limits of verbality, formality, figures of speech. Rhetoric doesn't consist only in the technique of tropes, for instance. First, rhetoric is not confined to what is traditionally called figures and tropes. Secondly, rhetoric, as such, depends on conditions that are not rhetorical. In rhetoric and speaking, the same sentence may have enormous effects or have no effects

at all, depending on conditions that are not verbal or rhetorical. I think a self-conscious, trained teacher of rhetoric should teach precisely what are called "pragmatics"; that is, the effects of rhetoric don't depend only on the way you utter words, the way you use tropes, the way you compose. They depend on certain situations: political situations, economical situations—the libidinal situation, also.

Q. Ever since Plato's opposition to rhetoric as a discipline, philosophy and rhetoric seem to have existed in a state of continual tension. Why does there seem to be tension between these disciplines? Aren't these disciplines—rhetoric and philosophy—necessarily bound together? Aren't they necessarily intricately and complexly tied?

A. Well, from that point of view I would be on the side of philosophy. The tension comes first from the fact that rhetoric as a separate discipline, as a technique or as an autonomous field, may become a sort of empty instrument whose usefulness or effectiveness would be independent of logic, or even reference or truth—an instrument in the hands of the sophists in the sense that Plato wanted to define them. So contrary to what some people think I think—for instance, Habermas—I would be on the side of philosophy, logic, truth, reference, etc. When I question philosophy and the philosophical project as such, it's not in the name of sophistics, of rhetoric as just a playful technique. I'm interested in the rhetoric hidden in philosophy itself because within, let's say, the typical Platonic discourse there is a rhetoric—a rhetoric against rhetoric, against sophists. I've been interested in the way concepts or arguments depend intrinsically on metaphors, tropes, and are in themselves to some extent metaphors or tropes. I'm not saying that all concepts are essentially metaphors and therefore everything is rhetoric. No, I try to deconstruct the opposition between concept and metaphor and to rebuild, to restructure this field. I'm not at ease with metaphor either. I'm not saying, "Well, we should just substitute metaphor for concept or simply be content with metaphors." What I say, for example, in *White Mythology* is that the concept of metaphor, first, is a metaphor; it's loaded with philosophy—a very old philosophy—and so we shouldn't keep the concept of metaphor the way it is commonly received. So I would distrust, suspect, the couple concept and metaphor. And I would, for the same reasons, be suspicious of the opposition between philosophy and rhetoric. To the extent that I am caught up within this couple, I'm a philosopher, but I try not to remain within this opposition. I try to understand what has happened since Plato and in a recurrent way until now in this opposition between philosophy and rhetoric.

Q. Let me ask you more about the sophists. Recently, several historians of rhetoric have sought to revive the legacy of certain "good" sophists—Gorgias, Protagoras, and Prodicus, for example—finding them lost exemplars of an anti-Platonism attuned to the ways that the contexts for rhetorical acts can shift. In your deconstruction of the *Phaedrus* in "Plato's Pharmacy," you seem to offer support for a sophistic stance toward rhetoric and philosophy. Yet, at times you seem to retreat from a full-fledged endorsement of the sophists. Would you elaborate on your attitude toward the sophists for these historians? Do you think that we know enough about them to conceptualize their legacy?

A. Your question implies the answer, and, in a way, I've already suggested an answer. I've resisted the way Plato attacked or imprisoned the sophists, captured the sophists, in the figure of the sophists. To that extent, it's as if I were simply counterattacking Plato from the position of the sophists. But as you've said, it's not that simple: if the sophists are what Plato thinks they are, I'm not in favor of the sophists; however, I think it's much more complicated. We don't have enough knowledge; the question of what the sophists really were is an enormous question. I wouldn't venture to simplify this. Considering how little we know of what the sophists were, I think today we must be interested in the challenge philosophy was to the sophists, as well as the challenge the sophists were, and still are in their modern form, to philosophy. This has had, again, a recurrent form in many epochs, including Nietzsche's and ours. So today, first, we should remember what happened between Plato, Socrates and the sophists—remember all the subsequent figures of this opposition. But also we must try not to reduce modern conflicts to this opposition. There are people who say, "Well, today we have to restore philosophy against the modern sophists." And usually deconstructionists are considered the modern sophists. Such people are reducing the complexity and the singularity of the situation. We're not in the same situation. We have, of course, to refer to these Greek situations because they are part of our heritage, but some essential things have changed, and we have to take these changes into account. There are no more sophists today and I would say no more philosophers in the given sense. So I'm not in favor of sophistics. But neither am I against the sophists, against Protagoras and the others. I would try to give an accurate analysis if possible of what is inherited, but also of what is new in our culture. And I think the battle between Plato and the sophists is not pertinent enough.

Q. Rhetoric is defined in many disciplines as Aristotle's "discovery of the available means of persuasion." Yet, in many English departments, the notion of "rhetoric" that has become increasingly familiar is the view promulgated by Nietzsche, Paul de Man, J. Hillis Miller, Barbara Johnson, and others. They seem to equate rhetoric with the cognitively disruptive interplay of tropes—the status of text as an allegory of its ultimate unreadability. Some rhetoricians tend to regard this notion as an undue truncation of what appears to be a Western rhetorical tradition. Would you agree with this judgment? By giving such importance to their own particular sense of "rhetoric," can these deconstructionists be accused of "rhetoricism"? Or does this set of questions unfairly characterize them?

A. This is a very delicate question since names are dropped. It's very difficult. As you know, I'm very close to the people you mention here, but at the same time I'm not doing exactly what they're doing with regard to rhetoric. All of them are attentive, and I think rightly so, to rhetoric. First, I wouldn't agree with this opposition. Paul de Man, for example, is interested in rhetoric also as a means of persuasion. And his theories precisely of grammar, rhetoric, tropes, and persuasion are very complex ones.

Q. So you don't think that this work necessarily subverts the ancient rhetorical tradition?

A. I would not simply reduce these people, these works, to a single, homogeneous set; however new these works are, they aren't simply inventing a new rhetoric or breaking with the tradition. Their relation to the tradition is more complex: it disrupts and it inherits at the same time. For instance, when Paul de Man speaks of "unreadability," he's not simply a rhetoricist (although in comparison what I'm doing is less rhetoricist than his work). There are so many differences here between de Man and myself that this is difficult to answer, but let me try an answer that would do justice to the complexity without really being able to engage in the full complexity of this subject. I would say, for instance, that de Man and Hillis Miller, differently, are very much, and I would say rightly so, interested in rhetoric in literature and in the problem of rhetoric. Sometimes it's as if rhetoric could have the last word for both of them, especially for Paul de Man. Then, perhaps, someone could speak of rhetoricism. Sometimes I'm tempted to say, "There is a danger of rhetoricism here—that is, of claiming to exhaust the text, the reading of the text, through the means of rhetorical questions." But at some point, what de Man and Miller do goes further than rhetoric. For instance, when de Man speaks of the aporia between performative and constative, when he speaks of unreadability and so on, he exceeds the classical field of rhetoric, although through a new problematic of rhetoric. Another example is when Hillis Miller asks questions, when he not only reads Victorian novels in a new way, in a deconstructive way, being attentive to all the rhetorical figures, but when he asks ethical questions, when he speaks of the ethics of reading, and so on; the ethics of reading cannot be reduced to rhetoric.

This doesn't mean that rhetoric is simply subordinate, not simply, but rhetoric is not the last word. Rhetoric is subordinate to something which is not simply rhetorical. When sometimes I've used the word *rhetoricism*, it was not simply in reference to rhetoric. I remember having used this word as an accusation. I was not referring to what we call "rhetoric" or to the attention given to rhetoric. On the contrary, I am in favor of the most rigorous and most generous attention given to rhetoric. What I'm suspicious of under the name "rhetoricism" is the authority of language.

Rhetoric comes from, as you know, a Greek word meaning *speaking*. So, the charge of logocentrism or phonocentrism is, by itself, a charge against rhetoricism—not the narrow field of what we call rhetoric, but simply the authority of speech, the authority of speaking. If you give absolute privilege to rhetoric you fall into what I call logocentrism or phonocentrism; that's what I meant when I spoke of rhetoricism. I was not charging anyone with being too attentive to rhetoric. I think we should be attentive to rhetoric and to language as much as possible, but the hegemony of speaking over anything else—writing, acting, and so on—is a kind of rhetoricism. So for me, rhetoricism in that context is synonymous with logocentrism or phonocentrism.

Q. Some of your remarks on Chinese characters in *Of Grammatology* suggest that logocentrism may be less prevalent in non-Western cultures. If so, can we turn to these other cultures as a model of a post-logocentric culture, or are we doomed to remain within logocentrism and struggle against it?

A. Well, for these very, very difficult questions there are many possible answers. Let me attempt an immediate answer, not a learned or scholarly answer. I wouldn't say that logocentrism, as such, is less prevalent in non-Western cultures. I would speak of "phonocentrism"; I would say that the phonocentrism of a culture linked to a technique of writing, which submits, for instance, writing to speech, is less prevalent in cultures in which non-phonetic writing prevails—the Chinese language, for instance. But I would dissociate here phonocentrism from logocentrism, because even in a culture which is non-phonocentric with respect to its technique of writing, the logocentric scheme may prevail with all its essential features, even all the oppositions, the hierarchies which are linked to logocentrism in Western cultures. So I would say that phonocentrism has prevailed in Western cultures. Logocentrism, however, is a universal structure.

That's the unlearned answer, using the word *logos* in the wide sense. Now, if you refer to *logos* in its Greek, determined sense, then, of course, logocentrism is only a Western phenomenon. Then we'll have to understand what logos is. Last week I gave a lecture on Heidegger and precisely on the tradition of logos, what he wrote about logos. I tried to show how Heidegger was logocentric, not because logos was considered the center, but because, for Heidegger, logos is a gatherer; it's something which assembles, unifies, gathers everything. Logocentrism wouldn't mean in that case that logos is at the center of everything, but that logos is the centering structure; it is the structure or the experience of re-gathering—that is, re-assembling around the circle, re-forming the circle, not being at the center of the circle but gathering instead of dissociating the authority of the one as opposed to the multiple, to the other. So from that point of view, if you interpret the tradition of logos—which, of course, you can't do improvising in front of these little tape recorders—then I would say logocentrism is essentially Western. Logocentrism literally, as such, is nothing else but Greek. Everywhere that the Greek culture is the dominant heritage there is logocentrism.

I wouldn't draw as a conclusion, as a consequence of this, that we should simply leave it behind. Perhaps modern China is Greek and as logocentric as any other culture. I wouldn't say that we have to "leave" logocentrism. It's something that we can't simply turn our back on and say, "enough." There's another way of, let's say, living with this memory and transforming it and thinking it, and to think of it is not simply living within it. You can travel all your life and go very far from Europe without stopping being logocentric, and you can live in Athens or in New York or in Rome and already have left logocentrism to some degree. I think that the deconstruction of logocentrism is not a matter of decision, it's not a matter of deliberate politics; it happens—it just happens.

Q. Have the non-Western cultures been an influence on your thought?

A. Unfortunately not. The *existence* of such cultures, the *fact* that they limit or delimit or make a pressure on our own, of course, has an influence. I can't simply sleep and ignore this. But if by "influence" you mean: do I really know from the inside a non-Western culture, then no, unfortunately; of course, I should but I don't. I would like to, but that's a limitation on my part. What is interesting to me—and unfortunately I'm not able to follow this work—is that there have been a number of publications on the relationship between deconstruction and some non-Western cultures—Buddhism and Zen, etc. So I read to some extent these books, but I can't really say they've influenced me.

Q. Final question: your work has been cited extensively by countless scholars from numerous disciplines. Such frequent citation necessarily increases the opportunity for misunderstanding or misrepresenting your views. Are you aware of any specific misunderstanding that you would like to take issue with at this time? Any analyses or critiques of your work that have been misinformed?

A. First, there are no simple misunderstandings. Each time you read a text—and this is my situation and the situation of every reader—there is some misunderstanding, but I know of no way to avoid this. Misunderstanding is always significant; it's not simply a mistake, or just an absurdity. It's something that is motivated by some interest and some understanding. Sometimes the most ferocious critics who react vehemently and passionately and sometimes with hatred understand more than supporters do, and it's *because* they understand more that they react this way. Sometimes they understand unconsciously, or they know what is at stake. Sometimes I think that this enemy, because he's so ferocious, so nervous, is more aware of what is at stake than a friendly ally is. So, sometimes misunderstanding is understanding, and the other way around.

After these preliminary cautions, I would say, very briefly, that the misunderstandings that I deplore most would be, in the broad sense, political and institutional. I think that the people who try to represent what I'm doing or what so called "deconstruction" is doing, as, on the one hand, trying to destroy culture or, on the other hand, to reduce it to a kind of negativity, to a kind of death, are misrepresenting deconstruction. Deconstruction is essentially affirmative. It's in favor of reaffirmation of memory, but this reaffirmation of memory asks the most adventurous and the most risky questions about our tradition, about our institutions, about our way of teaching, and so on. When people try to confine deconstruction in negative models as something nonpolitical, noninstitutional or as something confined to books, to speculative speeches, to what is in the library, when they interpret text as something which is written down and not in the generalized concept that I've tried to elaborate, I think it's a very serious misrepresentation. But it's the symptom of a resistance; it's not simply a mistake. It's precisely a resistance to what is happening through deconstruction. So I try to understand what this resistance is, where it comes from; and sometimes this resistance is at work within myself, within the people who are supposed to be in favor of deconstruction. These prejudices about the notion of text, the notion of writing, are as old as what I call "deconstruction," which is about twenty-five years old. From the beginning, I tried again and again to say, "Well, a text is not simply an alphabetic note or a book." And from this statement a number of consequences should follow. But from the beginning and from the most authorized voices in France and over here came not simply the misunderstanding but the deliberate effect of misunderstanding. They didn't want to understand. Foucault tried not to understand, and many people, distinguished individuals who really understood what was going on, tried to reduce the text to "the book," the writing to the "pen"—and with all the consequences of this reduction. If this mistake, this prejudice, could be left behind or deconstructed, then a number of consequences would follow.

Jacques Derrida on Teaching and Rhetoric: A Response

SHARON CROWLEY

When I talked with Gary Olson about the *JAC* interview with Jacques Derrida, I heard the term "deconstruction moonie" for the first time. If I understand correctly, the phrase refers to a person who uncritically subscribes to deconstruction as the authoritative way to interpret the workings of language and culture, and who does not easily brook dissent from this view.

Any deconstruction moonies who may be lurking in the halls will be disappointed, I'm afraid, by Derrida's responses to Olson's questions about rhetoric and teaching composition. Derrida persists in giving what he calls *"une réponse de Normand"*; "yes and no"; "on the one hand and on the other hand." This is not simply Gallic coyness, however. Despite (or perhaps because of) his status as an intellectual celebrity, Derrida is wary of simple answers to difficult questions.

In the interview, Derrida reminds readers of a couple of things that American deconstructionists are wont to forget. Prominent among these is his reiterated assertion of the importance of tradition. This apparently surprised Olson, but it shouldn't have. As Derrida observes, deconstruction cannot happen without a tradition to deconstruct. Those who read nihilism into deconstruction picture it as an advocacy for disorder, for deconstruction of tradition and culture. But this is a sheer impossibility. How is it possible, for example, to feel the necessity to deconstruct a literary canon if you have never felt the exclusionary pressures exerted by that canon? How is it possible to feel the necessity of opening up writing instruction to something other than instruction in formalism if you have never felt the oppression imposed on writers by instruction in traditional methods?

A deconstruction exposes and critiques reified ways of seeing, exposes them for what they are: interested. The reification of any way of reading (even deconstructive reading) is always motivated by institutional or cultural politics. As those of us who regularly find ourselves on the down side of English department politics know only too well, terms like "deconstructionist" and "poststructuralist" can be used to justify business-as-usual as easily as terms like "organic unity" or "canonical writer." In the interview Derrida expresses his suspicion of "self-appointed deconstructionists" who would appropriate his work to claim authority for their own interested ways of reading. He worries about this possibility since, like anything else in language, the name "deconstruction" can be put either to repressive or liberatory uses; "that's why you can't stop watching and analyzing. You can't simply rely on names, titles, or claims."

Deconstruction can't be worn like a new hat. It happens. It happens when certain cultural pressures work to reify some ways of seeing while other forces work to reify others. The tension which results between authorized and alternative readings of texts, or pedagogies, or cultures, or anything else, is necessarily deconstructive. To give a small example from the institutional history of composition instruction: so-called "process pedagogy" deconstructed some aspects of current-traditional rhetoric, in particular its suppression of the fact that the process of composing does not always repeat the spatial alignment of prose on a page. Teachers who were familiar with the oppressive and limited view of writing given by current-traditional rhetoric undertook its deconstruction because no one else was in a position to do so. This deconstruction of a reified writing pedagogy was naive and partial; that is, it was not undertaken with some deconstructive methodology in mind, and it offered a limited critique of the traditional writing classroom. But it was no less necessary for all that.

The advantage of deconstruction is that it permits us to oppose tradition to its suppressed alternatives, and from this opposition to generate yet other alternatives. As Derrida repeatedly implies in the interview, the oppositional assumptions we habitually make are too simple because they overgeneralize. Olson asks a series of either-or questions: should writing be taught in the disciplines or in a single department by persons skilled in rhetoric? Is writing a universal technique, or does it manifest itself differently in different disciplines? Are you on the side of the rhetoricians or the philosophers? Derrida refuses to take sides on any of these questions because both sides (all sides) have their uses, have things to teach us. Rather, he looks for new models which appropriate features from both alternatives, and his guidelines for constructing such models are drawn from ethics and politics rather than from metaphysics.

Derrida is reluctant to take sides on general questions because he is acutely aware of the situatedness of any debatable issue. He does not comment on the relevance of the ancient sophists to contemporary rhetoric partly because we know so little about them, but, more importantly, because their historical situation is not ours. Nevertheless, his refusal to accept nonsituated readings of any situation smacks of the sophistic. For example, he implies that universalized composition pedagogies aren't particularly desirable since there are always exceptions to any rule. One cannot condemn traditional teaching, exactly, because "there are very disturbing ways of teaching quietly and, apparently, according to the most traditional forms." Compositionists who unilaterally advocate the use of student-centered classrooms should not overlook the pedagogical potential of the traditional teacher-centered classroom, in the right time and place.

The problem with universalized pedagogies is that they disguise and compromise the context of teaching. French students are not American students; what may be said about composition in French in France may not necessarily be said about composition in English in America; the teacher who only lectures is not necessarily conservative or authoritarian. What is constant in the context of university teaching is the academy itself, with its carefully defined specializations and status hierarchies. A universalized image of the academy often motivates the creation of universalized pedagogies, whether these are intended to extend the hegemony of the academy or to work against its power in favor of students. Such pedagogies are useful to the extent that they may be modified by and in the local situation in which they are employed.

From where Derrida sits, a productive examination of pedagogy would begin with a deconstruction of privileged pedagogies, not necessarily to overthrow them, but to determine from whence they derive their authority. For example, a deconstruction of current-traditional rhetoric discloses that this rhetoric reifies the authority of the academy and works to silence or displace the authority of students and teachers. Or, radical criticisms of social constructionism charge that its (seeming?) reification of peer consensus is oppressive to minority voices. A deconstruction undertaken along these lines would seek to know why consensus has been privileged at this moment in composition's institutional history, and whose interests are served by such privileging.

A deconstructive reading of composition studies would not content itself with looking at pedagogies in isolation, however. It would ask larger questions about composition as an academic institution. It would ask, irreverently enough, why composition is blessed (or cursed) at this moment in its history with a plethora of competing pedagogies. It would ask further whose interests are served by infusing composition theory with deconstruction, with social constructionism, with Freirean neo-Marxism, or with any other perspective for that matter. It might even ask why the theoretical diversity and excitement that characterize the meetings attended and journals read by composition teachers are not shared by faculty who don't teach writing, or by the culture at large, all of whom persist in defining freshman composition as a course in grammar, spelling, punctuation, and usage.

Northern Arizona University
Flagstaff, Arizona

"Where Have You Come from, Reb Derissa, and Where Are You Going?" Gary Olson's Interview with Jacques Derrida[1]

JASPER NEEL

Students come to my classes these days wearing T-shirts that read, "Shit happens." The teenager who murders his girlfriend in the film *River's Edge* explains, "You're born, shit happens, and you die." He displays neither militancy nor anger. Students who adorn their bodies with the statement seem to regard it as a face-value explanation that random events occur and pass. "Shit" in this parlance is the most neutral available term. This "shit" is not offensive, revolting, ugly, or odoriferous. It functions as in, "We were at the mall doin' a bunch o' shit."

"I often repeat this," Derrida says matter of factly in the *JAC* interview: "deconstruction is not a method or a theory; it's something that happens—it happens." "The deconstruction of logocentrism," he repeats, "is not a matter of decision, it's not a matter of deliberate politics; it happens—it just happens." In this sense, deconstruction was at work for millennia before the Tel Quel group began publishing. It is an utterly neutral, natural phenomenon.

Residents of Memphis, Tennessee old enough to remember World War II are likely to remember Dr. Robert G. Lee, the longtime pastor of Bellevue Baptist Church. By 1950 Bellevue was the largest church in the central South and one of the largest churches in the nation. Dr. Lee's powerful sermon about Jezebel, "Pay Day Some Day," made him famous throughout the South. When called upon to advise young Southern Baptist ministers, Dr. Lee always admonished them to seek formal training. "Go to New Orleans," he would say with an arch smile. "Do what they tell you at the seminary there. Then when you graduate, just listen to the Holy Spirit and preach the Bible. The Holy Spirit hasn't had courses in homiletics or systematic theology, but He won't hold these courses against you if you listen to Him, and your congregation won't listen to you if you haven't had these courses."

"People who read me and think I'm playing with or transgressing norms," Derrida says, "usually don't know what I know: that all of this has not only been made possible by but is constantly in contact with very classical, rigorous, demanding discipline in writing, in 'demonstrating,' in rhetoric." He continues:

> My classical training in France has been a great influence—all those competitions that I suffered from. The French system was and still is terrible from that point of view; you have to go through a number of selective competitions which make you suffer to make you better. I'm politically against this system and I fight it; nevertheless, I had to go through it. Yet, however negative it may be from some point of view, it's good discipline and I learned a lot from it.

"I start with the tradition," he repeats. "If you're not trained in the tradition, then deconstruction means nothing. It's simply nothing."

Deconstruction, like shit, just happens. Deconstruction, like the best, most powerful fundamentalist preaching, depends on a conservative curriculum whose competitive, agonistic operation marks the student, thereby enabling the radical struggle for "freedom" that comes after graduation.

Deconstruction, one might say, is a catachresis—in Coleridge's sense of the term as well as Perelman's.[2] Derrida is what Herbert Spencer called a catastrophist.[3] For composition professors, deconstruction functions as a sort of catachrestic catastrophism. It is both an opportunity and a liability, a labile chance, if you will. Unfortunately (or perhaps fortunately) we cannot let it "just happen" because it both implies and demands a certain fundamentalism.

First the chance; then the l(i)ability.

Chance

We can use "Derrida," as he himself says, to argue that "writing is the essential performance or act." Indeed, we can hardly resist using him this way, for if writing *is* "the essential act," then writing sets existence in relief, thereby settling the existence-essence precedence problem rhetorically. Using Derridean deconstruction, however, requires composition professors to make their wager on a perfecta card. Winning never just happens; it always entails loss and implies responsibility. If we win, then we must admit that those who cannot write also cannot perform the "essential act" and thus have no access to existence; as a result, the Freireans immediately demand to know how we intend to build "cultural action" into our professional self-definition. If we win, then writing precedes epistemic, exceeds ontology, and spreads itself both as the horizon on which the "episteme" can appear and as the medium in which the "logos" can reverberate; as a result, the deconstructionists dismiss us out-of-hand as graphocentrists. Derrida, perhaps against his wishes, shows us how to manage both what we win and what we lose: we begin with the logos, immediately transgress this beginning, and then inhabit a continuous, self-conscious deconstruction.

"For Heidegger," Derrida explains, "logos is a gatherer; it's something which assembles, unifies, gathers everything." Logocentrism functions not as a center itself but rather as a "centering structure." Logocentrism allows authority both to gather itself and to resist the dispersion of the multiple. Through Derridean deconstruction, composition can live with logocentrism as a memory while transforming it into a pedagogy. The pedagogy may seem unchanged because order, unity, and correctness continue to operate much as they did before. The shift is subtle. The composition professor thinks (of) logocentrism rather than simply living (in) it.

The effect of the boundary enables this thinking (of) rather than simple living (in) logocentrism. "There should be a specificity," Derrida says; "there must be some specificity, something in the training of teachers in rhetoric, something in common." But there must also be "a crossing of the boundaries." Derrida uses the word "model" sixteen times in the interview, the word "norm" fourteen, the words "form," "formula," and "pattern" a combined total of six times. Boundaries—their necessity, their function, the operations they enable—allow the discussion of composition to occur. Deconstruction allows the emergence of such boundaries through a kind of unlimited oscillation—an arhythmic, erratic swaying back and forth across these boundaries.

This oscillation gives such utterly discredited notions as "cause-effect" back to composition, but with a difference (that is, a *différance*). When "cause-effect" returns through deconstruction, it returns as a trope with a history, a trope that provides two sorts of specificity. First, composition professors must know this trope's origin in Aristotle's *Rhetoric* (1399^b5; 1400^a30). Second, students must learn it *as* a rhetorical effect, as a line of argument that functions in the service of enthymemic proof. Deconstruction demands that the boundary generated by each specificity be transgressed. The ontic value of each boundary depends on such transgression. While the professor learns to read the *Rhetoric* against itself—as a sheaf of lectures, a weaving of Attic folk notions, a problem in and for history—the student learns to see cause-effect as a contradiction that often has the apparently innocent rhetorical effect of incontrovertible truth.

By interrupting the rhythm of oscillation and constantly erasing the boundary lines, deconstruction constantly unworks both the foundation and the justification of any pedagogy that might include "cause-effect." Without deconstruction, the oscillation becomes rhythmically consistent, thus allowing itself to be enclosed within a new, invisible boundary. Then textbooks, even whole courses, can operate under the unquestioned hegemony of such notions as "cause-effect." "I can imagine some perverse use of deconstruction in the hands of the authorities," Derrida warns. Such authorities could "maintain the given order by using apparently deconstructive arguments.... That's why you can't stop watching and analyzing." At least for the compositionist, deconstruction must always operate as a kind of (unwanted) surprise.

More importantly, deconstruction "solicits" the institution of "composition" itself, which turns out to be nothing more than the Derridean version of the Heideggerian logos. Composition implies a bringing together, a location. Deconstruction, in contrast, questions everything composition has enabled: synthesis, thesis, position, positing, even the implication "that you can distinguish between the meaning, the contents of the meaning, and the way you put these together." Deconstruction gives composition to composition professors and allows them to teach it by constantly making both the *com* and the *position* impossible. By dislocating the ontogeny of composition, deconstruction allows the composition of ontogeny.

With such unworking constantly at work, the composition professor can even grade papers. Grading papers, perhaps more than any other form of (mis)reading, depends on what Derrida calls a willed act of misunderstanding: "Each time you read a text—and this is my situation and the situation of every reader—there is some misunderstanding." Through deconstruction, the requisite misunderstanding that constitutes grading papers can present itself as it is: "not a mistake or an absurdity. It's something that is motivated by some interest and some understanding." Since misunderstanding cannot be avoided, deconstruction allows composition professors to foreground the motivation, the interest, the understanding, and the politics that authorize and inform their misunderstanding when they place a "mark" on a student's text.

We gain much by taking the opportunity of deconstruction. Within it we gain the security that writing is a teachable, learnable way to gather and unify existence. Through it we appear both as the authority who "knows" and as the one authorized to "mark." Because of it such landmarks as order and correctness still stake out an inhabitable territory where directions are possible. From it we learn how to construct our own discipline, our own specificity—a specificity that both identifies us and offers models and norms for our students. Most importantly, as a result of its continuing operation, we forever hold pedagogy, authority, location, and specificity in question, knowing that they never escape and are always undermined by the unfounded, unending process of construction. "All writing worth the name," according to Helen Vendler, "is the revolutionary effort toward freedom, away from the stereotypes of thought and language inherent in every belief system" (48). Derridean deconstruction allows composition professors to teach such writing.

L(i)ability

When we use Derrida, we unavoidably enable a composition haunted by the liability of "minima" and fraught with the lability of politics.

"Of course," Derrida assumes, "the minimal requirements in grammar, clarity of exposition, and so on can be addressed everywhere." "I don't think there is a model for teaching," Derrida says of pedagogy, "once the minimal requirements are fulfilled in terms of language, grammar, comprehension, and so on...." " While he does not complain himself, Derrida does see that the norms of writing "built through the ideology of the Third Republic" are no longer respected and that "we cannot recognize in children and young people now the same respect we had for spelling, and so on."

Diction, grammar, clarity, spelling? What presumptions operate here? How much has been dismissed as "basic" or taken for granted in the "and so on" that so casually and confidently ends each of these statements? No one could be so obtuse a reader or so enamored of Derrida as to miss the elitism that marks these "minimal requirements." Someone somewhere must establish the tradition and ensure the minima on which such blithely innocent elitism depends. Who? How?

In what he calls *"une réponse de Normand"* (both yes and no), Derrida proposes an intentionally contradictory model for the university composition professor: "You can't teach writing simply as a formal technique. Each technique is determined by the specific content of the field. So the one who teaches writing in law school should ... be informed about the laws and not simply a rhetorician." Derrida would have the compositionist trained in two specificities: the common core specificities of rhetoric (which at some point must include the minima) as well as the specificities of each field. It's a tough task, he shrugs, "but that's politics."

Well, not too many composition specialists need a lesson in politics, especially academic politics, to know where they are likely to rank after the struggle ends. In what imaginable political structure will the departmental hybrid, the rhetorician-*comme*-whatever, be credited with having undergone the "rigor," the "very classical training" in the "field" that Derrida claims for himself with such serene pride? What risk does the hybrid run? Will she be the watcher after minima, the enabler of the deconstruction to come? Will he in fact be the *pharmakos* through whose exclusion the field constitutes itself?

Who, for example, is Derrida talking to when he explains that rhetoric includes more than figures and tropes? Or that it operates in the *kairos*? Or even that it has political, economic, and libidinal dimensions? What imagined interlocutor needs to be told or reminded of this? No one who has read Derrida should be surprised that when the crunch comes, when rhetoric and philosophy stand against each other, Derrida comes down squarely on the side of "philosophy, logic, truth, reference, etc." His justification comes straight from the *Gorgias*: "rhetoric as a separate discipline, as a technique or as an autonomous field," he warns, "may become a sort of empty instrument whose usefulness or effectiveness would be independent of logic, or even reference or truth—an instrument in the hands of the sophists in the sense that Plato wanted to define them." Though rhetoric may be powerful, though philosophy never quite seems to escape it, though too much rigorous attention cannot be paid to it, Derrida the philosopher fears that you just cannot trust it. The rejections in *Gorgias* and *Phaedrus*, rhetorical though they may be, retain their "force and signification." While Derrida attempts to inhabit the opposition between rhetoric and philosophy so as to put that opposition in question, he does so (and has done so consistently for twenty-five years) as a philosopher. "I'm not saying," he makes unequivocally clear, "that all concepts are essentially metaphors and therefore everything is rhetoric."

How do compositionists respond to such goodwill, such frank good sense? Since "deconstruction *is* America," perhaps we need *une réponse de Missouri*. When Derrida assures us that "concept" exceeds "metaphor" and that some things escape rhetoric, our reply should be, "Fine. Let's wait for the first concept that is not a metaphor to present itself outside rhetoric."

What might that discourse sound like? Yes, I worry about it too, for I think it has the blithe sound of "minimal," "and so on," "an empty instrument." Not only have I heard that discourse in departmental meetings for fifteen years, I have also seen it written down—by Plato. The chance, in other words, is labile, fraught with liability. Can one hazard the chance, accept the lability, and yet escape the liability? Only if deconstruction can unwork itself; only if the Derridean strategy is separable from the Derridean project. The project, after all, depends on the most rigid, most prescriptive imaginable current tradition. Composition specialists *must* treat deconstruction as a theory that generates a method; the risk of letting it "just happen" is too great. "I hope," Julia Kristeva once said to a questioner, "I am not *correctly* following any line whatsoever."[4]

Vanderbilt University
Nashville, Tennessee

Notes

[1] The title of my response is quoted from the first line of *Phaedrus,* but I have replaced Phaedrus' name with the signature Derrida leaves at the end of *Writing and Difference.*

[2] The *Oxford English Dictionary* cites Puttenham (1589) as the first English user of the term, "Catachresis or the Figure of abuse." In 1820 Coleridge used the term as follows: "The proverb is current by a misuse, or a catachresis at least, of both the words, fortune and fools." The ancient Greek term meant "misuse of a word." Perelman uses the term as follows: "When the metaphorical expression is the sole way to designate an object in a language, it is called a *catachresis*: the '*foot* of a mountain' and '*arm* of a chair'" (122).

[3] In nineteenth-century scientific discussions, catastrophists, who generally held that some geological and biological phenomena occur because of sudden and violent disturbances of nature, were pitted against uniformitarians, who saw all developments in nature as part of uniform, continuous processes. Spencer, for example, wrote in 1879, "For a generation after geologists had become uniformitarians in Geology, they remained catastrophists in Biology" (iv. §17).

[4] See Verdiglione 73; Roudiez 1.

Works Cited

Aristotle. *Rhetoric*. Trans. Lane Cooper. Englewood Cliffs, NJ: Prentice, 1932.

Perelman, Chaim. *The Realm of Rhetoric*. Trans. William Kluback. Notre Dame, IN: U of Notre Dame P, 1982.

Roudiez, Leon S. Introduction. *Desire in Language.* by Julia Kristeva. Oxford: Blackwell, 1981.

Spencer, Herbert. *Data of Ethics*. New York: Appleton, 1879.

Vendler, Helen. "The Medley is the Message." *New York Review of Books* 18 May 1986.

Verdiglione, Armando. ed. *Psychanalyse et Politique*. Paris: Seuil, 1974.

Paulo

Freire

History, *Praxis*, and Change:
Paulo Freire and the Politics of Literacy

GARY A. OLSON

In true Marxist form, Paulo Freire appeals unabashedly to an "objective" reality that we all can come to know through careful, critical analysis. He has little patience for poststructuralist proclamations that reality is neither objective nor knowable. In Freire's world, everything, including the objective reality to which he so regularly appeals, is social. Of course, "there is an individual dimension of this social perception," but "the very construction of reality is collective." The social collective, the people—this is where Freire's heart lies.

Also in typical Marxist form, Freire tends to subsume the struggles of women within the class struggle. That he is becoming sensitive to charges that his writings and pedagogy are male oriented and his language sexist is abundantly clear from this interview: he takes pains always to say "he or she," for example, and he insists that he does "emphasize the fight against machismo." He even goes so far as to say that he can "feel like a woman" in women's struggles for equality, and he appears somewhat defensive, insisting that it would be "absolutely naive" for women to "reject my sympathy and my camaraderie because I am a man." Yet, Freire seems to downplay the women's movement, saying, "I always work together, men and women—the people" because "in the last analysis, men and women, we are, together, human beings."

These views, though, are consistent with Freire's larger world view, for he sees himself as a man *of the people*. And, of course, he has devoted his life to liberation of the masses through critical literacy. In fact, freedom is "one of the main issues of this century," and we all must continue to strive for more and higher levels of freedom because "without freedom, it's impossible to go on." But bringing freedom through critical literacy necessitates carefully conceived ethnographic research of a given community, and this means, again, becoming one with the people. That is, the ethnographer must learn to "respect the reality" of the people in order to minimize the distance between the people and him or herself so as to be positioned to intervene effectively in their reality.

Freire's constant striving to be thought of as a man of the people is evident in some comments made during a coffee break midway through the interview. Like many of his compatriots, Freire indulges liberally in numerous cups of powerful Brazilian coffee. He explains proudly that his own staff is quite communal when it comes to this indulgence:

> This is not public coffee. We do not put the expense of the coffee in the budget of the Secretary. *We* pay. We make a collection. Of course, I pay more than the others. First of all, I drink much more than anyone else, and I receive more people, and also I'm paid more than some. But I *will* tell you that there *are* people here who get paid more money than the Secretary—the lawyers, for example.

Freire prides himself on the democratic workings of his own office, even in such trivial matters; and he also reveals that though he is the chief executive, the Secretary of Education of São Paulo (one of the largest school districts in the world), others in the system are better paid, that somehow his high rank still does not cause him to transcend "the people": he is, forever, one of us.

Freire is preoccupied with "history," as is to be expected of someone steeped in Marxist philosophy. It is the task of the progressive educator, the progressive intellectual, to intervene in history, to move history forward. For example, Freire feels that the U.S. is beginning a new decade of activism in reaction to the social apathy of the past, and "one of the tasks of progressive educators, teachers, writers, and so on is to challenge, to push, to improve, to increase this trend." Change, like history itself, is a process; and we must understand that "the process of change starts exactly in the place that we would like to change." To intervene in history, says Freire, "we just have to start." And he even senses his own small part in history, expressing with joy and genuine humility his pleasure that "history is not waiting for my death in order to say, 'That man existed.'"

Perhaps it is exactly this kind of activism that makes his pedagogy so compelling. His notion of *praxis* as reflection plus *action* foregrounds the importance of students' adopting a "subject position," a position of agency, of action. This theme permeates the discussion here, as it does all of Freire's publications and interviews. He insists that students take an active part in their own education, that they be considered "subjects of the very process of education." Repeatedly, he contends that teachers must "respect the subjectivity of the students," that they must strive to increase curiosity at every turn. What truly makes someone critical, able to "read reality," is "insertion in the struggles in order to intervene in reality. It is *praxis*."

Nevertheless, this emphasis on students' participation, on students' action, on "respect for students and their contexts," does not mean that teachers should surrender authority to some abstract ideal of classroom democracy. In fact, Freire is quite adamant that his liberatory pedagogy does not translate to the teacher's relinquishing of authority. Quite the contrary: "The teacher has the duty to teach," to use his or her authority to good advantage. Despite attempts to read Freire as advocating the dissolution of the teacher's authority as a means of achieving a truly participatory, dialogic teaching environment, Freire argues that the teacher's authority *"has* to exist." The important point is that it should never "have such power that it crushes freedom."

Paulo Freire may seem at times a bit patriarchal, even as he pledges solidarity with women in their struggles, and he may appear somewhat out of step with contemporary epistemology in his tenacious appeal to objective reality and his unshakable faith that we all can come to comprehend and transform it; yet, he will always be especially important to compositionists because permeating his life and work is a sincere and abiding love for literacy, for freedom, and, most importantly, for students.

Q. Since the publication of *Education as the Practice of Freedom* in the early 1960s, you have written a considerable number of books and articles. Do you consider yourself a writer?

A. The other day a friend of mine asked me, "Paulo, do you think that sometime you could become a member of some academy of letters?" I said, "No." And he asked me, "But why? Do you have some prejudice?" I said, "No, I don't; it's just that I don't feel that I'm a writer." I would like very much to be a writer. Of course, when I publish books this is because I write good books. I write essays; I write about my *praxis*; I write about philosophy and the politics of education, but I don't make "literature." Whether I write well or not, whether I have good taste—I would like very much to have good taste in writing—is another question. Yet for me, this would not be enough to make me a member of an academy of letters. The novelists, the poets—they are writers for me. Maybe I'm wrong; maybe I have a narrow understanding of being a writer. I also have to tell you that in thinking like this I feel sad because I would like very much to be a writer. Maybe in some moments of my books—a certain moment of the analysis I am doing, and so on—readers could think they are reading a "writer." This is when I become most happy in writing. For example, in one of my short books that's already in English, *The Importance of the Act of Reading*, I think that perhaps there are moments that give the impression that somewhere inside of the educator is a sleeping writer.

Q. When you do write, do you revise often? Do you use a computer? Tell us about your writing habits.

A. I can tell you with humility, with humor, but not with irony, that I am underdeveloped. I am a man of northeast Brazil, one of the very precarious regions in the world, and I am almost seventy years old, so it's difficult to start learning some things, especially things concerning machines and technology. I believe in my hand, in the pencil, and in the white piece of paper before me. I believe in that. Then I start filling up the paper with my thought and transforming it into words. I don't even know how to type; I never use a typewriter. I am thinking about buying a computer for my wife to use to write her essays, her books—and also for me to use. But I don't believe that I will learn how to use it. It's very sad that the educator Paulo Freire would say such a thing. Yet I am convinced that all of us need to use computers. I see how my friends in the States—professors such as Ira Shor, Henry Giroux, Donaldo Macedo—produce their work with such discipline. They know how to use the machine, how to put it at their service. It's fantastic. They do much more than I because they use a very good instrument. My friends all tell me, "Paulo, you have to learn to use the computer." And maybe I will start, because I believe that in the last analysis there's always time for us to learn.

Q. In some of your publications, you have attempted to transcend the constraints of conventional text formats by experimenting with various dialogic forms. *Pedagogy in Process* is a collection of letters that together constitute a dialogue between you and revolutionary leader Mario Cabral; even the introduction is, in your words, a "letter-report" to the reader. *Learning to Question* is what you've called "a spoken book," a lengthy conversation between you and Antonio Faundez. And *A Pedagogy for Liberation* is a collection of "dialogues" between you and Ira Shor. Why have you found these experimental formats necessary?

A. Maybe before I perceived them as *necessary*, I saw them as *possible*. I remember that one day some years ago—in the 1980s, maybe '81 or '82—I asked myself, "Why not start *speaking* books instead of exclusively *writing* them?" Of course, I never thought that we should stop writing in favor of speaking books, but why not do the two things from time to time, and even simultaneously? Then I invited a young Brazilian educator from São Paulo to make the first experience with me. He accepted, and we started a dialogue, following a certain thematic issue, and we spoke a book entitled *On Education*. Immediately we did a second volume, and afterwards we started another. Today, I think I have five or six such books, some of them very good ones. The book with Ira Shor is for me excellent, not because of *me* but because of *us*. Ira is very critical, very lucid, and the book is very good. In every language, the book has had a good reception. And *Learning to Question*, with the Chilean philosopher Antonio Faundez, is also for me a very good book. I did that, as I said, not because I thought it should be done, but because I thought that it *could* be done, it was possible to do.

Q. Do you see these forms as a counterpart to your antihierarchical, dialogic pedagogy?

A. Yes, I think so. It has to do with the spirit of dialogue.

Q. When you were a young student, what were the most influential factors in the development of your own critical literacy?

A. Perhaps the moments which challenged me and invited me to think of a much more participatory education in relationships between educators and educatees were the moments in which I did not understand the teacher but nevertheless lacked the courage to ask questions because I felt myself inhibited vis-à-vis the arrogance of the teacher, the authority of the teacher. Maybe those negative moments challenged me and invited me to think of that *more* than the positive ones. At least, this is what I could tell you now.

Q. Drawing on the work of Karl Mannheim and others, you have espoused a social epistemology. You say in *Education: The Practice of Freedom*, for example, that "the *we* think determines the *I* think." Do you agree, then, with those who posit that knowledge, reality itself, is a social construct—a product of social consensus?

A. Yes, because the very perception of reality, the perception we have of reality, is a social one. Of course, there is an individual dimension of this social perception. It is obvious because I can perceive in some way and you in another way because of different reasons (which are all social ones). But the very construction of reality is collective.

Q. Fundamental to your liberatory pedagogy is "resolution of the teacher-student contradiction"—a dissolving of the authority hierarchy between students and teachers. Some compositionists attempt to do this in their writing classes through collaborative learning, asking students to meet in groups of three or four and jointly work on specific writing tasks. Does this method reflect your own pedagogical values?

A. Every kind of activity of educational *praxis* in which two, three, four, fifty, or one-hundred students are challenged to increase curiosity and to improve their understanding of how reality is becoming, every kind of action in which the subjectivity of the students is respected in its relationships with the objectivity of the object, every kind of educational *praxis* in which the students are considered also as being subjects of the very process of education has to do with me—or maybe I should say *I* have to do with *it*. I think that telling it to you in this way is better than trying to put these ideas into some scheme.

Q. Some compositionists argue that while collaborative methods *seem* democratic, they can easily cloak and even reinforce the instructor's authority and control over students. Thus, ironically, collaborative methods can reproduce ruling ideology even more effectively than traditional hierarchical methods. What are your thoughts on this matter?

A. Yes, this is very interesting because, in fact, you can get lots of different results starting from a very apparently good thing. And I think there is another aspect of this question which we should underline: dialogue and respect for students and their contexts do not mean that the teacher has to disappear or, in other words, that the teacher does not have to teach. It's impossible for me to imagine the existence of a teacher without teaching.

That is, the teacher has the duty to teach. The question for me is how the teacher uses his or her authority. I'm not against the authority of teachers. I am against the hypertrophy of authority against the fragility of students' freedom, and I am against the hypertrophy of students' freedom against the fragility of authority. For me, when some people say, "No it does not work well because inside all of this you can have again the authority of the teacher being stressed," I say, "No, the authority of the teacher *has* to exist." The question is that it never should have such power that it crushes freedom. Dialogue is not a tactic for denying authority, in my view.

Q. You say in *Pedagogy in Process* that "the impatient educator often transfers knowledge like a package while discoursing volubly on the dynamic nature of knowledge," while the overly patient teacher can lapse into passivity. How can we maintain a productive tension between patience and impatience?

A. Of course, I don't have a prescription for this. Nevertheless, I can state that we should live and act impatiently patient. If you are exclusively patient, you don't accomplish your tasks; you don't get the results of your dreams. But if you are exclusively impatient in order to make viable your dreams, maybe you will lose them. Being patiently impatient means having a very critical understanding of the limits of the practice. That is, we have to know that there is no practice which can be free from limits. The question for us is to know what the limits are. What are the ideological, economical, political, scientific limits? Then we have to deal with all of these in order to learn how to be impatiently patient.

Q. The concept of critical consciousness is, of course, central to your theory. There is a "critical thinking" movement in the U.S. in which students learn a kind of informal logic and acquire the ability to analyze and synthesize. Unlike your own context-specific critical pedagogies, however, such training is often directed toward atomistic dissecting of texts or arguments and is not linked dialectically to "action." How can we influence this movement to include your concept of *praxis* as reflection *plus* action?

A. I think the best way for us to have dialogue with these people is not just to try to teach them about that but to discuss with them how it is not even possible to get their own results without *praxis*—that is, without action plus reflection. Theoretically, it is not difficult to understand, for example, that becoming critical in the process of reading reality does not come about through a mere intellectual exercise. Through an intellectual exercise, I can increase and improve my power of speaking, for example, so that I speak fluently, beautifully even; but what makes me critical, what gives me knowledge, what teaches me how to read reality, how to reread reality is my insertion in the struggles in order to intervene in reality. It is *praxis*; it is practice. On the other hand, there is also another danger, which is to think that just practice or just action is enough to teach someone how to become critical. For me, the only way (which is already the critical way of doing things) is to experience the tension between theory and *praxis* without denying one or the other. Thus, I am never interested just in theory, just in *praxis*, but in the relationships between them. This is what makes me more critical.

Q. One important concern of compositionists is the use of standardized tests to evaluate writing ability and reading comprehension. Do you believe such tests are appropriate for evaluating reading and writing? Or do you think there are other, more productive ways to measure such things?

A. First of all, no matter whether the examinees are candidates for becoming medical doctors or sociologists, we have to keep in mind regional differences. That is, I can ask a question of a young man from northeast Brazil who hopes to become a medical doctor which I would not ask of a young man here. Nevertheless, there are questions which should be asked there and here. Secondly, since I was very young I have never accepted those tests that are a kind of guessing game. We introduced that here in the admission-by-competition examinations for teachers. I believe that candidates must have time and space for speaking or writing, for telling us finally how they think vis-à-vis a question. Maybe they won't be able to quote a famous writer or a famous philosopher. This does not matter. I want to see, *at this moment*, how his or her curiosity walks, what a student can do independently. One of the tasks of the university in preparing students to be professors, to be doctors, to be sociologists should be to teach them how to increase their curiosity, their desire to know. So these kinds of standardized tests are not for me. I don't believe too much in them.

Q. The last three decades have witnessed the development of numerous philosophical and critical systems that posit that there is no "objective" reality. Yet, throughout your own writings you consistently appeal to an objective reality that we all can come to recognize through a truly critical education. How do you respond to criticism that your theory is out of step with current notions of epistemology?

A. If Peter or John or Mary comes to me and makes a well-structured speech, telling me that there is no reality, and if afterwards Charles comes and says, "Paulo, your pedagogy is totally based on the analysis and transformation of reality, so how do you feel after that speech?" I'd say they are naive.

Q. In your literacy campaigns you begin with what Manfred Stanley calls "intelligently conceived and executed anthropological research on the objective situation." Some argue, however, that ethnographic research can never be objective because the researcher will always be an outsider, an other. What are your thoughts about the dynamics of ethnographic research?

A. Of course, one of the conditions for a researcher in the social field who dreams of finding something valid by the end of his or her research is to try to diminish the distance, which varies, between the researcher and the concreteness of the people he or she is studying. The ethnographer should become one of the others: it's not a question of degree; it's a question of becoming. Thus, I think it depends on the political choice and the political clarity of the researcher, which together condition his or her methods of work. It depends, because of this, on whether the researcher's political choice is a democratic one, whether he or she really believes in the possibility the people have to think, to speak, to know, to create. The ethnographer has to respect the people in their reality in order to be respected. In order to intervene in a reality, first you must respect this reality. That is, you have to try to understand it, to know it with the people. Then you can diminish the distance. Maybe by the end of the research, you are no longer exclusively a foreign person but, on the contrary, a person in the process of becoming. It's not a question that has to do exclusively with ethnography. Before being this or that, it's a political question.

Q. Are you familiar with E.D. Hirsch's concept of "cultural literacy"? He argues that literacy means more than mastering reading and writing skills; it also entails acquiring a level of knowledge about one's culture. While this may appear to be an attempt to situate literacy within specific historical, social contexts, it has become a concerted conservative effort to establish official canons of knowledge that everyone "should" know. How can educators resist such campaigns to establish official, prescribed bodies of knowledge?

A. Since the book came out and people began to talk about it, I have read it; but I am waiting for some time, given my limited time, to reread the book. First of all, I think we should accept the concept of cultural illiteracy and develop it, use it in a much more progressive way. We undoubtedly have cultural illiteracy in the States and here, and we need to fight against it. For example, one day I received a letter from someone in the States in which the writer said to me, "I am very sorry to be obliged to write to you in English because I don't have good command of Spanish." It's incredible that this man thinks I speak Spanish as my mother tongue. This is a kind of cultural illiteracy.

Also, there is a certain ideological aspect of this problem of cultural illiteracy. For example, sometimes you find among famous people and intellectuals a strong cultural ignorance and cultural illiteracy; and what is making them cultural illiterates, in the last analysis, is their prejudice against race, against class, against the nation. For example, when sometimes some Europeans or Americans think and speak wrongly about us, it's not exclusively because they don't know. They don't know precisely because they don't believe in us. Because they have the prejudice of being superior and, therefore, perceive us as inferior, they don't know anything about us and thus remain culturally illiterate.

Q. You have said that "in a class society the power elite necessarily determines what education will be, and therefore its objectives." Richard

Ohmann and others have argued that the formal education system, in its response to illiteracy, teaches only those skills that will help support the military industrial complex. How can the progressive teacher oppose such forces while remaining within the system itself?

A. Yes, this is exactly my case; for example, now I am the Secretary of Education of the city of São Paulo. It is really necessary to understand that we human beings are ambiguous beings. Reality makes us, from time to time, ambiguous, precisely because reality is also ambiguous. For example, a progressive teacher, a progressive thinker, a progressive politician many times has his or her left foot inside the system, the structures, and the right foot out of it. [Freire solidly plants his left foot to one side and his right to the other.] *Here*, he or she has the present; *here*, he or she has the future. *Here* is actuality, the reality of today; *here* is utopia. This is why it's so difficult, experiencing this ambiguity, for us to walk: we have to walk like this. [With a playful smile, Freire begins to waddle across the room.] Life is like this. This is reality and history.

Q. Many people in the U.S. believe that the nation is experiencing a "literacy crisis," and they point to what they see as the dismal condition of the educational system and a general decline in the level of literacy. This perception has contributed to a conservative "back to basics" movement. Just how does one implement a progressive pedagogical agenda in the face of such overwhelming public perception that the progressive educational movements of the 1960s were a failure?

A. In one of his recent books, Ira Shor has said many very interesting things about this regression you are now having in the States, this movement backwards. First of all, I think we have to understand how history is walking with us and because of us, while at the same time conditioning us to walk like this. There are reasons for that. For example, when I arrived in the States in 1969 to teach at Harvard, I found the youth in a state of rebellion. Harvard had been invaded. I met students with head injuries because the police had beaten them. One of them said to me, "Paulo, I thought we could never have things like this here, just in the Third World." I said, "No, you also have the Third World here vis-à-vis your First World. In some moments, you have the same thing we in the Third World have, but not constantly." We have to try to understand that history is like this. And I think that every five or ten years we have changes in the States. From the decade of annunciation of the presence of the students and the people, the popular movements in the streets, we go to a decade of almost total lack of interest, apathy; suddenly the students come back just to study, just to read. They say that the duty of students is just to read and write, to be on the side of the universities. The decade before, they thought that besides reading and studying they also could fight, that they could be "subjects." Maybe I am wrong, but perhaps now in the States we are starting a new decade that will attempt to overcome this apathy—a decade different from the sixties. If this is true, I think that one of the tasks of progressive educators, teachers, writers, and so on is to challenge, to push, to improve, to increase this trend.

This is the end of this century as well as the end of the millennium, and I think that one of the values which human beings have because they have fought historically for it is also one of the main issues of this century: freedom. There has been a test for freedom in this end of the century. For me, all the changes we are seeing and experiencing in the world today in Eastern Europe and with the Berlin wall are not an attempt to return to capitalism; that is a naive explanation, an ideological explanation. The result is a return to capitalism but that is not the main aspect. I think everything happening in Eastern Europe is a kind of ode to freedom. Maybe we could take advantage of this in the States, here in Brazil, everywhere, to speak about the beauty of freedom and the need for freedom. We are like we are now because of freedom. Without freedom, it's impossible to go on, even though we know we can never get absolute freedom because that does not exist. Freedom is also historical. When we reach a certain state of freedom, we immediately discover we have another one to attain. In the last analysis, reaching freedom means creating avenues to get more freedom. And I think that this is one of the issues of this century.

Q. You have distanced yourself from Ivan Illich's solution to oppressive education—to completely dismantle the schools—and you've applauded Mario Cabral's decision not to "close all the schools inherited from the colonial era" but instead to introduce "into the old system some fundamental reforms capable of accelerating the future radical transformation" of the educational system. Won't this compromise result in the same corrupt system but with a new face?

A. We have to understand change as a process. And once we understand change as a process, we also have to understand that the process of change starts exactly in the place that we would like to change. Many people speak about change and think it's possible to start such change in the ideal society. First of all, we can never get the ideal society. The ideal society perhaps is heaven, and we cannot speak about heaven now because we are inside of history; heaven is metahistory for those who believe. We have to change society starting from the society which we now would like to change. This demands tactics; it demands knowledge of the society that now for us is old; it means knowledge of what society should become, the society of our dreamed utopia. Also, there are many virtues we have to create within ourselves. We cannot just receive virtues from leaders or from God; we have to create them in our *praxis*—like humility, for example, like being patiently impatient, and all these things. We must also learn *how* to change, and that takes time, and it demands wisdom, which we get through the experience of becoming engaged in the very process of

change. Once again, there is no prescription; we just have to start.
Q. In your programs to develop adult literacy, do you take specific measures to respond to the needs of women?
A. Oh yes. I remember that in the 1960s when I was organizing some issues to create codifications to challenge the illiterate, I wanted to discuss with them the concept of culture in order to fight against the apathy, against the immobilization of mind that makes us not believe in the possibility of change. In organizing some figures, some pictures, I asked the artist to put a book in the hands of a woman who was conversing with a man, not in the hands of the man. My intention was precisely to provoke debate in the very male culture of northeast Brazil, a *machista* culture, to provoke men to understand that women not only have the right to read, to write, to improve their intellectual possibilities, but also that they *can*, that they are *able* to do so. And this is just one instance that I remember right now. Nevertheless, I never worked to prepare programs dedicated to women. I always work together, men and women—the people. But I do emphasize the fight against machismo, which I think is one of the weaknesses of our culture.
Q. In *The Politics of Education* you say, "I am in total sympathy with women's fantastic struggle, even though I cannot fight their battle. Although I am a man, I can feel like a woman." First, why *can't* you fight the battle for women's liberation? And, also, in what ways can you feel like a woman and what insight does this give you into women's struggles?
A. Even though I cannot take a leadership role in the women's liberation movement, mostly because I'm not a woman, my sympathy—more than my sympathy, my feeling of camaraderie with them—for me is politically important. I think that only in a naive perspective could women reject my sympathy and my camaraderie because I am a man. It would be absolutely naive from the political point of view, because as a man I add through my solidarity (real and not tactical solidarity) something politically to the women's movement.

Also, let me address your question about what insight feeling like a woman gives me into women's struggle. First, I am sure that all men have something of the woman in them, and all women have something of the man in them. The issue for me is that the *machista* culture has repressed men in such a way that we're unable to feel like a woman and that we're afraid to say things like this. When I came back to Brazil in the 1980s, I had a ninety-minute interview on national television, and a woman asked me about the struggle of women, and I said I also feel like a woman. Because of that I received letters and telephone calls, above all from northeast Brazil, from friends of mine asking me with some irony or humor, "But Paulo, is it possible that the time of exile changed you in such a way?" They weren't able to understand what it means philosophically speaking, and also politically speaking, when I say I also am a woman. I am first of all expressing my solidarity with women in their struggle, and I am also saying that scientifically it is true. The point is that to a large extent I became able to overcome the fears the culture had imposed upon me, and I am not afraid that people say, "Ah, look, Paulo does not know yet whether he is a man or a woman." No, I know that I am a man; I have five children and the possibility to be a father again. But I'm not a *machista*, and I don't feel bad because I recognize in me something which could be characteristic of men but also characteristic of women. In the last analysis, men and women, we are, together, human beings.

Q. You frequently say that *agency*, the "ability to act and intervene," is an essential precondition for acquiring knowledge; only "subjects" can know. Feminists often talk about women's need to attain "subject position." What steps do you believe women must take in order to achieve this agency, this position of liberation?

A. This is also a historical question. I am absolutely convinced that the way women fight in the States is not necessarily the same way that women in Brazil should fight. The methods of action, the understanding, the levels of domination, the power of male ideology—all these things are conditioned culturally, historically, and socially. I can only give a generic answer that does not necessarily apply to the States, or even to Brazil. I think that some of the conditions and preconditions and the values and virtues necessary for the liberation struggle of the oppressed people of a nation are also necessary steps for the struggle of women. First, struggle is an ethical value; we cannot separate ethics from the political activity of women's liberation. For example, I think there's a need for some humility during struggle; maybe when we are fighting and getting some results, we sometimes risk losing humility and becoming arrogant. I am not speaking as a priest, but as an educator and a politician. I think that losing humility in the process of fighting and becoming more or less arrogant is not a good tactic.

Second, I think that even though the liberation of women has to do with men, in my point of view men are not necessarily the enemy of women. It's quite different from the struggle between classes, for example. I understand that during the struggle women sometimes have to adopt an attitude which perhaps gives the appearance that they are excluding men from all aspects of history; but this is not possible. I understand, but this cannot be. For example, I understand scientifically that in some moments of the struggle, women cannot allow the presence of men in their meetings. It is obvious because historically men have controlled things, and sometimes the presence of men can influence things in a bad way. There are many things like this that women have to do. Maybe I am wrong concerning the point of view of women, but the world they dream of cannot be just a world of women; that would be bad. For me, it would be a very ugly world. The world *I* dream of is the world of *us*, men and women. With this, I am not saying that I discriminate against relationships between women and women, men and men. No, I'm absolutely open to this. In my point of view, it's a right; it's ethical; but it cannot be thought of as a generalization. For me, then, the world that women want is a free world with the collaboration of all of us.

Q. Do you believe that the discourse of the women's movement has influenced the discourse of liberation in general? In what ways?

A. I am not able now to tell you in which ways, but I can say that the discourse of liberation—despite whether it is more or less naive or critical, despite whether it comes from this or that group or this or that class of people or nation—once it is heard, it has the possibility of exercising influence. Sometimes it works against the wishes of those who speak the discourse. The human word, human speech, is not something which crosses history without consequence.

Q. In *Conscientization and Deschooling*, John Elias says that one weakness of your work is your "failure to consider the role of the church in maintaining the existing level of political and social awareness among the people." He says that you see the church as part of the solution when it's "really an essential part of the problem itself." How do you respond to this criticism?

A. I think the churches have been both problem and solution. The problems in themselves are not the solutions; that is, the solutions for the problems come from outside of the problems. Sometimes the church brings the solution; sometimes it worsens the problems. The question for me is to see when the churches are helping or not. I am not a fanatic in favor of or against the churches. For example, I think that historians of Brazilian politics now, and in the next century, have to recognize that the progressive churches in Brazil were absolutely important in the struggle of the Brazilians in overcoming the military coup d'état. It cannot be denied. Nevertheless, in 1964, immediately after the coup d'état, the National Conference of Brazilian Bishops published a proclamation to the nation applauding the military for having saved Brazil from communism. If it was not unanimous, it was almost. You see how history works? These bishops, during the process of seeing priests, nuns, workers, and peasants being tortured and killed, little by little became conscientized. It was not Paulo Freire who conscientized the bishops; it was history. And then, in some moment, the bishops changed and began to become opposed to the military. You see two moments—the same church, the same bishops. This is what history is: we have the same church with different positions in different moments. Today, perhaps, the much more conservative wing of the church is becoming the majority. It is like this, and I never have a sectarian position. I am always open to reunderstanding the facts according to the context.

Q. Many people all over the world admire and support your work. Some, however, have criticized various aspects of both your theory and pedagogy.

Are there any criticisms or misunderstandings of your work that you would like to address at this time?

A. Sometimes there are criticisms that are not correct, but I think the critics are exercising their rights in criticizing me. Sometimes, however, the criticisms reveal a bad reading of me and sometimes not even a reading of me but a reading of others who did not read me well. Since the beginning I learned something very important, and my first wife Elza helped me a lot in this: in order not to be criticized, not to be coopted, it is absolutely necessary that you do *nothing*, and this is a very high price. I also learned that we must be humble vis-à-vis criticism, even those that are not correct ones. I thank you for the chance you're giving me now to refer to some of them, but I won't do that. I will make some defense of criticisms when I write a new book or article.

What I would like to say in closing, though, is that I feel happy. I have had the privilege in life, while still alive, to receive recognition from institutions, from the universities, and from many people. That is, history is not waiting for my death in the order to say, "That man existed." So I am happy. These things don't make me arrogant, but undoubtedly they make me happy as a human being. You cannot realize how beautiful it is for me when in different parts of the world I am recognized—when, for example, a young man or a young woman working in a shopping center asks me to write an autograph in one of my own books which they happen to have in their pocket. One day in Athens, Greece, I was walking in the street and a man who was selling something in the streets came to me and said, "Professor Freire, I saw you yesterday on television. I want to tell you that your books are very important also in my country." And he asked me to autograph his book. A merchant in the street! Scenes like this I have had all over the world, and it is for me a reason to be happy, but not to be proud.

Freirean Pedagogy in the U.S.: A Response

JAMES A. BERLIN

The relevance of Paulo Freire to the work of writing teachers cannot be exaggerated. Far from being a narrow and doctrinaire Marxist, or liberation theologian, or "Third World literacy worker," as is often charged, he is first and foremost a widely read scholar and committed teacher who has spent his life exploring the intersections of theory and pedagogic practice. His intellectual roots are extensive: Althusser, Aquinas, Buber, Chomsky, Fromm, Goldman, Jaspers, Mannheim, Marcel, and Marx, to name just a few. His travels have been no less diverse, including teaching stints in Brazil, Chile, the U.S., Switzerland, Canada, Guinea-Bissau, Angola, Cape Verde, and São Tomé and Príncipe. Not unexpectedly, then, his recent thought takes into account the poststructuralist and postmodern critiques of language and culture, and his work from the start has insisted on the historical and social situatedness of all theory and practice, including his own. Throughout his intellectual and physical journeys, however, Freire's central and abiding preoccupation has been the teaching of ways of reading and writing the world, and his work has always emphasized the central place of this activity in the life of a society.

Reading and Writing the World
Freire provides a rich rationale to support those who argue that literacy ought not be treated as a merely instrumental "skill," a useful tool in the mastery of more significant and substantive academic subjects. For Freire, to learn to read and write is to learn to name the world, and in this naming is found a program for understanding the conditions of our experience and, most important, for acting in and on them. Everywhere reminiscent of Kenneth Burke, Freire insists that language is at the center of our knowledge of ourselves and others. Language, furthermore, is a social construction, a constantly changing set of formations whose meanings emerge as people engage in written and spoken dialogue with each other. Language then is always prior to individuals, always already in place as it works to form consciousness, to shape subjects.

Freire, however, is no determinist (or poststructuralist indeterminist, for that matter) who regards individuals as mere effects of language. While he would never deny that the concrete material and social conditions of our experience shape and limit us, he also sees in the mediating power of language the possibility for the change and transformation of these very conditions. While language indeed serves as a means of control and domination, it can also serve as an instrument of liberation and growth. Language—in its mediation between the world and the individual, the object and the subject—contains within its shaping force the power of creating humans as agents of action. Each individual occupies a position at the intersection of a multitude of discourses, which Freire, in the manner of Barthes, calls codes. These codes can define subjects as helpless objects of forces—economic, social, political, cultural—that render them forever isolated and victimized by the conditions of their experience. These discourses can also, however, form individuals as active agents of change, social creatures who acting together can alter the economic, social, and political conditions of their historical experience. The codes, scripts, or terministic screens that define individuals as helpless ciphers can be replaced by narratives that enable democratic participation in creating a more equitable distribution of the necessities and pleasures of life.

This outline can be seen as a brief defense against those who see in Freire an innocence about the poststructuralist and postmodern insistence on the indeterminacy of value and the impossibility of action. As Freire is too kind and too tactful to mention in his interview with *JAC*, such arguments are often very effective in maintaining existing power structures. Indeed, they are commonly offered by the organic intellectuals of ruling groups, power brokers who are quite willing to concede that, since there are no foundational principles for validating any given economic and social order, we may as well keep on dancing to the tunes we know best. That no distribution of the necessities and pleasures of life is inherently better than any other is a strong argument to stay with present arrangements, since change may simply make matters worse (although "worse" here is obviously a highly problematic concept).

Freire's position is significantly at odds with this one. He is first of all a foundationalist, a Catholic who sees in the cruel inequities of our time a violation of the essential importance of every individual. However, as the numerous applications of Freire have shown—most conspicuously in the work of Ira Shor and Henry Giroux—one does not need theology to answer those who are politically paralyzed by the consequences of a world without certain truth value. This response echoes the oldest of reactions to this vexing question, one offered by the sophists, particularly Protagoras, some 2,300 years ago (see Havelock). If there are indeed no external validations for our actions, then we must invent them contingently as we go along. Furthermore, since no one person or group can then claim to know more about "truth" than any other, all must be allowed to deliberate and decide in freedom on the nature of these provisional formulations. Communal decision making is crucial here since any decisions about economic and social and political arrangements will affect the community as a whole. Only after all the arguments for any action are considered will a decision be made, and then it will be made by all, for all. Of course, these arguments will not be based on ontological principles, but will instead debate the consequences of decisions for that which the community has decided is in its best interests—these interests themselves being historically contingent and always open to discussion and revision. This conceptual scheme, of course, requires a utopian vision, a notion of a good and just society, "the society of our dreamed utopia," as Freire says. But, again, this vision is continually subject to discussion, debate, and alteration. A world without certainties thus creates the need for a radical democracy and a radically open rhetoric.

Empowerment and the College Writing Class

It requires little imagination to see that writing and reading teachers hold a central place in Freire's political thought. They are offered a unique opportunity to help make students agents of change and betterment. They can just as easily, however, become a part of a dehumanizing status quo. Schools and (especially) colleges in the U.S. have usually leaned in the direction of the latter, encouraging the banking model of education—the teacher as repository of a commodified knowledge to be deposited in the empty receptacle of students' minds. And since Reagan, this model has become nearly unassailable. One of the main institutional sites for resisting this notion recently has been the college writing class.[1] Against the argument that writing is a matter of skills and drills, or self expression, or privatized cognitive act, social epistemic rhetorics of various hues are arguing that writing is a public and communal enactment of a political interaction. Teachers in this group point to the historical role rhetorical education has played in civic affairs—for example, in ancient Greece—as well as to the traditions of political rhetoric in U.S. schools and colleges, ranging from Fred Newton Scott and Gertrude Buck, to Warren Taylor, to Richard Ohmann and Ira Shor (see Berlin). These teachers, furthermore, take into account the encounter between politics and poststructuralism, exploring in Freirean fashion the intersections of language and power.[2]

The large number of students in composition courses who today beg to be told in detail what to write and how to write it (an inevitable product of the banking model) are disappointed in these classrooms. They are instead asked to locate and address the conflicts and contradictions they find in their own social and political experience, presenting in their essays an account of this engagement. Here, at the point of encountering difference and discord, we can see how much Freire's pedagogical project has to contribute to the writing class in the U.S.

Literacy: Experiencing the World

The classroom in which writing and reading are considered communal performances of political behavior is preeminently participatory and democratic. It is, of course, disconcerting that a nation so conspicuously proud of its democratic and activist legacy is currently so reluctant to extend the fruits of this legacy to its schools. For example, notably lacking in the report of the 1989 governors' summit on education was any mention of citizenship preparation. A literacy that is without this commitment to active participation in decision making in the public sphere, however, is one that cannot possibly serve the interests of egalitarian political arrangements. For democracy to function (as we are now being reminded in Eastern Europe), citizens must actively engage in public debate, applying reading and writing practices in the service of articulating their positions and their critiques of the positions of others. The inability of citizens to write and read for the public forum thus defeats the central purpose of democracy: to ensure that all interests are heard before a communal decision is made.

Freire relates this silencing of citizens through literacy education to the formation of subjects as agents. Without the language to name our experience, we are the instruments of the language of others. As I am authorized through active literacy to name the world as I experience it (not as others tell me I should experience it), I become capable of taking action, of assuming control of my environment. In more direct terms, literacy enables the individual to understand that the conditions of experience are made by human agents and thus can be remade by human agents. This process of making and remaking, furthermore, is conducted in communities, in social collections. For Freire, however, the individual must never be sacrificed to any group-enforced norm (as he underscores in this interview). All voices must be heard and considered in taking action, and the integrity of the individual must never be compromised.

Freire has come to stand for a position many of us in English studies have been forwarding for quite some time: in teaching people to write and read, we are teaching them a way of experiencing the world. This realization requires that the writing classroom be dialogic. Only through articulating the disparate positions held by class members can the different ways of experiencing the world and acting in it be discovered. These differences organize themselves around class, race, gender, age, and other divisions, and it is the responsibility of the teacher to make certain that they are enunciated and problematized.[3] At the same time, those of us who have experienced the dialogic classroom know how reluctant many students are to engage in public debate. Years of enduring the banking model of education have taken their toll so that, like the unschooled peasants that Freire tells us about, our students often refuse to speak. They would rather sit quietly and take notes that they later will reproduce exactly for the exam. When pressed to active dialogue, they frequently deny the obvious social and political conflicts they enact and witness daily. For example, the majority of male students I have encountered at Purdue have in our first discussions assured me that race and gender inequalities no longer exist in the U.S. and simply do not merit further discussion. Any inequalities that do remain, they insist, are only apparent injustices since they are the result of inherent and thus unavoidable features of human nature (women are weaker and more emotional than men, for example), or are the product of individual failure (most homeless people refuse to work hard and so choose to live in the street).

It is at the moment of denial that the role of the teacher as problem poser is crucial, providing methods for the questioning that locates the points of conflict and contradiction. These methods most often require a focus on the language students invoke in responding to their experience. The teacher attempts to supply students with heuristic strategies for decoding their characteristic ways of representing the world. Here we see why the literacy teacher, the expert in language, is at the center of education in a democratic society (and in this case not because English studies has historically been used in U.S. schools to reinforce hegemonic ideological positions). The methods of questioning that the teacher poses are designed to reveal the contradictions and conflicts inscribed in the very language of students' thoughts and utterances. The teacher's understanding of the structuralist and poststructuralist assertions about the operations of language in forming consciousness here comes to the fore. At the minimum, this involves an examination of the various hierarchical binary oppositions on which the key terms in any discourse are based, the various connotative levels on which these terms function, and the larger narrative patterns of which the terms form a part.[4] The movement is thus from the concrete and specific conditions of the student's experience to the larger economic, social, political, and cultural systems into which these conditions coalesce. A student's attitude toward women in the workplace, for example, is often a part of a larger conceptual formulation regarding reproductive responsibilities, the family, work in the community, and the realities of economic conditions that govern our lives.

The relation of the teacher and students is of course crucial at this point. Although, as I have pointed out, the classroom is to be democratic and participatory, this does not mean that the teacher surrenders all authority. As Freire here points out, the authority of the teacher is never denied. On the other hand, it should never be exercised so that it destroys the student's freedom. The teacher must resist the obvious institutional constraints that in the typical college classroom make the teacher the center of knowledge and power and that deny the student's active role in meaning formation. In the Freirean classroom, the teacher shares the right to dialogue while never relinquishing the authority to set certain agendas for class activities. Certain matters are always debatable—for example, all positions on issues, whether the teacher's or students'—but certain others are not—the participatory and dialogic format, the search for contradictions, the analysis of codes. As Freire says, the teacher must be "patiently impatient," displaying neither complete passivity nor complete dominance in discussion. From my experience in the writing classroom, I know that the successful use of the problem posing and dialogic method usually leads to increasing participation by students. Often, by the middle of the course, students are themselves problematizing the assertions of their peers, the teacher becoming only one of many problem posers in the classroom.

I will not deny that my students at Purdue have demonstrated resistance of various kinds.[5] What Ira Shor calls "desocializing students"—that is, making them conscious of the concealed conflicts in their language, thought, and behavior—is never pursued without some discomfort. This resistance has as often taken the form of passivity as it has of active and open opposition to locating dissonance in our coded responses to such areas of discussion as schooling, work, play, and individuality, and their relation to class, race, and gender formations. Working together, the graduate student teachers in my mentor group and I have developed devices for dealing with this resistance. One of the most effective is to explain at the outset that the course will involve writing about the contradictions in our cultural codes. Since this will require that students participate in disagreement and conflict in open, free, and democratic dialogue, the students are asked to draw up a set of rules to govern members in their relations to each other. These rules are then published and made available to students. The device has had the salutary effect of including students in the operation of the class from the very start, thus averting passivity as well as inappropriate reactions.

Freirean Pedagogy in the U.S.

The success of Freirean teaching in the U.S., as in Brazil or Guinea-Bissau, depends on teachers knowing their students. The critics of Freire are right in arguing that the teaching materials used with Brazilian peasants are not appropriate for U.S. college students. They are wrong, however, in presuming that Freire ever suggested otherwise, as his emphasis on the role of teacher as ethnographer indicates. The teacher must understand the unique economic, social, and cultural conditions of his or her students in order to arrive at the appropriate form and content that dialogue will assume. Extensive knowledge about the students' backgrounds enables sound planning about the topics, questions, and comments that are most likely to set a meaningful encounter in motion. The aim of the course—enabling students to become active, critical agents of their experience rather than passive victims of cultural codes—is the same in all situations; but the "tactics," to use Freire's term, are always open to change.

And so the final purpose of the course is to develop citizens who are actively literate, that is, critical agents of change as social and political activists—in this way realizing the highest democratic ideals. This conception of the writing class has been under fire lately. At the University of Texas at Austin, for example, a majority of English department members voted in 1989 to restructure the required freshman composition course as a class in writing about cultural differences, including race, gender, class, and ethnic designations. Despite the strong support of the English department for this offering, a vocal minority of faculty members within as well as outside the department protested, enlisting the support of former Texas students in pressuring the university president and college dean to ban the course. Much to everyone's surprise, the president and dean capitulated to their protests, ordering that the course be put on hold for this year. Furthermore, as of this writing (December 20, 1990), its status for next year is still uncertain, and this despite the fact that recently a majority within the English department again voted to offer it. The nation that prides itself on being the most free and democratic country in the world (as Reagan repeatedly reminded us) has somehow spawned a group of intellectuals who balk at the idea that a course in rhetoric might encourage students to exercise actively their rights and responsibilities as citizens in a democracy.

Despite a heritage that from Jefferson to Emerson to Dewey has insisted on education as first and foremost a preparation for active citizenship, many professionals somehow find subversive the notion that reading and writing might be taught by focusing on public discourse in a democracy. Ironically, these same intellectuals are fond of citing historical practices in support of their position. Yet, most educational precedents established by democratic states, from ancient Athens to twentieth century U.S. public schools, directly contradict them. Freire, who smiles at the conception of a cultural literacy in the U.S. that would ignore the most obvious facts about its South American neighbors (the language of Brazil is Portuguese, not Spanish), would find the Texas scandal equally absurd, although not unfamiliar. After all, his pedagogy has been forbidden more than once by regimes who could not tolerate critical literacy in their midst. However, these governments, unlike ours, made no commitment to democracy and freedom of expression, or to being the "melting pot" of the world. And so Freire is installed as Secretary of Education in São Paulo, democracy is established in much of Eastern Europe, and a course in cultural differences at the University of Texas is postponed—indefinitely. The more things change abroad, the more they remain repressively the same at home.

Purdue University
West Lafayette, Indiana

Notes

[1] Counterparts in the public schools can be found among the advocates of the whole language approach.

[2] Two excellent examples of the work of this group are the essays collected by Patricia Donahue and Ellen Quandahl, and by Mark Hurlbert and Michael Blitz.

[3] In passing, I should mention that those who have found Freire suspect in his response to feminism should be encouraged by this interview, particularly in his separation of gender struggles from class struggles.

[4] For examples of this kind of activity, once again see the collections by Donahue and Quandahl and by Hurlbert and Blitz.

[5] In the Hurlbert and Blitz collection, C.H. Knoblauch and Cecilia Rodríguez Milanés have each reported similar experiences.

Works Cited

Berlin, James A. *Rhetoric and Reality: Writing Instruction in American Colleges, 1900-1985.* Carbondale: Southern Illinois UP, 1987.

Donahue, Patricia, and Ellen Quandahl. *Reclaiming Pedagogy: The Rhetoric of the Classroom.* Carbondale: Southern Illinois UP, 1989.

Giroux, Henry. *Theory and Resistance in Education.* South Hadley: Bergin, 1983.

Havelock, Eric A. *The Liberal Temper in Greek Politics.* New Haven: Yale UP, 1957.

Hurlbert, C. Mark, and Michael Blitz. *Composition and Resistance.* Portsmouth: Boynton (forthcoming).

Shor, Ira. *Critical Teaching and Everyday Life.* Chicago: U of Chicago P. 1987.

A Response to Gary Olson's Interview with Paulo Freire

C.H. KNOBLAUCH

It occurs to me that an interview is precisely the wrong rhetorical setting in which to elicit serious critical reflection from an educator who thinks in the concrete and contextual ways that Paulo Freire does—an educator who cherishes situated dialogue as the discourse of free society. Interview is static, simplified, deferential (as a rule), and abbreviated, resisting the give-and-take, the fluid, mercurial, serendipitous movement of conversation. Questions are not themselves subject to question; responses are not subject to close engagement that might lead to greater clarity or to modification. Add to these limits the fact in this instance that important cultural differences are involved: an American interviewer framing questions, consciously or not, in terms of the values, assumptions, and preoccupations of American educational life; an interviewee who is "a man of northeast Brazil," a teacher whose politics and pedagogy have been formed by social circumstances of a place and time. I intend no offense to the interviewer or to other respondents in this volume who find interview a comfortable medium for thought. Nor do I suggest that Freire must necessarily have been uncomfortable in this setting—I don't know whether he was or not, or whether he is struck or not by the ironies of miscommunication that are troubling me. I simply regret the absence of negotiated meaning here, particularly where crucial concepts are involved—freedom, dialogue, reality, objectivity, authority, oppression, subjectivity, cultural literacy, critical pedagogy. And I regret the missed opportunities to explore with concentrated attention the issues of feminist and deconstructive criticism that are named here too casually, and with too much assurance that each speaker understands the other, and with too much potential for unproductive judgments either of Freire or of those critical positions.

Social *Praxis* and Ethical Paralysis

Since I *am* uncomfortable, let me remark on some of what I find confusing in the interview—not to abuse the participants for being unclear, or to straighten them out as though I knew what they should have meant, but to pursue my own understanding of the themes they introduce. Keywords are a good place to start, since the text presumes, wrongly I suspect, some agreement on the subtleties of pivotal terms. The interviewer opens his introduction with references to "objective reality," claiming that Freire is a "true Marxist" in his belief that "careful, critical analysis" can yield the understanding of social life that leads to constructive *praxis*. Freire's "objective reality" is contrasted with a "poststructuralist" contention that "reality is neither objective nor knowable." The interviewer later suggests that Freire "may appear somewhat out of step with contemporary epistemology" in his faith that we can know and transform the world, a judgment he presses during the interview by appeal to "criticism" of Freire's views presumably from a deconstructive vantage point. Freire's response to the criticism is oblique and dismissive: if someone made a "well-structured speech" telling him "there is no reality," and then another person asserted that his pedagogy is based on "the analysis and transformation of reality" and asked him how he felt about the speech, he would say "they are naive," meaning presumably both the person who made the speech and the person who asked him the question. Neither Freire nor the interviewer pursues the matter; under the circumstances, further examination would have been impolite.

The issue here is an important one, belonging not to the esoteric discourse of ontology but to a public conversation about educational ethics. The issue is, precisely, how the critical educator establishes an ethical ground for *praxis*, how the imperative for social change is validated by appeal to what we can claim to know about undemocratic social conditions. Unfortunately, the interview doesn't really allow the issue to surface. Instead, some heavily coded oppositions are insinuated without clarification or scrutiny. The politeness of interview closes off talk. On the one hand, I hear in Freire's dismissal the impatience of a teacher immersed in the "realities" of Brazilian peasant life (which include gross poverty, illiteracy, social disenfranchisement, and political oppression), who is not about to tolerate self-indulgent intellectualizing aimed at trivializing his commitment to social change. On the other hand, in the interviewer's hint about outmoded epistemology, I hear claims for the deconstructive critic as more sophisticated about the unstable, figurative character of language, more sensitive to the ideological struggles implicit in competing statements about the world, and correspondingly less "naive" about the reliability, the disinterestedness, of anyone's version of "objective reality." These opposed characterizations are not to my mind unhelpful because of implausibility: I can imagine each serving as a substantive critique of the other. Freire's imperatives raise questions about anyone's right to claim superior insight; the skepticism of poststructural thought raises questions about its capacity for moral vision. But the oppositions are unhelpful because the interview leaves both of them skeletal and isolated. In their unmediated starkness, Freire is a "typical Marxist," heroic in his commitment but overly positivistic in his view of the world; the deconstructive critic is subtle about ideological constructions of "the way things are" but relativistic to a point of ethical paralysis.

This isn't the place to investigate details of Derrida's or Freire's intellectual position. But it is worth recalling, on the one hand, that Derrida's arguments have maintained from the start a clear mandate for educational and other cultural critique, notwithstanding the paradoxical subversion of even their own philosophical axioms. (Derrida has been associated with the Group for Research on Philosophical Teaching in Paris since 1974.) And it is apparent, on the other hand, from Freire's reports of his work and working conditions that his intellectual framing of educational imperatives deserves more than condescending disregard as a nostalgia for presence, an unexamined attachment to metaphysics, or even an oversimplified reading of social life. Stray comments in the interview suggest as much. "We human beings are ambiguous beings," Freire says. "Reality makes us . . . ambiguous, precisely because reality is also ambiguous." And elsewhere: "The construction of reality is collective. . . . The perception we have of reality is a social one." Freire is plain enough, here and elsewhere, about the interpretive nature of knowledge, the provisional character of our understanding of things, the importance of negotiating our renderings of "objective reality" mindful of the ideological tensions that always attend such a conversation. But the fact that "reality" lacks an ontological status, a divine origin, an ahistorical stability, does not make it subjective or unreal. The fact of cultural difference and change does not make culture an intellectual phantasm. The figurative nature of language ensures that the array of social institutions that language articulates will always be "ambiguous," not simply referential; but the collective agreements about meaning for which those institutions stand have palpable substance as well as real force in conditioning the lives of people for better and for worse. Freire is also straightforward, therefore, about the need for clear-headedness in the face of obfuscating language designed to maintain existing power arrangements, and about the need for moral vision in the midst of collective struggle to alter those arrangements and constitute democratic society.

Reality and Language Games
    Freire would situate this issue in his own culturally specific terms; let me situate it in the necessarily different terms of American society, where a comparatively high degree of literacy makes possible legislative and judicial language games designed to maintain economic hierarchies by sleight of hand. It seems to me, for instance that recent characterizations of American affirmative action programs as "reverse discrimination" offer a crudely direct illustration of linguistic obfuscation that must be challenged for its self-serving manipulation of "objective reality." The critical educator is not permitted to take refuge, with the average college sophomore, in a cozy view that "everything is relative," that this renaming of the right to employment comfortably demonstrates the impossibility of determining responsible courses

of legislative action. The "reality" is that people who have long possessed economic power, and possess it still, see their privilege jeopardized by affirmative action and seek to protect themselves by a cynical appeal to "fairness" proclaimed at the very moment that those to whom fairness has been long denied have found means to pursue it. In Freire's terms, it is politically "naive" to accept the seductive claims of "reverse discrimination," naive not to recognize the special interests at work and the sociohistorical circumstances that serve to validate the fact of injustice.

The *topos* underlying reverse discrimination arguments is "the abuser claiming to be abused." Bluntly parallel reasoning occurs in the hypothetical instance of a person who attempts to rob another and who then charges assault when the intended victim fights off the attack. This analogy is, of course, too crude. The arguments employ subtler terms, contending that the abuse is vaguely historical, that the abuser's parents, or parents' parents, or distant relatives, or fellow citizens, or a shadowy entity like "the economic system" is at fault, so that, in effect, there is no abuser—only an abuse. The idea of collective responsibility is acceptable to Americans in the harmlessly abstract terms of, say, original sin; or better still, in the congratulatory terms of an achievement—say, "improved" race relations—for which "everyone" gets (and claims) credit; but it is inconvenient in the context of employment rights. So, a subtler parallel to the reasoning might be the hypothetical case of a person who knows about a robbery, accepts its perpetration, profits from its gains, and then claims false arrest when charged as an accessory. Of course, this comparison is also fraught with imprecision and would never convince those whose best interests depend on not being convinced. That is part of the point: arguments can readily be made to sound reasonable in defense of the concept of reverse discrimination; counterarguments can be endlessly rendered inadequate in the legislative language game. My analogies can be slowly picked apart until those who most need to find them deficient are satisfied that they have been neutralized. But Freire would insist that certain "realities" remain, however clever the language games, that we can understand them viscerally as well as intellectually, that the life experience of large numbers of people attests to them: some groups enjoy economic privilege while others do not; those groups have been responsible for the imbalance in historically discoverable ways; democratic values require a redistribution of privilege that entails making the more advantaged less so if there is to be any hope of making the less advantaged more so. It is not possible to remain long committed to social change if these "realities" are subjected to a deconstruction that rests content with identifying their ideological sources (of course, they have such sources) as though no underlying principle of fairness existed or could be determined. At the same time, to be sure, it is not possible to safeguard against the substitution of one tyranny for another if the commitment to equal opportunity is not persistently reexamined to ensure that its aims retain their integrity. This, I think, is the deeper issue at stake in the opposition between Freire's beliefs and the assumptions of poststructuralism.

Freire and Feminism

Another important but largely suppressed issue in the interview is the relationship between Freire's work and feminism, a relationship that seems at best obscured and at worst falsified by the failure there to address questions of cultural difference. It is clear that the struggle for women's rights, just as any liberatory movement, is necessarily conditioned in its aims and tactics by social and historical circumstances. Even within American culture that fact has become clear of late as women of color and of working class background have critiqued the *praxis* of upper-middle-class white women who frequently occupy relatively comfortable university positions and whose images of freedom imply the advantages of their socioeconomic standing. Freire's (I think awkward) representations of his political solidarity with women—his ability to "feel like a woman," his belief that "all women have something of the man in them" and vice versa, his rejection of "machista culture" (secure in the biological fact of his fatherhood)—all suggest to me a defensiveness bred of efforts, in the interview and elsewhere, to evaluate his record by inappropriate sociohistorical yardsticks. It isn't that Freire should escape critique for the gender bias in his writing (any more than white women should escape critique for biased appropriation of feminism); it isn't that cultural difference is enough to cast a protective mantle over "machismo" in Brazil or elsewhere; it is only that different places make for different struggles, so that the question of social responsibility pertaining to the freedom of women must be concretely situated. Freire observes that "the way women fight in the States is not necessarily the same way that women in Brazil should fight." He adds that "the methods of action, the understanding, the levels of domination, the power of male ideology—all these things are conditioned culturally." I would add, on his behalf, that what is true of the ways in which women must struggle is true as well of the ways in which men are to struggle alongside them. Freire's fight has been against the politically oppressive conditions of profound illiteracy in Third-World countries. There is a mark of gender upon those conditions in "the very male culture of northeast Brazil." But profound illiteracy has not been a distinctively feminist issue in Brazil in quite the way that, say, primitive or nonexistent childcare facilities for working parents is a distinctively feminist issue in American society. Freire's commitment to "the people" has entailed a struggle alongside of women, but not one framed in feminist terms.

One judgment that Freire makes about the relationship of sympathetic men to the fight for women's rights intrigues me however for its applications to American feminist *praxis*. He argues that he "cannot take a leadership role in the women's liberation movement" but that his camaraderie is politically important to women. Questions arise. What constitutes leadership in the circumstances of American life? What roles are appropriate for men in those circumstances? What constitutes camaraderie? Freire doesn't answer these questions, and one senses their relative insignificance in the face of his vision of "the people," a collective of men and women currently united as the subjugated population in a class war. Answers in the American context might be different. It is possible to observe, among American men of liberal politics, a certain *me-too-ism* (for lack of a better expression) where women's rights are concerned, born (at best) of their embarrassment at social practices that have finally been made visible to them. *Me-too-ism* takes different forms. A defensive form is the insinuation of equivalent oppression: "If women have been imprisoned in the home, we men have been imprisoned in the office and missed the development of our children." An offensive form is the frequently sincere but mischievous request to "do something for" the women's movement, a desire rich in mixed motives that cannot help but include a bid to reestablish the intellectual and social control that feminism has critiqued in the first place. Freire's judgment here is worth considering: political solidarity is one thing; political interference, whatever the motive, is another. Solidarity entails many responsibilities for American men: first, to do no (more) harm, a sophisticated and exacting obligation that requires a radical reconstituting of long habitual social practices; second, to make room for, to step aside for, to be changed by, the fact of *difference*, not alikeness, that feminism is struggling to articulate. American feminism is not about an equality rooted in likeness; it is about an equality rooted in the respect for difference. For that reason, it is properly a movement by, no less than for, women. Sisterhood is as crucial a concept in America as The People is in Brazil.

Local *Praxis*

However this issue might be argued, my larger point is that it must be framed in culturally specific ways, just as other problems posed in the interview—about authority, or collaborative learning, or cultural literacy—must be similarly framed. We do not look to Freire, nor would he have us look to him, for the answers to *our* questions. What Freire has done about related problems or different ones in his own circumstances is not applicable in narrow tactical or methodological terms, as he has insisted on many occasions. His work is valuable to us for the larger vision of freedom that it embodies, the democratic commitments it has sought to realize in specific, localized social action. We have plenty to keep us busy in our own locales, even the restricted social space of the American university or school, mindful of Freire's point that "the process of change starts exactly in the place that we would like to change." We should not be "naive" about the power or the ingenuity of those in the school setting who want things to remain just as they are: advocates of a "cultural literacy" far different from Freire's concept of it, including the Department of Education, who want to use myths of monolithic culture and the American melting-pot to ensure the suppression of appeals for institutionally sanctioned diversity; or the National Association of Scholars, working within universities to ensure that the ideology of the political right remains unchallenged by others, arguing indeed (language games are everywhere) that the articulations of critical pedagogy are "ideological" but that the largely invisible, and certainly pervasive, curriculum of the right is intrinsically reasonable and devoid of political content; or other academics who patronize critical educators as nostalgic for the 1960s and enacting only a facsimile of countercultural *praxis* in the "safe" conditions of the university—as though that social space exists somehow outside the "real" world so that the working to change it has no actual consequences either for the "world" designated as real or for the educators themselves; or popular media, including a recent issue of *Newsweek* (December, 1990), that critique liberation pedagogies for advocating narrow-minded "political correctness," a form of thought control (schools, to be sure, have erred more than once recently in their zeal to curtail freedom of speech in the name of ethnic, racial, or gender sensitivity), as though they could be nothing better than that, as though prevailing and normative school curricula were not far more effective in their own forms of political correctness and thought control because of their calculated silence about, or unreflective belief in, their own politics. This is the setting for our work. Freire's educational philosophy, his concept of *praxis*, can guide critical educators in the United States; his victories can offer them hope of constructive social change; his difficulties can remind them of their own; his solidarity with them can support their efforts. Past that, if we wish a democracy, our burden is to continue to make one.

State University of New York
Albany, New York

Clifford

Geertz

The Social Scientist as Author: Clifford Geertz on Ethnography and Social Construction

GARY A. OLSON

Clifford Geertz says it all in one crisp, succinct sentence: "I'm probably a closet rhetorician, although I'm coming out of the closet a bit." For over three decades, Geertz has been attempting to steer anthropological scholarship away from a rigidly scientific model and toward a humanistic, interpretive, hermeneutic model—apparently with great success. Perhaps it is Geertz's preoccupation with seeing science and scholarship as *rhetorical*, as socially constructed, that makes his work so eminently appealing to many of us in rhetoric and composition. Geertz sees rhetoric as *central* to his own life and work. From his college days as an English major at Antioch College and a copyboy at the *New York Post* to 1988 and his *Works and Lives* (where he "reads" the work of four major anthropologists as if he were a literary critic explicating canonical texts), Geertz has been consumed with questions of language, rhetoric, interpretation.

For years he has pondered exactly what makes a text in anthropology persuasive. As he explains in this interview, it's not simply a matter of presenting a body of facts; it has much more to do with the author's ethos, with the power of his or her presentation. This is why, according to Geertz, a kind of New Critical close reading of texts is essential. All texts in the social sciences are in one way or another "fictions," constructions, and we need to treat them as such, not as inviolable, unassailable statements of scientific truth. Treating research reports and the like as "texts," be they in anthropology or in rhetoric and composition, does not diminish their usefulness or even their "truthfulness"; rather, it opens these texts up to a richer, more significant interpretation that leads to broader understanding of the subject at hand.

Geertz sees rhetoric and composition as similar in many ways to anthropology, especially in the relative youth of both disciplines and in the fact that neither has "a distinct subject matter" or a "real method" of research. Members of both disciplines share the fate of fields that "don't track something in the real world very closely": a great deal of anxiety over disciplinary identity. Speaking of anthropology and, by extension, of composition, Geertz says, "There's a sense that somehow we don't have an identity, that somehow the field doesn't hold together internally." But to Geertz, an atmosphere of pluralism, diversity, debate, and conflict is productive because it keeps a discipline intellectually vital: "If you want that certainty, and if wobbling around in the water bothers you, then you should go into chemistry, not anthropology—and, I have a feeling, not into rhetoric and composition either."

Understandably, then, Geertz recommends the same modes of inquiry for composition that he does for anthropology. While he's unwilling to rule out *any* research modes, even experimentation, he gravitates toward interpretive modes, such as ethnography, that will lend insight into the workings of human activities. Yet he rails against notions of ethnographic research that assume that researchers must be objective, detached, scientifically uninvolved in the community under investigation. To represent ethnography "as though it were a laboratory study of some sort" is, according to Geertz, "almost in a kind of positivist sense *false.*" Instead, he continues to champion a studied self-reflexivity, or what Renato Rosaldo has called the "positioned observer"—a recognition that "you *are* somebody: you come out of a certain class; you come out of a certain place; you go into a certain country; you then go home; you do *all* of these things." As if to underscore the importance of this recognition, Geertz is preparing a new book, *After the Fact*, in which he is surveying the work of his long career in an attempt to "reconceptualize" his life's work in terms of research conducted not by some impersonal, objective "scientist," but "by human hands—that is, *mine.*"

Geertz is particularly frustrated with attempts to maintain a sharp distinction between the humanities and the sciences. Not only is such an artificial distinction "false," but it is used to make value judgments between "what is legitimately rigorous and objective and what is soft and stupid." Geertz believes we should "deconstruct this dichotomy and be done with it," especially since this very distinction has often been made regarding his own work, with critics charging that he is "not a reasonable scientist." Such critics, Geertz counters, are succumbing to a simplistic two-cultures notion that fails to account for the complexity of the intellectual universe.

It will be of little surprise that Geertz considers himself a social constructionist, that he believes "meaning is socially, historically, and rhetorically constructed." He stops short, however, of calling himself a poststructuralist, thinking of himself instead as a "late modernist under pressure." Yet Geertz does find poststructuralist perspectives useful, and he has always opposed the structuralists for their essentialism and hyperrationalism. And though he agrees with the critiques of the New Critics, he has a special affinity for the kind of close textual analysis they championed.

Clearly, what makes Geertz especially influential in composition scholarship is that throughout his career he has wrestled with the very same issues that we ourselves have: the nature of interpretation, the role of rhetoric, the nature of persuasiveness, the social construction of meaning, the relative value of various modes of inquiry, the role of the researcher in ethnographic research. In many ways Geertz is, as he rather proudly admits, a rhetorician; and in many ways his life's work has been a sustained and impassioned study of rhetoric, its uses and abuses. Clifford Geertz may very well think of himself as a "novelist manqué," but to many of us in rhetoric and composition he is a rhetorician *accompli*.

Q. It's often been noted that your prose, even in your more technical anthropological writings, is very readable—even, at times, *entertaining*, in the best sense of that word. In your recent book, *Works and Lives*, you examine the notion that ethnography itself is "a kind of writing, putting things on paper." In what ways do you think of *yourself* as a writer?

A. In all kinds of ways. I started out to *be* one; that's the first answer. I wanted to be a novelist and a newspaper man. As an undergraduate, I had the notion—maybe an antiquated one by now—that one could work on a newspaper and write novels in the evening. I went to Antioch College and majored in English, at least in the beginning, with the intention of doing something like that. In high school I had edited a newspaper and a literary magazine—the usual sort of thing. So I wanted to be a novelist. I even wrote a novel (though I didn't publish it) and some short stories. Antioch had a co-op program so I went to work for the *New York Post* as a copyboy. Then I decided I didn't want to be a newspaper man; it was fun, but it wasn't practical. After a while I shifted into philosophy as a major, but I never had any undergraduate training at all in anthropology and, indeed, very little social science outside of economics. I had a lot of economics but nothing else. Anthropology wasn't even taught at Antioch then, although it is now. And except for a political science course or two and lots of economics, I didn't have any social sciences. So I was in literature for at least half the time I was there, the first couple of years, and then I shifted to philosophy, partly because of the influence of a terrific teacher and partly because in a small college you can run out of courses. Then I got interested in the same sort of thing I'm interested in now: values, ideas, and so on. Finally, one of my professors said, "Why don't you think about anthropology?" That was the first time I had thought seriously about being an anthropologist, and then I began to think about it and I went to Harvard and so on.

So I came in preformed as a writer and put writing aside for awhile because I had to learn what anthropology was all about and do research and get a kind of union card as a working anthropologist. But, yes, I really am a novelist manqué. (Some of my enemies would say I'm still a novelist—a fiction writer anyway.) So it's not accidental; I've always had that bent, I guess, and I still do. I think of myself as a writer who happens to be doing his writing as an anthropologist. I've often been accused of making anthropology just into literature, but I don't believe I'm doing that. Anthropology is also field research and so on, but writing is central to it.

Q. Would you describe your writing process? For example, do you spend substantial time gathering information and synthesizing it before you draft? Do you prepare an outline, revise extensively, use a computer?

A. I've spent a lot of time in the field—almost a dozen years in Southeast Asia and North Africa—where I don't do any writing at all. I can't write in the field. I write a lot of field notes, but I can't compose anything. I once started to write a book review in the field, but that didn't work. I just can't do it. I think there's a much greater separation in anthropology, especially among field anthropologists, than in a lot of social sciences between the research and the writing—at least as I do it. You do two or two-and-a-half years in Java in which all you do is live with the people, write down everything, and try to figure out what the hell is going on; then you come back and *write*—out of the notes, out of your memories, and out of whatever is going on in the field. So, for me at least, it's a fairly divided life. I don't write in the field; I write after I return. Mostly, *here* I write and *there* I research.

As far as *how* I write, there's no single answer. I hesitate to confess this in public because I think it's a very bad way to do things, but I'll do it anyway: I don't write drafts. I write from the beginning to the end, and when it's finished it's done. And I write very slowly. That may seem odd, because I've written a lot, but I've often been in situations like this one here in Princeton where I've had a lot of time to write. I never leave a sentence or a paragraph until I'm satisfied with it; and except for a few touch-ups at the end, I write essentially one draft. Once in a while people ask me for early drafts, but these drafts just don't exist. So I just go from line one to line X—even in a book. I have an outline, especially if it's a book, but I hardly pay attention to it. I just build it up in a sort of craft-like way of going through it carefully, and when it's done it's done. The process is very slow. I would not advise that other people write this way. I know people who can write a first draft and not care whether it's idiotic. They'll write "blah, blah, blah," and put zeros to hold space for something to be filled in later. Good writers do this. I wish I could too, but for reasons that are probably deeply psychological, it's impossible. I usually write about a paragraph a day, but at least it's essentially finished when it's done. And all of this is not due just to the computer, because I've only used the computer for a year or so. I write by hand; even now I write by hand. I just type text into the computer so I can print it out and read it.

Q. In discussing what constitutes persuasive discourse in anthropology, you've observed that the persuasiveness of a text does not rest on the accretion of facts and details but on "the ability of the anthropologist [or any writers] to get us to take what they say seriously"—that is, on what rhetoricians call the writer's *ethos*. Exactly what factors do you think make discourse particularly persuasive? What is it about a given text that makes us take the author and the text seriously?

A. In *Works and Lives* that's a question I *asked* rather than tried to give a definitive answer to. So my first response is that I don't know. If you look in anthropology, the diversity of kinds of texts that have been persuasive and have had purchase in the field militates against any simple conclusion. In *Works and Lives*, I really wasn't trying to establish a canon; rather, I was trying to say, "This seems to be the canon; why do we believe Evans-Pritchard and Lévi-Strauss and Malinowski and Benedict and some others?" I think the answer to your question is itself empirical, and I think it's empirical in a discipline that is yet to come—that is, rhetorical analysis in anthropology. We need to think more about the nature of rhetoric in anthropology, and that's what I tried to begin. There isn't a body of knowledge and thought to fall back on in this regard.

Q. Is it that we just know persuasive writing, good rhetoric, when we see it?

A. I think people *are* making judgments, but I don't think they know what basis they're making them on. In recent years, there's been more and more writing about anthropological writing, but still there's not that much. You could name a half dozen books and another dozen articles and pretty well exhaust the stuff that's worth reading. It's not a vast field. I'm sometimes amused by people who are furious about *Works and Lives* because they think it's an abandonment of the field to literature. I respond, "It's the only book like this I ever wrote and probably the only one like it that I ever will write. The field is not really dissolving into this; most anthropologists are doing straightforward ethnography, and should do it." So in that book I tried to examine how at least these four people managed to be persuasive, and it turned out to be a little bit different each time. Even the factuality problem is not that simple. It certainly is true that just the assembly of facts is not going to make a text persuasive; if it were, there would be a lot of very dull books that would be a lot more famous than they are. Somehow, the sense of circumstantiality and of power in reserve (if an anecdote or an example doesn't sound strained but sounds like you've got fifty others and this is the best one you chose) are factors that are rhetorically important. I guess I want to dodge the issue, mostly because I just don't know the answer.

What I want to see get started is a lot more reflection about these matters. Book reviews in *The American Anthropologist* hardly ever concern themselves with rhetoric. The most you ever hear is, "It's well written," or "It's lousily written," or "It's obscure," but no real sense of how the book is put together. You almost never get anything about how composition occurs, how the text is constructed, how the argument is developed, and why it is or isn't persuasive. There's very little about "writing" in that sense. So we're operating in the dark. Yet at the same time, and this is what started me with the kinds of concerns addressed in *Works and Lives*, there's a fair consensus in the field about what the canonical books are. We aren't in that much of a debate about them. We may like or not like what A or B says, but nobody is going to say that Lévi-Strauss is not an important anthropologist or that Evans-Pritchard or Malinowski wasn't influential. Most people would say that these are significant people. But we just don't know *why* their works are persuasive.

Q. So you'd like to see more self-reflection on the part of anthropologists, especially about how anthropological texts are constructed.

A. Yes, that's the point of "literary criticism" or "rhetorical analysis" in anthropology—not to replace research, but to find out how it is that we are persuasive. It is odd in anthropology, because if you read a book by me on Java or some other place, you either take it or leave it. You don't know anything about the place. You could read another couple of books and probably get more confused, but there's no way of matching it to "reality." (If the correspondence theory of truth ever does work, it doesn't work here.) If I write about the Balinese cockfight, who knows what's what? A few readers might be able to make *some* comparisons, but the average reader is just left with the text and with what I'm saying about the subject. So why the cockfight piece has been popular, why that took hold, is interesting to me. Why certain papers, certain articles, certain pieces, certain books, certain writers have a kind of persuasiveness, why we believe them, is curious. Again, we don't know anything about the Nuer, the people Evans-Pritchard wrote about. I've never seen a Nuer, and I never will probably, and ninety percent of the students won't. Maybe a few will, but even they will go at a different time from the original investigator—E-P. If there's ever a place where you *can't* argue that you can put the facts over here and the text over there and see if they fit, it is surely in anthropology.

Also, a lot of books that have been influential don't meet the usual stereotypes of why we believe them. They're *not* very factual. I gave an example of Leach's *Highland Burma* book, which I do think is very good, but he doesn't have much in the way of facts in it. And there are lots of others. Why do we believe Leach, or at least more so than we do other people? It isn't really theory, because anthropological theory is not that impressive, in my view. I don't think we know, and I think the way to know is what I at least was trying to do and what some other people are trying to do: to look at the texts as a close reader. I was trained in the fifties, so I was trained as a New Critic. Close reading is important to me. Though I agree with many of the critiques of the New Critics, I often remember what literature was like before the New Critics, when people stood up and talked about Shelley's "soul" and such things. I still have a fair amount of nostalgia for New Critical discipline and for close reading, and there hasn't been that in anthropology. It's beginning a bit, but it's still minuscule. So, close reading is what I want to happen, and if it happens enough, perhaps in twenty years I could answer your question—though, of course, I won't be around then. At the moment I can't answer it because I don't think we have a body of knowledge yet.

Q. Certainly, a feasible kind of project for someone in rhetoric and composition would be to look at various anthropological texts and apply a kind of rhetorical analysis to them.

A. That's the kind of thing I wanted to do. I wanted to get other people interested in doing this because, like practitioner history, practitioner criticism isn't always the best sort of thing. Anthropologists have certain commitments to what they're doing and they have certain distortions. I would hope that one of the results of *Works and Lives*, whether anybody likes the readings given there or not, is that those outside the field would be stimulated to look at anthropology as textual construction.

Q. In discussing textual construction, you've drawn on the work of Foucault and especially Barthes to distinguish between an "author" (and a "work") and a "writer" (and a "text"). What crucial distinctions do *you* see between the two concepts?

A. The Barthes piece actually impresses me more than Foucault's. Barthes' distinction, and I think it means something to me, is that for him, if I remember correctly, a writer is someone who wants to convey information. That is, language or writing is a code: I want to tell you how many days a week the Balinese have rituals, and I'm just trying to convey information. The other image is that it's a theater of language; that is, you're trying to convey a sense of what things are like, and you want to use language itself as a mode of construction. Again, this is what's interesting about anthropology in this regard: anthropologists can't really opt for either of these. Obviously, I can't give up telling you how many Balinese there are and what they do and getting it right. On the other hand, I do want to convey something of the inner significance of Balinese culture, and that demands a theater-of-language kind of authorship. There, all kinds of other things come into play because voice and signature and things like that really play a role that they perhaps don't to the same extent in communicative writing. That is the axis upon which I wanted to try to see what an author in anthropology is. I think the question of what the relationship between author and text is has never really been raised before in anthropology.

Q. Perhaps this is the distinction you were searching for before about what really makes a text persuasive. Of course, it's still a vague distinction.

A. And it won't be persuasive if the writer's side is missing either. There are lots of "literary" books (in the bad sense) in anthropology that nobody believes because readers just don't feel the writer really understands what the X indians or the Y natives are all about, and they feel, therefore, that the text is in the bad sense a "fiction." On the other hand, it *has to be* something of a fiction: it has to be *made*; it has to be *constructed*. That's the mule image that I gave. We have to be both of those things. That's what interests me about the Barthes distinction; he was concerned at least somewhat with this problem. [In *Works and Lives*, Geertz speaks of "the North African mule who talks always of his mother's brother, the horse, but never of his father, the donkey" as an example of how we suppress parts of our heritage "in favor of others supposedly more reputable."]

Q. In the preface to *Works and Lives*, you say that the work of Kenneth Burke was that book's "governing inspiration at almost every point," and often in the past you've cited his work. In what ways has Burke's scholarship been an influence on yours?

A. Burke *is* important to me. I first encountered his work as an undergraduate in literature. There are lots of things about Burke that I like. I guess the main thing is the notion of symbolic action—the notion that writing is a form of action and that action is a form of writing or a form of symbolic behavior; that you can take (and I've done this; the Balinese cockfight piece is an example) a ritual or a repetitive event as a text, even take the state as a text, to "read" action in symbolical terms as Burke was one of the first to do (at least that I ever ran into); that writing, on the other hand, is itself a form of action, that it has a pragmatical/practice dimension and that's what it's about. Burke healed the division between what goes on in the "real" world (activity) and what goes on in the "unreal" world (that is, writing about it) without fusing them. There's a marvelous line of his that often gets quoted, "Having children by marriage is not the same as writing a poem about having children by marriage." You can see that both having children by marriage and writing a poem about having children by marriage are forms of action and forms of symbolic action. *That's* what I get out of it, and the whole emphasis is on rhetoric. Two people have been really liberating in my mind for what I was doing; one is Wittgenstein and the other is Burke. As a very young man in college, I read Burke—before he was a secular saint, before everyone was reading him. Even then I thought this is what literary criticism ought to be.

Q. In "Ideology as a Cultural System," you make a case for "the study of symbolic action" (in Burke's sense) as an important interpretive, analytical tool of sociologists, especially those examining ideology; and you show how ideology draws on metaphor and other tropes to socially construct a complex web of interrelated meanings. In the decades since you wrote that essay, there has been, of course, intense interest in tropology, especially among poststructuralists. Do recent discussions of tropology shed new light on the project that you were articulating back then?

A. Sure. I think what is true is that what seemed then a rather odd thing to say now seems a rather banal thing to say. That's happened. People have begun to do more of this, even in anthropology—I'm not just talking about literature. Certainly, the whole notion of tropology has become more and more important, but what I see is that when I wrote "Ideology as a Cultural System," as far as anthropology or social science in general was concerned, even the stuff that did exist, like Burke and the beginnings of what later became deconstruction, had no effect. So I don't see myself as being ahead of the world in doing this but as mediating to anthropology or the social sciences. I'm not even alone in that, but if I was ahead of the game at all, it was in saying that we ought to look this way. Later on I wrote specifically about looking toward literature and these kinds of matters, saying that we should stop looking at levers and hydraulics and such things and start thinking in that symbolical way. What has come along, of course, is hermeneutics, which has enriched this stuff immensely because it encouraged us to study it. I just called for it and others have begun to organize the discussion of it. I find some of this scholarship useful, even though I have some reservations about far-out versions of it.

Q. So do you see yourself as a poststructuralist?

A. No, I don't. I'm certainly not a structuralist, as I early on was hostile to structuralism; it's a kind of hyperrationalism that I oppose.

Q. But you don't see yourself as involved in the same project as the poststructuralists?

A. I don't see myself as a poststructuralist. Someone recently wrote about me, saying I was a late modernist *in extremis*, which may not be too far off. Maybe *in extremis* is a little extreme, but I'm certainly a late modernist under pressure. I still regard myself as that. I'm not sure what I mean by all this, except that I'm unwilling to let signifiers float entirely freely, and I'm unwilling to have a scrapbook approach to the composition of texts, and so on. So while I've learned an enormous amount from the poststructuralists, I'm not willing to be categorized as one.

Q. You've said, "Human thought is consummately social: social in its origins, social in its functions, social in its form, social in its applications." Such comments and your work in general have led some compositionists to call you a leading "social constructionist." Do you consider yourself a social constructionist?

A. Yes, that one I'll buy. In fact, I'm writing a review right now of three books on feminism and science, and it's about social constructionism. Yes, I would say I'm a social constructionist, whatever that means. Like most people I hate to adopt labels, but the whole business about the social construction of meaning seems to me to be right. Your question about what's happened since I wrote "Ideology"—all that has happened. Again, I think it was there in Burke and in all kinds of things, but it has been thematized, analyzed, brought forward; and I do think that meaning is socially, historically, and rhetorically constructed. If you want to call me anything, call me that. I don't think there is a field or a movement called social constructionism that I *belong* to, but I'm sympathetic to that notion.

Q. The concept of social construction is quite important in rhetoric and composition right now since language is, of course, central to anything that's being socially constructed.

A. That's what I wanted to see in *Works and Lives*. I wanted to see how anthropologists socially constructed people, which doesn't mean that they're all wrong, or they're all made up—that's part of a very advanced sort of poststructuralism I don't want to buy. I'm not willing to say they just made it up. I just gave some lectures, the Harvard Jerusalem Lectures, that will be compiled in a book called *After the Fact*, and it's essentially an argument for a social constructionist view of anthropology—in fact, explicitly so. It's sort of a looking back at my work over forty years and figuring out how I constructed the images of Morocco and Bali—how I constructed them and what foundations I had for doing so. So I'm trying to do that. (I guess it's an attempt at self-historicizing or something of that sort.) So yes, I don't mind the term *social constructionist*, except that I don't like labels in general.

Q. In *Local Knowledge* you discuss Richard Rorty's concept of *normal* and *abnormal* discourse, and you suggest that the terms *standard* and *nonstandard* discourse would be more appropriate. You explain that your "preference for standard/nonstandard stems from a dislike of the pathology overtones of normal/abnormal (itself a revision of Kuhn's rather too political-sounding normal/revolutionary) and from a dislike of pure types, dichotomous dualisms, and absolute contrasts." Your sense of the concept of nonstandard discourse seems more useful than Rorty's grander notion of abnormal discourse (in *JAC* he said abnormal discourse is a "gift of God") and seems more in line with how compositionists use it. Would you elaborate on your understanding of standard and nonstandard discourse?

A. The main reason I didn't like the normal/abnormal business is that both in my field and in general it has all the overtones of abnormal as *sick*. I don't like the medical model applied in general, so I wanted to get away from that. It's amusing that Richard, who is a diehard atheist, is talking about "gifts of God." Nonstandard discourse is something that reaches beyond the conventionalities of ongoing discourse, and in anthropology you almost always have to do that. We always have two problems when we write about others—the Javanese, for example. One is making them sound like Martians, like they're just wired so differently that we can't understand them; the other is making them sound just like ourselves. If you use standard discourse, you do end up making them sound just like ourselves—or like Martians—because those are the only alternatives. So you need to develop some sort of mode of description or argument that mediates between the two extremes; and this mode is nonstandard. Generally, I'm not wildly experimental, but my own writings in anthropology are certainly nonstandard. They're not wild or off the edge of the map or anything, but they aren't the way most anthropologists write. And certainly when I started they weren't. There are more people doing it now.

Q. Your writings are nonstandard because they're not part of the conventional discourse of the discipline?

A. Yes, there's been mimicry of the sciences in an attempt to sort of be fashioned after them—you write an introduction, then the findings, then the conclusions. I've written—not only me but more and more other people have written—in a much more off-the-wall sort of way in an attempt, among other things, to cope with that endless dilemma of not making the Balinese or the Moroccans or the Javanese sound like they live on the moon but also not making them sound like they live next door. They don't do either of those things. To cope with that dilemma I think some sort of experiments in prose are necessary, some sort of departure from received canons of description.

Q. So you don't see abnormal discourse as something that happens only once every few decades or so with some sort of major find, but as something that happens all the time with certain people in certain circumstances.

A. More so. One thing about terms like *standard* and *nonstandard* is they come in degrees. There are people who write much less standard discourse than I do. Some of the people to the intellectual left feel that I'm still writing linear prose, which they see as a big mistake. (I should be putting things in all capital letters and that kind of thing.) I don't think necessarily that nonstandard prose is always better than standard prose or standard writing. I just think that in anthropology and the social sciences the received canons are limiting. So yes, I do think it's something that goes on all the time, and it goes on in degrees. Every once in a while, somebody really revolutionizes the way things are done; most of the time, they inch up on it and after a while you notice that it's really done in quite a different way than it was before. It's always amusing to look at how something early in the twentieth century was written in anthropology and how it's written now. You can see that somehow there's been an enormous shift in how it's done, but yet you can't put your finger on someone who actually did this—there's no Joyce, for example. But that can happen, too. One of the small problems with Tom Kuhn's work (which I like very much; Tom's a good friend of mine) is that because he dealt with physics and with particular events in physics, he did tend to have a normal/abnormal radical distinction. I don't think that model fits so well in biology, for example. But shifts can be more gradual, and the concept of standard/nonstandard has to be relativized that way.

Q. In "The Growth of Culture and the Evolution of Mind," you discuss some of the difficulties in studying the concept of mind. Recently in *JAC* Noam Chomsky complained of a "pernicious epistemological dualism," in that "questions of mind are just studied differently than questions of body." Do you agree that in studying the mind scholars have tended to ignore the role of biology and what Chomsky calls "innate structures"?

A. I agree with Chomsky in almost nothing. That's too strong—he's made major contributions in studies in syntax and so on, but in philosophy and in philosophy of mind I certainly don't agree with him, for the same reasons I don't agree with Lévi-Strauss. They share the same kind of hyperrationalism that I don't. When it comes to innate structures and so on, I'm very skeptical.

Q. He apparently feels quite frustrated with this movement away from biology toward social forces. He said, "Look, if you're going to study puberty, you don't study peer pressure." When I chuckled, he said, "You're laughing. Why do people laugh nowadays when I say that? You would automatically go, for something like puberty, to biology. So why don't you do the same for the study of the mind?"

A. I don't disagree with the notion that we need to consider the body as well as the brain. That's what I argued for years ago in the "Evolution of Mind" article, and I still argue for that. I recently gave a talk in which I said that I think advances in neurology are going to make an enormous difference in the way we think about mind. So there Chomsky and I don't disagree. Where he and I would disagree is that he has an intensely nativist view of the structure of the brain and mind which I think wildly over simple. Also, he's an odd man to be making that point, because he doesn't study the brain; he studies computers and language. He's been criticized by a lot of people on the grounds that if you really want to study the brain, you need to study the brain and not project your theories into it in a deductive way, which is what I think Chomsky does.

I think what's known about neurology is still scattered and uncertain, but, yes, I think we need to know about the body. As you say, I've written about it, though I haven't written about it recently. Certainly, I'm not a dualist in that sense. I think genuine investigations into the structure of the brain or the structure of the nervous system should help us understand thought. What I am opposed to is two ways of approaching the subject. One is Chomsky's kind of innatism, where you postulate a central processing mechanism—the problems with that are enormous. The whole central processing view of psychology, I think, is quite unworkable. That's one way to do it. The other way is sociobiology, which is highly adaptationist. And when you protest, as I have on a number of occasions, against one or both of these with some vigor, the countercharge is that you don't care about the body or biology, which is false. It's just that I think that neither neo-Darwinism nor neo-rationalism is the way to go.

Q. So obviously you also wouldn't agree with the evolutionary epistemologists, such as Karl Popper?

A. No, I wouldn't.

Q. Do you think they're having much influence?

A. Well, Chomsky, of course, at one time did. He isn't as influential as he was, at least in social psychology and certainly in anthropology. Sociobiology is a trickier business. Popper—no. I don't think he's had much influence in America.

Q. You mentioned that you're writing a review of some books on feminism and science. Do you believe that Western culture in general and U.S. society in particular have made substantial progress toward gender equity?

A. I think there have been some advances, but what I think has happened in a rather short period (When was Betty Friedan's book published? One always tends to date it from that) is an enormous development of thought and self-reflection about gender, and not only among feminists (though particularly among them) but among everybody. Everyone, I think, is much more conscious of these matters than they were, and that's certainly an advance. And gender consciousness has become involved in almost every intellectual field: history, literature, science, anthropology. So in that sense, I think there's been an extraordinary advance. I suppose there's also been some progress in the marketplace because there are many more women working; so there has been *some* correction, I suppose, of gross inequality—but there are also many gross inequalities still left. What *is* different—I guess because I'm an anthropologist I think about culture—is that the culture has changed. I do think the attempt to raise consciousness has in that sense succeeded. People are very aware of gender concerns now. There is much greater legitimacy of investigations from the point of view of gender concerns in everything, again, from literature to science. Also, there has been more consciousness about sexual harassment in the workplace. But whether or not things have gotten radically better *there* is not something I'm really able to say.

Q. So it's both yes and no: our consciousness has been raised somewhat, but we still have quite a way to go.

A. Well, again, I live in a university environment and *there* it's changed. There are many, many more women present. That's not to say that equity has occurred, just that it has compared to what it was. When I first came here twenty years ago, there was only one woman professor at Princeton. Now there are a lot; there's a critical mass. The women are there and they're influential. Whether it's like that in the banking industry, I honestly don't know.

Q. Chomsky said that "for cultural reasons, the move away from patriarchy is a step upwards. It's a step toward understanding our true nature." Do you agree that the elimination of sexism is an "evolutionary" step, and that there's a "true" human nature that we *can* approach?

A. I certainly think that it's an advance; it's a moral advance of major proportions that needs to be sustained. I would not myself formulate it in terms of "human nature" or evolution toward some intrinsic essence of man—generic man. I just don't think that way. But I don't have any disagreement with the notion that it's a moral advance. I can't briefly say why, but it wouldn't have to do with the fact that we're getting closer to our nature. My arguments would all be from arguments of moral justice and equity and things of that sort, not from somehow approaching some preexistent inner essence that we are evolving toward. That sort of language always bothers me because everybody has his or her own notion of what that essence might be. You've got people peddling this stuff on every street corner (and I'm not speaking of Chomsky here). So I certainly don't disagree with the ethos of the statement, but I wouldn't put it the way Chomsky did; that's not the way I would argue for it.

Q. Has feminism had an effect in anthropology itself? Has feminist inquiry, for example, changed how you do things or how anthropologists do things?

A. Yes, very much so. It's had an enormous influence. Anthropology in general has always been fairly hospitable to female scholars, and even to feminist scholars. There's always been a number of women who have been really quite influential in the field—not only Mead and so on. They weren't always feminists in the modern sense of the word, but some of them were. There have been enormous advances in the number of women who are teaching—though, again, the process is far from complete. Has feminism made us all more conscious? Yes, I think it has. Feminist critiques of anthropological masculine bias and so on have been quite important, and they certainly have increased *my* sensitivity to that kind of issue. I think feminism has had a major impact on anthropology. We were talking before about making discourse less scientistical; feminism has been something of an assistance in all that: some of the support for that has come from feminism.

Q. Because rhetoric and composition is a highly interdisciplinary field, drawing on work in anthropology, linguistics, philosophy, psychology, and so on, the whole range of modes of scholarly inquiry—from experiment to ethnography to theoretical speculation—is available to us. Currently, compositionists are engaged in an important debate over which modes of inquiry are most appropriate for the making of knowledge in our field. Do you feel that it would be advantageous for a discipline like composition to use a multiplicity of modes of inquiry, or should it rely primarily on one or two modes that seem especially productive?

A. It's hard to give advice to a discipline I have so little knowledge of, but I'm an inveterate fox and not a hedgehog, so I always think you should try everything. My intuition would be yes, try multiple approaches to these matters. I'm a little at a loss because I don't quite know what they are and what the problems are and what ones, if you were a hedgehog, you would cling to.

Q. Well, let me give you an example. Some think that since our roots are in the humanities, we really ought to work with our strengths and do theoretical, speculative kinds of scholarship. But we do have a very strong science orientation in the discipline, and so others argue that we should conduct empirical research, even experiments with control and experimental groups and randomized selection of student writers, and so on. Then there are all the different modes in between, many drawn from the social sciences, including, and especially, ethnography, which has emerged as one of our major modes of inquiry. I'm not trying to get you to take sides in *our* debate; I'm just curious about what your intuition tells you about these matters.

A. It's hard for me to believe that a field like rhetoric and composition has arrived at such a state of paradigm consolidation that it would know which way to go with some certainty. One has to be somewhat critical and not just do any silly thing, but I would think, especially since it seems to be a discipline still very much in the process of formation, that it would be unwise to have premature closure on anything—certainly not ethnography, or even experimental research. I myself think that experimental research would probably not be of much use, but that doesn't mean you shouldn't do it. It just means that if it were me, I would find that a step in the wrong direction.

I also think that we ought to break down these kinds of large-scale distinctions between the humanities and social sciences, not in the sense of absolutely having no differences, but we at least ought to make them permeable. Certainly, there is a difference between doing literary criticism and doing chemistry. I'm not trying to say it's all together in one great big mishmash, but the notion that these fields don't have anything to say to each other or offer to each other strikes me as odd. For a field that looks to be somewhat interstitial like rhetoric and composition (it seems somewhat like anthropology: a bit of a mule, a bit of everything), it would seem very unwise to hedgehog and to say you're not going to do certain things. At the same time (I guess I'm getting into the "on the one hand and on the other hand" about this) if you have some things that are vital, you need to support them. As I say, it's a field I don't know much about.

Q. The reason I ask this question is that some people—for example, many of my graduate students and also well-known scholars in the field—feel somewhat insecure when they see all the bickering—some arguing we need hard "fact," others urging us to go with our strengths, to stay with theory because "experiments aren't going to tell us anything worth knowing." As a result, many in the field often become dismayed over this seeming chaos.

A. That resonates. Anthropology is like that. Some professors and especially younger anthropologists have the notion that anthropology is *too* diverse. The number of things done under the name of anthropology is just infinite; you can do anything and call it anthropology. (That's perhaps a little extreme.) In my field I have always argued for the pluralistic approach to things rather than solidification into some particular line (even my own line) of work. But there is a great deal of anxiety. I think it is true that scholars, both young and old, are overly anxious about pluralism, diversity, conflict—younger ones especially because when they're first getting into a field they want to know what it is they're supposed to know, but older ones, too, because they somehow yearn for a lost paradise when everyone knew what they were doing. I think that's the nature of things, and I don't think things are moving toward an omega point; I think they're moving toward more diversity anyway. So being an inveterate pluralist (of course, I don't know anything about rhetoric and composition), my instincts are always against people who want to fasten some sort of hegemony onto things. I myself don't feel that an atmosphere of debate and total disagreement and argument is such a bad thing. I think it's a good thing; it makes for a vital and alive field.

There may be a similarity between rhetoric and composition and anthropology. I know this is true for anthropology, and I ask *you* whether this is true for rhetoric and composition: because anthropology never has had a distinct subject matter (of course, primitives and so on, but that doesn't really give you much to go on) and because it doesn't have a real method, there's a great deal of anxiety over what it is. People keep asking how anthropology is different from sociology, and everybody gets nervous about that. There's a sense that somehow we don't have an identity, that somehow the field doesn't hold together internally. That leads to the rise of ideology as a way of unifying it. One of my former teachers said anthropology is a poaching license; it's just everything and anything. People for whom that produces anxiety want to close it up, and I think it's often true of fields that don't track something in the real world very closely or that have a long theoretical tradition. I think that if you don't like that kind of anxiety, you should go into organic chemistry. I don't want to pick on chemists. I'm sure there are lots of disputes in organic chemistry, and real fights, but at least you know what organic chemistry is: you know who the old organic chemists are, and you know who the new ones are; you know what the traditions are, and you know what the methods are. If you want that certainty, and if wobbling around in the water bothers you, then you should go into chemistry, not anthropology—and, I have a feeling, not into rhetoric and composition either.

Q. I've never thought of these similarities between anthropology and rhetoric and composition, but I think you're right. A colleague of mine just read *Works and Lives* and said to me, "I must confess that I'm really a closet anthropologist. I'd much rather be doing what Geertz is doing in this book."

A. Well, I'm probably a closet rhetorician, although I'm coming out of the closet a bit.

Q. The work of Shirley Brice Heath has served as a model for many compositionists interested in conducting ethnographic research. Are you familiar with her work?

A. Yes, but not as well as I should be. I read *Ways with Words*, and it's extraordinarily good. I think what she's doing is very very good, very very interesting.

Q. Do you think this is the kind of research compositionists should pursue?

A. Yes, I would like to see more of that sort of thing being done. I certainly would not like to see it being closed off by people who think you should have control groups and so on. They can do that type of research, too; but yes, I do think that this is the kind of research that should go on.

Q. For example, compositionists might (and do) study how people who are growing up in ghettos are writing in their own environments, or they might study writers in corporate environments, and so on—writers in their own environments.

A. I certainly would like to see somebody do that, whether it's rhetoric and compositionists or not, but somebody ought to be doing it. (Of course, Shirley Brice Heath is an anthropologist.) Indeed, I call for something like that in a paper called "The Way We Think Now," which is an attempt to say we should have an ethnography of the disciplines and begin to think about that sort of thing. It addresses some of the issues we talked about in relation to Chomsky: about different notions of how to study mind and how to study intelligence. Its main argument is that we need to get some understanding of representations and of the ways texts are put together and of the ways thought patterns go in the disciplines. I was brought to the subject by being here at Princeton, because after a while I realized that the way in which mathematicians and physicists and historians talk is quite different, and what a physicist means by physical intuition and what a mathematician means by beauty or elegance are things worth thinking about. I'm interested in trying to think about those things in a cultural anthropological way. You also find in talking to mathematicians and physicists that they're really conscious of writing differences; even though they would all claim that truth is truth and writing doesn't really matter, they also are aware of the fact that there are different styles and that rhetoric is important.

Q. You write that the "establishment of an authorial presence within a text has haunted ethnography from very early on.... Finding somewhere to stand in a text that is supposed to be at one and the same time an intimate view and a cool assessment is almost as much of a challenge as gaining the view and making the assessment in the first place." Since ethnography is emerging as probably our key scholarly mode of inquiry, what steps can an ethnographer take to achieve this balance between being in the text and being perceived by readers (given the typical expectations of readers of research) as sufficiently detached so as to have authorial credibility?

A. Actually, most of that kind of problem has centered on the question we usually refer to as "reflexivity." In *Works and Lives* I have some sardonic things to say about some attempts in that direction, though I think it's the direction to move. It's very hard to do this. On the other hand, a recent book by Renato Rosaldo talks, in terms that I think are better than reflexivity, of the "positioned observer." At least in the kind of anthropology that I and people like Renato and others do—as I've said, there are lots of kinds of anthropology—we are part of what we study, in a way; we're there. And it seems to me almost in a kind of positivist sense *false* not to represent ourselves as being so—false, or at least an imperfect representation. Now, I've never done it. Well, in the piece on religion in Java and in the cockfight piece and in a few other pieces I'm there, I'm self-represented; once in a while I've done it. But I've never really thoroughly done it, and I've written a lot of books which are written from the moon—the view from nowhere. I am persuaded that at least for some works, for a lot of works, we've really got to get ourselves back into the text, to have ourselves truly represented in the text. I've always argued that in part I'm represented in my texts by my style, that at least people won't think my books were written by anybody else, that there's a kind of signature in them. But I think Renato is right: we have to go further than that; we have to situate ourselves within the text. In the book I'm writing now, *After the Fact, that's* what I'm trying to do. It's not confessional anthropology, and it's not about what I was feeling or something of that sort; it's trying to describe the work I've been doing with myself in the picture.

Q. So you're going back to your earlier pieces and analyzing them?

A. I'm going back to my whole career—not the pieces so much, just to the work—and trying to reconceptualize it in these terms. I'm trying to restate it as work that was done by human hands—that is, *mine*. As I say, I think in my earlier work there are places where this occurs, and in my writing style even more so; but I think one needs to go further, and the whole problem is that it's very difficult to do. Now, I don't like confessional anthropology. Part of the confessional anthropology came out of the sixties when, for example, I had a hard time convincing students that they were going to North Africa or someplace to understand the North Africans, not to understand themselves. I'm in favor of people understanding themselves, and that's in a certain way what anthropology's about; but you really want to know what the *Moroccans* are like, and I still do that. That's what my vocation seems to be to me. But these people are right (as I say, thinking on these lines has advanced a bit) that you can't do that as though you were, again, on the moon. We need to find ways of bringing ourselves in. There are different ways to do it, and there are some silly ways to do it. People take photographs with their own shadow in them; that doesn't seem to me to be a particularly marvelous solution. The whole question is how to do this without being awkward. Take ethnographic cinema. A friend of mine did a movie on Nepal and is inclined as I am toward this line of thought, but she finally kept herself out of the film because the other ones in the series where the anthropologists tried to get themselves literally in the picture were awkward and silly. It's a very hard thing to do, and I think it's something, getting back to writing, that we don't know how to do rhetorically. We don't know how to do it effectively. We're getting better, perhaps, and there are some successes and some failures and some semi-successes. In any case, what I'm doing now is that I'm really trying to see whether I *can* do it unawkwardly. But it's a writing task, as far as I'm concerned.

Q. Assuming that we *can* get to a point where we can do it smoothly, would you say that what really needs to change, perhaps, is the expectation that an ethnographer must be somehow detached?

A. Well, these expectations are *wrong*. Evans-Pritchard is a good example. There's very little of E-P as a person in what he does. And Lévi-Strauss either. None of the people in that generation—Malinowski did a bit, but the others didn't—brought themselves into the picture. It was not considered the thing to do. But they of course *were* in the picture. That's the point. Maybe that's a fair representation of looking through a microscope; I'm not sure. But it isn't a reasonable representation of what I've been doing for forty years. I really did live among these people; I did talk to them. They did react to me; I did react to them. This is again Renato's notion of the positioned scholar. You *are* somebody: you come out of a certain class; you come out of a certain place; you go into a certain country; you then go home; you do *all* of these things. To represent it as though it were a laboratory study of some sort, in the traditional sense, seems to me to misrepresent it. So the expectations that have been formed, and that have been formed by ethnographic writers, that the anthropologist is not involved in what's going on, are false. It's not really a veridical picture, in a very simple sense of *veridical*, of what anthropological research is all about. How you undo that preoccupation with a sense of distance and so on is difficult to know. More and more people are trying, especially the younger group.

Q. What about those people who want to write off that kind of ethnographic writing, whether it's in your field or mine, as not being rigorous simply because you *are* there?

A. I don't see why such research is necessarily less rigorous. I would agree that a lot of it isn't very rigorous, including my own, but I don't see any reason why it *can't* be rigorous. That's exactly what we need to do: to rethink how ethnography has been written, how it might be written. And I think the only way to do that is interpretive. As I said earlier, that's what I hoped *Works and Lives* would stimulate, not so much agreement with my particular readings (though that would be nice). It's an interesting book because with my colleagues it provides a kind of vocational Rorschach test: some love the Evans-Pritchard chapter and don't like the Lévi-Strauss, and others have the exact opposite reaction. I think we need to do more of that kind of reading and more thinking about the problems of text construction, text building, and not start from preconceived notions of what ethnography ought to be. That's why even my use of Barthes and Foucault was tentative; it was a way into the topic, but the real heart of it was to get to a position where I could say something cogent or at least apparently cogent about actual texts.

Q. You describe a "pervasive nervousness" among ethnographers in an atmosphere of "deconstructive attacks on canonical works, and on the very idea of canonicity as such; *Ideologiekritik* unmaskings of anthropological writings as the continuation of imperialism by other means; clarion calls to reflexivity, dialogue, heteroglossia, linguistic play, rhetorical self-consciousness," and so on. Does this poststructural atmosphere undermine ethnography as a mode of scholarly inquiry or strengthen it by encouraging perpetual self-critique? Or both?

A. I think the critique has been and is very valuable. It has shaken up those of us who were a little dissatisfied and didn't know why and, even more valuably, those who didn't even know they were dissatisfied. That's not the same thing as saying I'm always happy about the actual critiques. These people have raised issues that really can't be evaded, that have to be dealt with. I think they've raised them more effectively than they've dealt with them, but I think they've raised issues that you just can't laugh off, including reflexivity and problems of representation and of the relation of power in representation. These are issues that we can no longer pass off with genuflections to the scientific method. In that sense, such critiques have been immensely valuable. I read something by an English anthropologist—I can't remember who—who said that in his view the life of postmodernism in anthropology would be short but its effect would be profound. I think that's about right. Poststructuralism has had an enormous influence. We can't go back to what we were, and I think those kinds of critiques are very valuable. I don't know which way to move entirely either, so I can't be too harsh with the poststructuralists. What does sometimes happen is a certain kind of self-indulgence which I'm not too happy with (it's easy to sort of wing it). I guess I'm positive about the critique, less positive about response to the questions it raises. But even those are sometimes suggestive, and I find a lot there.

Q. Are you equally satisfied with the whole ideological awareness agenda of Dell Hymes?

A. I think ideological awareness is very important in anthropology. We do come from somewhere. One of the things I'm trying to do in *After the Fact* is to think about how I function as an anthropologist in a certain time. From the 1950s to the 1990s, there was a tremendous change in the ideological framework under which I operated, not so much in my own ideology (though some in that too) but in the ideological ambiance of 1950 and the cold war, and 1990 and the end of it—not to mention a lot of things in between, including changes that have gone on in the Third World: the whole notions of optimism and pessimism, development and nondevelopment, changes of relations between the Third World and the rest of the world, internationalization, and so on. Yes, we do have to be conscious of those factors and think about them. I'm not quite sure what of Dell's you're referring to, but I like Dell's work in general. We don't always coincide ideologically, but I have no objection to the notion that ideology is important.

Q. It's a common assumption, expressed often in the popular press, that the U.S. is experiencing a literacy crisis. Some scholars, however, argue that rather than massive illiteracy there are multiple literacies competing against one privileged literacy that helps maintain white, male culture in general and the military/industrial complex in particular. What are your thoughts on this subject?

A. I know very little about the multiple literacies discussion. One of the problems is I don't teach anymore so I don't quite know. I don't find in the people I do teach, when I do teach at Princeton, that they can't read anymore; they do.

Q. As well as they used to?

A. Yes, and they may even be better in some ways. I don't feel that we're going to hell in a handcart. What *is* happening is that this country is becoming much more plural than it was, and we can't make believe that it's the same as when not only white males but only a certain class-segment of *them* went to college. Now we've got all kinds of people, and we have to develop a new way of educating them. That doesn't necessarily mean educating them to our standards either. So there are obviously new problems of how to teach writing and modes of literacy that just didn't appear before now, and I don't think they can be evaded. I'm trying to think about this business of plural literacies; the rhetoric about the military/industrial complex I find to be "rhetoric" in its bad sense. I think attention to such matters as registers in language is very important; it's the sort of thing that Dell *is* interested in, along with a lot of other people. I'm all in favor of trying to see how people do put language together—how they write, how they talk, and so on—and trying to come toward them in some way in order to enable them to participate in literate culture. I don't have the notion, though, that everybody has to write in some single academic style.

My daughter teaches Native Americans in the Southwest. She teaches on a Navajo reservation, so she faces this sort of thing on the firing line. She's concerned with how to get Native American kids to be effective with the written word. Neither is a solution: just trying to make them into whites, or just saying they're Indians and so they're intuitive and they understand the world and that's all we need to do. She has to *teach* them. That kind of pluralism is inevitable. American society, insofar as it ever was, has been particularly homogeneous, certainly in the educational class side of things. There was the WASP ascendancy and so on, but that's gone and it's gone for good. How many Spanish speakers are there now in the nation? There's no sense in making believe that such diversity isn't what we're faced with. I don't think the response to it is to try to construct some kind of high old tradition, but I also don't think we can just say that any old way will do. Most of these things we won't know how to do until we work with them. Of course, I myself live in a fairly homogeneously literate world (not that we write well or anything), and I don't come up against illiteracy much.

Q. You say in the preface to *The Interpretation of Cultures*, "At a time when the American university system is under attack as irrelevant or worse, I can only say that it has been for me a redemptive gift." Do you still have faith in the university system, especially considering recent reports critical of the quality of education in the U.S.?

A. Yes, I do; but I'm not mindless. There *are* problems, and they're serious ones, and it's a continual fight to keep things going. Universities, and schools in general, are being asked to do an enormous number of things they never had to do with a much more complex population than they ever had to do it with. But certainly I'm against the Allan Bloomean sort of business. I really don't find *that* a reasonable response to what's going on. I think the American university system still seems to be the best system in the world. I haven't done a systematic study, but it still seems to me extraordinarily good. It has had some blows, and it will have more. It does have lots of problems, but I meant that business about it being a redemptive gift. I thought I ought to say that at least once. Perhaps because I'm in a somewhat unrepresentative part of academia, it looks better here than if I were teaching in the Bronx or somewhere else. But, I do still think we're not doing that bad.

Q. A great many people in and out of anthropology support your project. However, your work has generated a fair amount of criticism, such as recent critiques by Paul Shankman and others. Are there any important misunderstandings of your work that you'd like to address at this time?

A. Yes, but I don't quite know what to say in a few well-chosen words. I think the perception of there being a deep gulf between science and the humanities is false. Those who have that false perception tend to want to put me on one side or the other—usually on the humanities side, saying that I'm not a reasonable scientist. I resist that. I really don't think that's the way to think about it. The notion of what science is both varies from discipline to discipline and changes in time, and the attempt to make a simple distinction between what is legitimately rigorous and objective and what is soft and stupid is a dichotomy or dualism that *could* stand a little poststructural analysis. I really think we should deconstruct this dichotomy and be done with it. Much of the worst misunderstanding of my work comes from people who are trapped in that conceptual framework. It's everywhere. (It's perhaps a little stronger in anthropology in Britain than it is in the United States, but it is strong in the United States, too.) I'm speaking of the notion that, for example, literature is one thing and science is another, that they are eternally different, that they don't change, that they mean the same thing in any field. When I resist these notions, and when I resist the imposition by anthropologists (not by physicists) of hard-science notions on anthropology where I think they're inapplicable, or where they don't even work, I'm often interpreted as being anti-science or unrigorous. And I think that's just wrong. Of course, some criticisms are quite cogent, so don't get me wrong; I don't want to reject everything anyone has ever said about me. But when critics divide the world into real scientists and real (or "unreal," usually) humanists and decide that this gulf is an absolute—the two-cultures notion—I think that all of what I do and a good deal of what other people in the social sciences do just drops through the cracks because it's a *third* culture, a *different* sort of thing. Many of these critics really have yet to grasp that, and when they don't grasp it then they misread. Because they see a departure from what they learned, they make distinctions between explanation and understanding that really are not sustainable. They make all kinds of distinctions that I think are not sustainable and, therefore, misread both the intentions of my work and, indeed often enough, what is actually said on the page.

Q. Well, you must get terribly frustrated by the increasing specialization of the university system then. Doesn't it tend to militate against that kind of broad cross-disciplinary interaction?

A. Well, one thing this social science school here tries to do is go the other way: to *not* make those sharp distinctions. When I and a few others first started with this kind of work, I really did feel peripheral and marginal, or discriminated against. Now there are a lot of us around, and—this is parallel to the question of feminism—the battle has been joined in a way that it didn't used to be. It used to be just a weak protest against a massive establishment. I don't feel that way now. As I've said in some other place, "I think we're gaining on the bastards." So I don't think that things are really so frustrating.

Q. So you expect this interdisciplinarity to continue?

A. Yes, I see it all over. Your journal is full of this very interdisciplinarity. There's a lot of it. It's not a matter of dissolving, and it's not even a matter of interdisciplinarity; it's a matter of being open to something outside your tradition as strictly defined. Even economists (who were almost always the most self-sufficient) are beginning to be more permeable towards it. One example is Don McCloskey's work in *The Rhetoric of Economics*, in which he's beginning to look at something besides just what he learned at Chicago in microeconomics.

During my ten years at Chicago, I taught the introductory graduate course in anthropology a number of times; it's a critical course for the making of anthropologists. I kept trying to get them, not without success, to see that people who are officially "anthropologists" are not their only ancestors and are not the only people they should be reading. I got them to read a lot of people: Cassirer, Suzanne Langer in those days—people who would not otherwise be on anthropology syllabi. It wasn't that I was trying to get students out of anthropology, or get them to be amateur philosophers. Today I find in the field that everybody's read Richard Rorty, and some have even read Charles Taylor—which is even better. I find it much less of a provincial discipline in some ways than it had been. I don't want to sound *too* upbeat; it isn't *that* marvelous. As you say, there are a lot of people who react very strongly against all of this and against me for promoting it. I guess I'm aging, but again, if I look at '50 and '90, forty years of it, I think things are better. From where I stand, things look better.

The Somewhat Unitary World of Clifford Geertz

LINDA BRODKEY

Reading the interview with Clifford Geertz, I was reminded of "The Lecture," in which Erving Goffman, after dismissing other more obvious explanations, concludes that during a public lecture, speaker and audience "join in affirming that organized talking can reflect, express, delineate, portray—if not come to grips with—the real world, and that, finally, there is a real, structured, somewhat unitary world out there to comprehend" (194). What Goffman says about a social contract underwriting public lectures might be extended not just to interviews, but to all spoken or written efforts to produce a world in words. While we may find some words more convincing than others and therefore some worlds more "real" than others, I hesitate to dismiss even an implausible or terrifying wor(l)d view—out of hand—since I literally cannot imagine a world without words. I suspect that Geertz also believes that because words matter, we must accept them all as valid material tokens of human struggles to chart a course through reality.

For me, and no doubt for many others as well, Clifford Geertz is a set of texts. And in each of them he abides by the social contract (limns a world) of which Goffman speaks. But during the *JAC* interview, Geertz occasionally glances behind that tacit claim at what Goffman concludes is an even more compelling "tacit claim that valid pictures are possible" (195). And so, when Geertz concludes the interview with, "From where I stand, things look better," I take him to mean that after forty years he still believes in anthropology, and hence in the possibility—as he puts it when speaking of his current project, *After the Fact*—of writing it "as work that was done by human hands—mine." That Geertz sees writing as the anthropologist's work is not news (he has been saying so at least since *The Interpretation of Cultures*), but that he sees writing as rhetoric is if not news, then newsworthy.

Rhetoric and Contingent Value

If things look better to Clifford Geertz, then maybe they should look a little better to us, too, and not simply because he has publicly invited us to stand alongside him and consider what he sees from the vantage point of a cultural anthropologist. What he is looking at cannot but interest those who study and teach writing, for Geertz points to no fewer than three projects for rhetoric and composition: studying the texts anthropologists write; imagining the texts they might write; and writing ethnographies. Having already given some thought to each of these prospects (*Academic Writing as Social Practice* and "Writing Critical Ethnographic Narratives," for example), I have more than a passing interest in what might be learned from representing writing and writing pedagogy from cultural perspectives. And while I have a preference for the last project—for ethnographic studies of writing—like Geertz I think ethnographies are written and read and, ultimately, valued *as* texts.

Nearly everyone who studies ethnographic texts *as* texts comments on how boring they are. In one of the most astute literary explanations I've read, "Fieldwork in Common Places," Mary Louise Pratt attributes their unexpected dullness to the anthropological denial of its kinship with travel narratives and with its romance with science, which typically relegates all narrative or personal material to the margins—to introductions or personal memoirs or notebooks. Indeed, Geertz's wonderful anecdote about the mule might be read as a gloss on "Fieldwork in Common Places," for Pratt at least implies that anthropologists who suppress narrative (the lowly donkey) tend to "go on" about science (their remote but more respectable equine relation) and succeed not in impressing us with science, but in boring us, instead, with their all too tedious "scientific" observations.

Geertz suggests in the interview, however, that the dullness might also be explained in rhetorical rather than narrative terms. Speaking about what may make some prose persuasive (namely, the anthropological texts taken up in his most recent book, *Works and Lives*), he says,

> It is certainly true that just the assembly of facts is not going to make a book persuasive; if that were true, there would be a lot of very dull books out there that would be a lot more famous than they are. Somehow, the sense of circumstantiality and of power in reserve (if an anecdote or example doesn't sound strained but sounds as if you've got fifty others and this is the best one you chose) are factors that are rhetorically important.

I find the statement linking circumstance with example or anecdote the more provocative for the ironic realization that published anthropologists face the same problem student writers confront: convincing readers that they *really* know what they are talking about. William Labov says that storytellers ward off the question, "So what?" by evaluating their own narratives, by directly or indirectly letting readers know why a story is worth listening to (366). Perhaps, Geertz means something like "evaluation" by the phrase "circumstantiality and a sense of power in reserve," that writers who do not produce essays and books that readers find worth the work of reading also provoke the dreaded "So what?" and know that most readers answer the question in the negative (even if teachers and editors do not) by refusing to read.

Persuasiveness is a rhetorical notion. Considering his affection for the New Criticism ("I still have a fair amount of nostalgia for New Critical discipline and for close reading"), I wonder if Geertz is more interested in a set of canonical anthropological texts by which he is persuaded than in rhetorical principles of persuasion. By the phrase "circumstantiality and power in reserve," however, Geertz may mean something on the order of a "representative anecdote," even though when he talks about Kenneth Burke's influence, he elaborates only the more general "notion of symbolic action." Without denying the importance or influence of symbolic action to Geertz as a writer of anthropology or to modern rhetoric as a field, I think that Burke's "anecdote," which tries to account for the appeal of certain kinds of explanations, may come closer to specifying the terms on which some works create the "sense of circumstantiality and power in reserve" that Geertz singles out as critical to persuasion. Of course, since it's Burke making the argument, there is a simultaneous unraveling of the notion, since the "representative anecdote" represents not a literal but a symbolic reality. But then I presume that Geertz doesn't mean that a writer must actually have fifty other examples, but that the particular example or anecdote seems so "representative" that we believe there must be plenty more where that came from.

I think of rhetoric as a theory articulating the complex social practice of producing *and* receiving spoken and written texts. In other words, I am inclined to view description as the most powerful dimension of rhetoric, and so I value rhetoric mostly for what it tells me about epistemology. Whether any extant rhetoric could also be used to determine the precise value of particular texts is something not only Geertz, but nearly everyone who studies and teaches writing would like to know. No doubt, our practical reasons for wanting to know have to do with grading and assessment, but, surely, a more inclusive intellectual warrant for theory, research, and practice is pedagogy, since it is in teaching that most of us commonly exceed the theoretical and empirical limits of our knowledge of writers, writing, and written texts. Questions about what makes particular ethnographic texts persuasive and how to write "honest" ethnographies are questions for axiology, that is, questions explicitly dealt with by theory of value but only broached in even the most egregiously prescriptive of contemporary rhetorics.

In "Contingencies of Value," Barbara Herrnstein Smith argues that both the absolute and relative aesthetic value believed to inhere in some literary texts might better be explained as a contingent value. For Smith, then, aesthetic judgments along with all other human acts of evaluation are

> the evaluator's observation and/or estimate of how well that object, relative to others of the same implied category, has performed or is likely to perform certain particular (though taken-for-granted) functions for some particular (though implicitly defined) set of subjects under some particular (unspecified but assumed) set or range of conditions.
> (20)

I mention her argument for an axiology based on contingencies because in much the same way that we have been trying to transvalue writing (writing pedagogy) in English studies, Geertz and others are trying to transvalue writing (written texts) in anthropology. And I think Geertz and we could do a good deal worse than think about contingencies that may make it difficult for our colleagues to value writing in any of the ways we do, or he does.

Transvaluing Writing

The writing process movement, if not also cognitive research on composing, seems to have transvalued the status of composition in at least some departments and/or institutions—specifically, to have legitimated a range of undergraduate and graduate courses and possibly even the field itself. And writing-across-the-curriculum programs may also have contributed to the transvaluation of writing pedagogy, though too few institutions are willing to use their considerable fiscal and human resources in support of these labor-intensive and costly interdisciplinary curricular reforms. Because efforts by Geertz and others to transvalue writing in anthropology deal more explicitly with the reception than the production of texts, they have encountered more concerted resistance. By the early 1980s, a fair number of anthropologists besides Geertz were reconsidering the place of writing in the field, more specifically, in narrative and rhetorical terms (see, for example, Marcus and Cushman), but by the late 1980s, writing had become the occasion for one of the most heated debates in anthropology. Geertz sees the debate about writing as derailing over what he says anthropologists "refer to as 'reflexivity,'" which I think may also mean his uneasiness with the split or divided subject of poststructuralism, but which he thinks may finally be put back on track with notions like Renato Rosaldo's "positioned observer."

When Geertz invites us to consider how ethnography might be written, he is not asking whether anthropologists should teach writing as cognitive processes or social practices—as we might—but is instead wondering what we might have to say about "the positioned observer" which would, as he puts it, allow anthropologists "to get ourselves back into the text, to have ourselves truly represented in the text." We probably do know more about personal essays than most academics because we teach them, or have taught them, and know them (or I do) as low-status, high-risk essays, if only because a teacher is inescapably judging a writer's life (if not also the writer) in the course of evaluating a personal essay. I am made so uneasy by my experience of grading personal essays that I don't assign them.

Yet, Geertz is absolutely right to say, "We are part of what we study, in a way; we're there. And it seems to me almost in a kind of positivist sense *false* not to represent ourselves as being there—false, or least an imperfect representation." Anyone who has written an ethnography knows that she or he has literally constructed it and that in so doing has not written all the other possible ethnographic texts. There is something to the point to be learned from Marianna Torgovnick, a literary feminist who characterized her writing self in a recent book, *Gone Primitive*, as "a person with feelings, histories, and desires" and hence her prose as "more direct and more personal" than in her previous books (27). It's largely a matter of remembering, if I understand Torgovnick, that when you write literary criticism, or anthropology, you are representing only yourself, since no one literary critic can represent Literary Criticism, no anthropologist can speak for Anthropology and, for that matter, no compositionist can represent Rhetoric and Composition.

Geertz may be more right than he knows when he whimsically suggests that only organic chemists can know organic chemistry in the way, for example, that many of us were taught by the New Critics to know literary criticism as a discipline, as an already established set of problems the answers to any of which would necessarily contribute to the cumulative and collective knowledge of literary criticism. Undoubtedly, there are many reasons why Geertz doesn't know cultural anthropology with the kind of certainty that he, and we, imagine an organic chemist to know organic chemistry. But judging by what he says later on about poststructuralism, Geertz might well give it as one of the reasons "scholars, both young and old, are overly anxious about pluralism, diversity, conflict"—whether in anthropology, rhetoric and composition, or any other zone of what he calls "a third culture," in which science and humanism are not as polarized as C.P. Snow once defined them and as some so called traditionalists, who insist on policing disciplinary borders, persist in believing.

Geertz is wary of poststructuralism, however, and inclined to embrace Barthes' distinction between writer and author rather than Foucault's. He refers to himself archly as "a late modernist under pressure" and shortly after says, "I would say I'm a social constructionist, whatever that means." Geertz is reluctant to go further than that, not only because he's grown too accustomed to "wobbling around in the water," his trope for the intellectual uncertainty with which he and other anthropologists practice anthropology, but because he has a penchant, which most anthropologists share with structuralists, for synchrony. It's a preference for space over time, I think, that at least partially explains his objections to poststructuralism: "I'm unwilling to let signifiers float entirely freely, and I'm unwilling to have a scrapbook approach to the composition of texts, and so on. So, while I've learned an enormous amount from the poststructuralists, I'm not willing to be categorized as one." Free floating signifiers and scrapbooks are hypertexts, and poststructuralism is the theory most suited to describing what is undoubtedly at once a temporal and spatial experience of text (see John Slatin). I find most poststructural notions to be primarily temporal rather than spatial, which makes it exceedingly difficult to move from theory to research to practice. My own efforts to track, say, shifting subject positions in actual texts invariably convert what I imagine as temporal events into spatial episodes (see "On the Subjects of Class and Gender in 'The Literacy Letters'").

It's not that I think Geertz is indifferent to time or history, or that I am, but that the methods (close reading, deconstruction, taxonomy, narration) used to "test" or even practice poststructuralism spatialize the temporal relations critical to theory, and so one tends to conclude, as Geertz does, that "the critique has been and is very valuable" but that to say so is not "the same thing as saying that I'm always happy with the actual critiques." We may be better poised than we know, given what we teach and who we teach—not to mention the theories and research methods we collectively know and use (if the journals tell us nothing else, it's that no one theory or method any longer typifies the field)—to construct methods that are at once empirically valid and pedagogically viable.

Ethnographic Analysis of the Academy

In addition to inviting us to analyze ethnographic texts and reflect on how they might be written, Geertz suggests that we write our own. He mentions ethnographies of literacy in passing but talks in more detail about the need for "an ethnography of the disciplines": cross-disciplinary cultural studies of "how to study mind and how to study intelligence," so as "to get some understanding of representations and of the ways texts are put together and of the ways thought patterns go in the disciplines." Given my own interest in academic writing, I can think of no research I would rather see launched than full-scale ethnographic studies of the academy. Bearing in mind his later remark, however, that the anthropological reception of *Works and Lives* "provides a kind of vocational Rorschach test," I think we are just as likely to discern intellectual tensions within as between disciplines. This is certainly true in English and anthropology, two departments (I hesitate to call them disciplines) where theories have altered how people teach and write. Geertz says as much himself about the effects of feminism and poststructuralism on anthropology, and many of us have observed, first hand, similar changes in literary studies and, in turn, shifts in attitudes toward writing in some English departments.

Were we to follow up on Geertz's suggestion, I think we might expand the parameters of *discipline* to include publication, for publication is the *sine qua non* of the academy, and it's the occasion on which academics are most likely to declare their intellectual allegiances. Among other things, we need studies of academic presses and journals to supplement the work already begun in sociology (for example, see Coser et al.), for we know little about how editors select books and articles for publication; about how they select books to be reviewed, or reviewers; surprisingly little about the selection of referees, or their reading practices; about the editorial boards of presses and journals, and their practices. These are obvious but important questions in composition, a field which claims students can be taught to write for professors of anthropology, literature, biology, and philosophy. The argument for that claim would be all the stronger were we able to describe reading and writing practices of anthropologists, literary critics, biologists, and philosophers in any detail.

Such ethnographic work might also help clarify what sometimes seems contradictory about the conceptualization of writing and writing pedagogy in composition theory, research, and practice. Although all are ways of talking about (or so I believe) writers, writing, and written texts, tempers are rising. By way of example, Maxine Hairston in a letter to *College English* recently dismissed a raft of essays she doesn't like as poorly written, which doesn't say much for Geertz's hope that if anthropologists only knew more about texts as texts, they wouldn't just praise them as "well written" or dismiss them as "lousily written" or "obscure."

There are gaps between theory, research, and practice in composition, but they need to be bridged by arguments, not claims, for like anthropology this field "is moving toward greater diversity" not "an omega point." Many of us welcome the proliferation of theories, since they remind us, as little else does, that we are positioned observers: "You are somebody: you come out of a certain class; you come out of a certain place." I take Geertz to mean that a field is known not from a vantage point at all, but is perhaps known a little better by those who see the limitations of their own positions than those who mistakenly believe that what they see is all there is.

University of Texas
Austin, Texas

Works Cited

Brodkey, Linda. *Academic Writing as Social Practice*. Philadelphia: Temple UP, 1987.

——. "On the Subjects of Class and Gender in 'The Literacy Letters.'" *College English* 51 (1989): 125-41.

——. "Writing Critical Ethnographic Narratives." *Anthropology and Education Quarterly* 18 (1987): 67-75.

Coser, Lewis A., Charles Kadushin, and Walter W. Powell. *Books: The Culture and Commerce of Publishing*. New York: Basic, 1982.

Goffman, Erving. *Forms of Talk*. Philadelphia: U of Pennsylvania P, 1981.

Hairston, Maxine. "Comment and Response." *College English* 52 (1990): 694-96.

Labov, William. *Language in the Inner City*. Philadelphia: U of Pennsylvania P, 1974.

Marcus, George E., and Dick Cushman. "Ethnographies as Texts." *Annual Review of Anthropology* 11 (1982): 25-69.

Pratt, Mary Louise. "Fieldwork in Common Places." In *Writing Culture: The Poetics and Politics of Ethnography*, Ed. James Clifford and George E. Marcus. Berkeley: U of California P, 1986.

Slatin, John M. "Reading Hypertext: Order and Coherence in a New Medium." *College English* 52 (1990): 870-83.

Smith, Barbara Herrnstein. "Contingencies of Value." *Critical Inquiry* 10 (1983): 1-35.

Torgovnick, Marianna. "Experimental Critical Writing." *Profession 90* (1990): 25-27.

Clifford Geertz on Writing and Rhetoric

Lisa Ede

The *JAC* interview with Clifford Geertz provides elegant confirmation—if anyone needed it—of the reasons why this "closet rhetorician's" work has drawn the attention of many in composition studies. Geertz, along with such scholars as Donald McCloskey (*The Rhetoric of Economics*), James Boyd White (*Heracles' Bow: Essays on the Rhetoric and Poetics of Law*), and Dominick LaCapra (*History and Criticism*), has helped catalyze what has been variously called the "rhetorical turn," the "turn to interpretation," or the "epistemological revolution" in the social sciences. Geertz has helped map the changes that postmodern life and thought have entailed. Essays like "The Way We Think Now" and "Blurred Genres: The Refiguration of Social Thought" have functioned for many as intellectual signposts, enabling scholars in a variety of fields to make provisional sense of the intellectual ferment surrounding them.

Composition and Pluralism

Geertz is an articulate scholar whose work transcends the boundaries of his own discipline; he is also a self-conscious stylist who has reflected for some time about what it means to be a writer, an author. Thus, not surprisingly, there is much in this interview to interest compositionists. Geertz's description of his own composing process, for example, stands as a striking reminder of the way in which our field's writing-as-process-not-product "revolution" has too often hardened into a repressive orthodoxy. If Geertz enrolled in a freshman composition course today, would his teacher insist that this "essentially one draft" composer couldn't possibly write an effective essay unless he revised numerous times? And would Geertz—who describes himself as writing "from the beginning to the end, and when it's finished it's done"—be forced to manufacture messy-looking freewrites and rough drafts to please his composition teacher, as some students now do?

Geertz is a forceful advocate of the usefulness of ethnographic research; this interview includes a number of comments directly applicable to those conducting such research in composition studies. Unlike many scholars, particularly social scientists, Geertz is also acutely aware of the extent to which a project like *After the Fact*, his current effort "to think about how I function[ed] as an anthropologist in a certain time," is as Geertz says "a *writing* task" (emphasis added). What more elegant affirmation could those engaged in writing-across-the-curriculum efforts ask for? And Geertz's reasoned and reasonable comments on multiple literacies, on the futility of trying "to construct some kind of high old tradition" to which all students must submit, are certainly heartening. It is reassuring to know that this internationally-known scholar working at the prestigious Institute for Advanced Studies is "against the Allan Bloomean sort of business."

Geertz sees a number of similarities between anthropology and composition studies. Both are relatively new disciplines; both are inherently interdisciplinary; and in both there is at times "a great deal of anxiety" over what the field is. Describing himself as an "inveterate fox," Geertz suggests that scholars in composition studies should not become dismayed over our field's seeming chaos. Instead, we should "try everything," avoid "premature closure on anything." This advice appeals to my own pluralistic sensibilities. But there's pluralism—and then there's pluralism. Pluralism can encourage healthy diversity and conflict; the resulting "atmosphere of debate" can, Geertz observes, "make for a vital and alive field." However, pluralism can also be a dodge; it can leave important questions not just unanswered but unasked.

Geertz comments, for instance, that even in a pluralistic discipline scholars must be "somewhat critical and not just do any silly thing." This sounds quite genial and commonsensical, but how do we finally determine in specific cases what comprises a reasonable versus a "silly" (or possibly even dangerous) research effort? And to what extent might the apparent openness and flexibility of pluralism mask strongly entrenched intellectual, emotional, and political commitments? Geertz himself notes that if scholars in composition believe that certain things are "vital," they therefore "need to support them." How do we determine whether scholars are reasonably and appropriately supporting their beliefs through professional argument or whether they are attempting "to fasten some sort of hegemony onto things"? Conversations in *JAC*, recent letters in the "Comment and Response" column of *College English*, and well-publicized arguments over the proposed freshman composition curriculum at the University of Texas at Austin indicate that there can be considerable disagreement over questions such as these.

So I find myself both attracted to and suspicious of Geertz's call for pluralism and for reconciliation between the humanistic and social science research models currently contending for dominance in many fields, including composition studies. Like Geertz, I don't like to think that scholars in the humanities and social sciences "don't have anything to say to each other or offer each other." But how do scholars with strongly divergent assumptions and methodologies forge a synthesis without resulting in "one big mishmash"? And does pluralism automatically ensure diversity and conflict, as Geertz seems to suggest? Couldn't it also mask the agreement to disagree politely, rather than to confront differences?

I have no answer to these questions; I simply want to point out that Geertz's genial, liberal approach may have the limitations of, well, genial liberal approaches. The questions that Geertz has clearly given much thought to—whether fields like anthropology and composition studies can be too diverse, the benefits and dangers of pluralism—are questions that we must continue to ask. We must also recognize that terms like "pluralism" themselves require critical scrutiny, lest we rely upon commonsensical (and hence unexamined) understandings of their meaning.

It was Geertz who first taught me to look with particular attention at that which seems most commonsensical, most obvious. It is there, Geertz notes in "Common Sense as a Cultural System," that we can often see how a culture or discipline "is jointed and put together," that we can discover assumptions so strongly held and so broadly shared that they remain unstated and thus uncontested (Local Knowledge 93). Reading Geertz's essay helped Andrea Lunsford and me realize, for instance, that it is hardly an accident that English teachers have assumed single authorship to be the norm. Rather, English teachers, like others in the humanities, have long held the pervasive commonsensical assumption that writing (particularly "real" or belletristic writing) is inherently and necessarily a solitary, individual act. Once we recognized the power that this largely unexamined assumption held for teachers of writing, we realized that our study of collaborative writing, *Singular Texts/Plural Authors: Perspectives on Collaborative Writing*, needed to examine the concept of authorship itself. It is no accident that Clifford Geertz is mentioned in the first paragraph of our study.

Precisely because it is so obvious, the wisdom of common sense can be hard to recognize, much less analyze. "There is something," Geertz comments in "Common Sense as a Cultural System," "of the purloined-letter effect in common sense; it lies so artlessly before our eyes it is almost impossible to see" (92). As I worked on this response, I found myself wondering if there might be one or more purloined-letters hiding in plain sight in Geertz's interview that might productively be analyzed. I would like to devote the rest of this response to one such potential purloined letter: Geertz's conflation of "rhetorical analysis" and "literary criticism."

Geertz's Conception of Rhetoric

Despite his fondness for and understanding of Kenneth Burke, Geertz's rhetoric seems grounded in the conservative tradition of technical rhetoric. In identifying rhetoric with literary criticism, in assuming that rhetorical analysis involves the New Critical close reading of texts, Geertz implicitly characterizes rhetoric primarily as formalistic analysis. Geertz asks many sophisticated questions about the relationship of authors and texts—questions that certainly need to be asked by those in the social sciences who have looked to science, not the humanities, for models and methods. But in exploring the factors that "make discourse particularly persuasive," Geertz focuses on such traditional concerns as "how composition occurs, how the text is constructed, how the argument is developed, and why it is or isn't persuasive."

These concerns are part of rhetoric's domain, but rhetoric—and certainly rhetoric as it is evolving in response to poststructuralist critical theory—involves more than traditional textual analysis. A number of theorists have drawn on rhetoric's emphasis upon and grounding in the rhetorical situation to argue that rhetoric can provide a means of analyzing the textual production of identities and of social relations. This view of rhetoric is articulated by Terry Eagleton, who closes his well-known *Literary Theory: An Introduction* by calling for a return to rhetoric, which he characterizes as follows:

> Rhetoric in its major phase was neither a "humanism," concerned in some intuitive way with people's experience of language, nor a "formalism," preoccupied simply with analyzing linguistic devices. It looked at such devices in terms of concrete performance. ... It saw speaking and writing not merely as textual objects, to be aesthetically contemplated or endlessly deconstructed, but as forms of *activity* inseparable from the wide social relations between writers and readers, orators and audiences, and as largely unintelligible outside the social purposes and conditions in which they were embedded.
> (206)

Rhetoric, as articulated by Eagleton and others, is concerned with and provides opportunities to explore the contingencies of history and ideology. Thus characterized, rhetoric goes beyond purely textual matters such as "how the text is constructed, how the argument is developed, and why it is or isn't persuasive" to consider the interplay of culture, politics, and ideology in the production and legitimation of texts.

Geertz's description of his current project, *After the Fact*, indicates that he recognizes the importance of reflecting on issues such as these. In attempting to look back on his previous studies in order to "describe the work I've been doing with myself in the picture," Geertz potentially at least is moving from an exclusive focus on the relationship of authors and texts to an examination of the anthropologist's rhetorical situation. In order to examine "the ideological framework" under which he operated from the 1950s to the 1970s, Geertz may need to go beyond a concern for "reflexivity" in order to address the larger questions of the nature of the subject and the relationship of the text to the historically, politically, and ideologically contingent world in which it is situated. The fact that Geertz has found postmodern discussions of "problems of representation and of the relation of power in representation" to be "issues that we can no longer pass off" bodes well for his inquiry. I, for one, am looking forward to the publication of *After the Fact*, knowing that, as always, I can anticipate not only a good read by a sophisticated and witty stylist but also a challenging exploration of "The Way We [or at least one thoughtful, articulate anthropologist] Think Now."

Oregon State University
Corvallis, Oregon

Works Cited

Eagleton, Terry. *Literary Theory: An Introduction*. Minneapolis: U of Minnesota P, 1983.

Geertz, Clifford. *Local Knowledge: Further Essays in Interpretive Anthropology*. New York: Basic Books, 1983.

Geertz, Clifford. *Works and Lives: The Anthropologist as Author*. Stanford, CA: Stanford UP, 1988.

Richard

Rorty

Social Construction and Composition Theory: A Conversation with Richard Rorty

Gary A. Olson

There is no doubt that Richard Rorty is one of the most influential and innovative American philosophers writing today. He is perhaps best known for *Philosophy and the Mirror of Nature*, his critique of traditional epistemology. His newest book, *Contingency, Irony, and Solidarity*, promises to generate debate about the relation of epistemology and politics. Recently, Rorty's work has been of interest to compositionists, particularly those concerned with collaborative learning, social constructionism, and what James Berlin has called "social-epistemic rhetoric." The following interview with Professor Rorty may surprise many compositionists in that it suggests that we have constructed a collective interpretation of Rorty's views that is oddly disjunctive with his own positions.

Perhaps most startling to composition theorists, especially those who think of Rorty as a leading social constructionist, is that Rorty does not recognize the term *social constructionism* as referring to any intellectual movement that he is aware of. Nor does he see *social constructionism* as sharing the same fundamental assumptions as *new pragmatism*, as Kenneth Bruffee and others have suggested. Rorty seems sympathetic to social constructionism in a general way, but, as he says, "that's about as far as it goes."

Rorty also responds to Bruffee's concept of writing as "social talk re-externalized." Rorty comments that while Bruffee's theory "seems true enough," the theory is too general to be applied profitably to the composition classroom. In fact, Rorty is "suspicious" of theoretical justifications for practice like Bruffee's rationale for collaborative learning and peer tutoring.

Rorty seems singularly unconcerned about the cultural/ideological positions that have been proffered as correctives to Bruffee's theory and that, by extension, are critiques of Rorty's own pragmatist positions. He sees no danger of peer groups' promoting Orwellian "groupthink"; he side-steps Greg Myers' Marxist critique; and he doesn't seem to think of *gender* as an important factor in the socio-dynamics of a discourse community's "conversation."

Also surprising are Rorty's opinions about the objectives of freshman English. He calls the writing-across-the-curriculum model, in which students are taught how to join in the conversations of their particular disciplinary discourse communities, "a terrible idea." In fact, for Rorty the goal of freshman English is to teach students to "write complete sentences" and "get the commas in the right place." Clearly, freshman English, in Rorty's view, is a necessary evil, not a means of empowering students to engage in real meaning making.

Thus, it seems fitting that Rorty shares E.D. Hirsch's desire for renewing cultural literacy, arguing that for a society to work citizens must have a sense of "loyalty" to the nation and a sense of cultural "tradition." Consequently, he sees Hirsch's cultural literacy as a cohesive force promoting loyalty, even patriotism. In fact, Rorty's own personal patriotism emerges in his response to leftist political criticism of his views. He calls the United States "a spectacular success story of the growth of democratic freedom" and "still the best thing on offer."

Rorty sees no theoretical inconsistency in his defending the call for increased cultural literacy. Although Rorty has argued repeatedly that knowledge is "socially justified," he supports the cultural literacy movement's efforts to codify knowledge into an accepted canon of texts and facts. He seems oblivious to the argument that if certain "knowledge" is slipping away from mass consciousness and therefore must be recalled and installed formally in an official canon, then such knowledge is, according to his own definition, no longer socially justified—no longer knowledge. Or is it? Perhaps by "social justification" Rorty really means "institutional justification."

Clearly, this interview suggests that it may be necessary to reassess our understanding of Rorty's positions and their relevance to social constructionism and composition theory. Perhaps this conversation will encourage a closer reading of Rorty's work and a more careful application of his ideas.

Q. The advertisement says, "When E.F. Hutton talks, people listen." *Your* published work seems to have a similar impact on the scholarly community: when you *write*, people *read* it. How would you describe your own rhetorical style? Do you think of yourself as a writer?

A. I enjoy writing, but I have no idea of what the effect of the style on the audience is. I think, like most people in this line of work, I write to please myself.

Q. Are you conscious of yourself as a writer when you write?

A. Well, I'm conscious of striving after turns of phrase and that kind of thing. I spend a lot of time polishing things up.

Q. In "Philosophy as a Kind of Writing," you say that for philosophy "writing is an unfortunate necessity," and you comment that "philosophical writing, for Heidegger as for the Kantians, is really aimed at putting an end to writing." You then point out that for Derrida "writing always leads to more writing, and more, and still more." What do you believe is the role of writing, the role of rhetoric?

A. Well, insofar as one defines rhetoric by contrast with logic, I suppose that the ideal of the logician is to make both metaphor and idiosyncratic stylistic devices unnecessary. And the kind of attack on traditional positivistic philosophy of science that we've had in the last thirty years or so adds up to the claim that not even in science is there this disjunction between logic and method on the one hand and rhetoric on the other.

Q. In "The Contingency of Language" you argue that "only sentences can be true, and that human beings make truths by making languages in which to phrase sentences." In this essay, as in most of your work, you have a great deal to say about language, but you don't often focus specifically on *written language*. Drawing on the work of Michael Oakeshott and Clifford Geertz, Kenneth Bruffee argues that writing is a "technologically displaced form of conversation." Bruffee argues, "If thought is internalized public and social talk, then writing of all kinds is internalized social talk made public and social again. If thought is internalized conversation, then writing is internalized conversation re-externalized." Does this concept of writing correspond with your own?

A. What Bruffee says seems true enough, but I'm not sure what it shows. It comes down to saying that all thought, discourse, and, *a priori*, all writing take place in some social context, and that's certainly true; but I'm not sure what Bruffee would say follows from this.

Q. I believe he's trying to establish a theoretical rationale for writing and for the teaching of writing, and so he puts it in the context of mirroring the kind of knowledge-making process that *you* suggest is in play in the larger arena.

A. It doesn't seem to me that one can draw many conclusions about how to write from something that general. There are all kinds of utterly unconversational modes of exposition which are handy for some particular pedagogic or other purpose.

Q. Do you consider yourself a social constructionist?

A. What's a social constructionist?

Q. Bruffee attempts to define social constructionism this way: "Social construction understands reality, knowledge, thought, facts, texts, selves, and so on as community-generated and community-maintained linguistic entities—or, more broadly speaking, symbolic entities—that define or 'constitute' the communities that generate them." And he continues, "Social construction understands knowledge and the authority of knowledge as community-generated, community-maintaining, symbolic artifacts." Is that a position that you're sympathetic with?

A. Yes, that seems true enough.

Q. Is *social constructionism* really just another name for *new pragmatism*?

A. I think that the only things they have in common are opposition to an idea of knowledge as accurate picturing of things as they are in themselves, and that this conception of knowledge is the subject of attack by a dozen schools.

Q. You don't, then, specifically consider yourself a social constructionist?

A. Well, when I read people like Peter Berger, I feel sympathetic, but that's about as far as it goes.

Q. Several scholars have suggested that you have generalized for all knowledge what Kuhn suggested for scientific knowledge—that it is a social construct. Do you see your work as an extension of Kuhn's?

A. Yes, I guess so. I'm not sure that Kuhn would like the idea, though. That is, he and I have been trying to define our differences over the years, and I keep trying to drive him in the direction of blurring the distinctions between science and non-science. I'm not sure that he's quite as ready to do that as I am.

Q. Your ideas on the social nature of language, knowledge, and discourse communities have influenced rhetoric and composition studies significantly. Bruffee draws on your work to establish a theoretical rationale for collaborative learning. He argues that placing students in peer groups in writing classrooms is an effective way of teaching writing because it mirrors the process by which, as you posit, knowledge is created and maintained—the "social justification of belief." Others disagree, claiming that even if knowledge is created and maintained as you suggest, it's a big leap to organizing classrooms into several mini-discourse communities. What are your thoughts on this subject?

A. I guess if the way Bruffee does it works, fine. I don't see why it shouldn't work, but there's no way to find out except trying. In general, I guess I'm suspicious of theoretical justifications for practice. I would want to look at how well the practice comes off first and worry about the rationale later.

Q. So you would suggest that *praxis* precedes theory?

A. Well, obviously they play back and forth, but in as concrete a case as this it seems to me that you can just see whether a pedagogic experiment succeeds; if it doesn't, that may leave the theory intact or it may not, but the thing to do is find out whether it actually works.

Q. Some scholars recoil from the idea of peer groups in the classroom because they feel they promote Orwellian "groupthink"—that they suppress differences and conflicts and promote conformity. How would you respond to this critique?

A. I should think that it's overstated to suggest that they lead to groupthink. I should think, the worst they could lead to is committee prose. It's a familiar phenomenon that when you have to have all members of a committee agreeing on the text of a report, you get something bland. That would seem more of a danger than any enforced conformity.

Q. The next question is somewhat related. Marilyn Cooper suggests that your discussion on the discourse of hermeneutics (in *Philosophy and the Mirror of Nature*) is "idealistic," and that your consideration of intellectual communities only in terms of "intellectual beliefs and discourse conventions" conceals many *cultural* factors that affect ability to participate in community discourse—such as political, moral, economic, class, and, I might add, gender factors. As Cooper points out, "Even if the epistemological assumption of external standards of knowledge is dispensed with, not everyone has equal access to the discourse." What are your thoughts about these socio-dynamics of equal access?

A. It seems perfectly true that there are all kinds of difficulties getting in on any given conversation, but I don't see what it has to do with idealism. That is, I take it that the idea of democratic politics and equalization of opportunities is just to fix it so that these hindrances to access are minimized, but what notions you have about the nature of inquiry don't seem to be much affected by whether you live in a society which imposes hindrances or doesn't impose hindrances.

Q. Greg Myers would go a step further. He argues that these cultural factors—social class and race, especially—are the very heuristics by which people come to know. As Myers suggests, "Ethnocentrism and economic interests... are the whole systems of ideas that people take for granted and use to make sense of the world." Again, how do these cultural factors fit into your hermeneutical framework? You seem to suggest that perhaps they may not have as much of an impact as some of these people believe.

A. I don't think one should minimize the impact, and I think Myers has a point: that a large part of what one does in setting up a system of thought or a set of principles is a matter of defining one's own group over against other groups—the people on the wrong side of the argument over against the good people on your side. But, again, I don't see what conclusion one can draw from this except that we all, Marxists and everybody else, divide the world up into the good and the bad.

Q. Most of the critiques of collaborative learning have been from this kind of cultural, social framework; gender is another factor, it would seem to me, that limits interaction in any given discourse community. And, of course, feminist scholars suggest that women's positions in large discourse communities are problematic because social expectations of women must necessarily modify their rhetorical stances in a community. In other words, if they fulfill expectations of "female" discourse, then their discourse is devalued; however, if they seek to appropriate "male" discourse—male ways of speaking, talking, and thinking—they're invalidating their own experience as women and exposing themselves, perhaps, to ridicule. Can your account of normal and abnormal discourse shed light on the problem women have in creating a credible *ethos*? Or do you think that this issue, too, perhaps is not as important as it appears?

A. No, I think it's important all right, but I think that the history of oppressed groups ceasing to be oppressed so much has been a mixture of the oppressed showing that they can speak the language of the oppressors just as well as the oppressors can and, on the other hand, also being able to say something that the oppressors have never thought of before. I think all movements of liberation have fought on both fronts simultaneously, so it doesn't strike me as a great big dilemma. I should think some feminists are good at simply doing the kinds of things that men have traditionally done as good or better, and other feminists are good at doing things that no man or woman has thought of doing before; the later tend to be identified as something distinctively feminine, at least at first, and then with luck they just become absorbed in the general experience of the culture.

Q. Some scholars have used your notions of discourse communities to argue that the job of freshman English is to teach students the discourses of the academic disciplines rather than the traditional "essay" which students are traditionally taught in first-year English. Other scholars, such as James Kinneavy, remind us that students should also learn to talk with people outside of their discipline-specific communities. Would you agree that your hermeneutical position suggests the former, or do you think this kind of discipline-based instruction should be the concern of freshman English?

A. Tell me a little more about what the proposal for discipline-based instruction looks like.

Q. Rather than teach the traditional academic essay that for decades and decades has been the model that students have imitated in freshman classes, some compositionists now are saying, "That's an artificial form; no one in the real world really writes those things to begin with. What we ought to be teaching students is how to enter the particular discourse communities of their fields. So, let's forget this traditional, artificial essay; let's teach them the normal discourse, if you will, of whatever field the student is going into."

A. The suggestion that they learn the normal discourse in the field suggests that, as freshman, they try to pick up the jargon of a particular discipline.

Q. And the rhetorical forms, too.

A. It strikes me as a terrible idea. I think the idea of freshman English, mostly, is just to get them to write complete sentences, get the commas in the right place, and stuff like that—the stuff that we would like to think the high schools do and, in fact, they don't. But as long as there's a need for freshman English, it's going to be primarily just a matter of the least common denominator of all the jargon. Besides, I don't see how freshman English teachers are supposed to know enough about the special disciplinary jargon.

Q. Well, there is a movement across the country in several universities to try to train teachers to move around in the various disciplines and help students apply rhetoric to any field; it's called writing across the curriculum.

A. I think that America has made itself a bit ridiculous in the international academic world by developing distinctive disciplinary jargon. It's the last thing we want to inculcate in the freshmen.

Q. Do you share E.D. Hirsch's desire for increased "cultural literacy," a sharing of a common vocabulary and a common body of knowledge?

A. Yes, I think he's perfectly right about that. The effect of the present system is to keep education for kids from relatively well-educated, middle-class families who pick up the common knowledge of society as a whole. And kids who come from other kinds of families don't have a chance to pick it up in school.

Q. But wouldn't it seem that the passing away of the kind of knowledge that Hirsch hopes to recall suggests that that knowledge is no longer "socially justified"? For example, Richard Ohmann suggests that we do, indeed, share a common culture, albeit one so superficial that perhaps we're afraid to acknowledge it, one based on the messages of the mass media, and so on. It seems that if you have to try to "save" a particular kind of knowledge or a particular body of knowledge, then perhaps it's no longer valuable for one reason or another. In other words, perhaps even according to you own system, it's not really even knowledge itself any more.

A. What Ohmann presumably suggests is that you can keep a democratic tradition going without any historical self-consciousness on the part of the citizens of the democracy about how their society arose and how it differentiated itself from alternative social forms. This seems to me very dubious. I should think what Hirsch has going for him is that in order to have a sense of citizenship in a country, one has to have enough historical perspective to see that this arose out of certain conditions for certain reasons and has been maintained for certain reasons against other alternatives. And that kind of historical self-consciousness I don't think anybody's going to get out of the mass media.

Q. Clifford Geertz has argued that a social conception of knowledge makes conventional education almost impossible—that, as he says, the "enormous multiplicity of modern consciousness renders the image of a general orientation . . . shaping the direction of culture . . . a chimera." You, however, have suggested in "Hermeneutics, General Studies and Teaching" that education should offer students "a sense of tradition, of community, and of human solidarity." How can tradition, community, and solidarity be realized in education, and why should education seek these particular ends?

A. I think that you have to have some sort of loyalty to the, well, it really comes down to the nation, in order to care enough to vote, to care about who's elected, to care about what policies are adopted, to think of yourself as a citizen. Without that sense of the tradition to which you in your political role belong, I don't see how anybody is going to take social criticism or suggestions for reforms seriously. The fact that our culture is becoming increasingly varied and cosmopolitan doesn't strike me as a great big change. It's always been pretty varied and cosmopolitan. The changes Geertz speaks about seem to me to have been going on fairly gradually for a couple of centuries, and I don't see that they create any special problems.

Q. But would you suggest from this that in the educational setting students first ought to be taught what you call normal discourse? I know you, at certain times, have suggested that students need also to understand how to go about abnormal discourse, but I suppose you're saying that first it's important that they learn this normal discourse, this sense of community, this sense of solidarity and tradition.

A. Yes, I think of abnormal discourse as a gift of God rather than anything anybody gets educated for or into. It seems to me that the normal division between secondary and tertiary education is and should be the line between getting in on the normal discourse of the tradition in the nation and the community to which you belong, and higher education is a matter of being told about all the alternatives to that tradition, to that discourse. But that isn't necessarily going to move you into one of these alternatives; it's just going to make it possible, if you have an imagination, for that imagination to work.

Q. So you don't really see the role of education as trying to teach people to engage in abnormal discourse?

A. That isn't the way I'd put it. I think higher education should aim at fixing it so the students can see that the normal discourse in which they have been trained up to adolescence (or up to age eighteen, or something like that) is itself a historical contingency surrounded by other historical contingencies. But having done that, whether they remain happily imbedded in the normal discourse of their society or not is something teachers can't predict or control.

Q. Besides other avowed pragmatists, what theorists do you feel particularly sympathetic to nowadays; what theorists are particularly worth reading?

A. I think I just look for people who seem to be strikingly original—Harold Bloom in literary criticism, for example. There are people whose individual voice is so distinctive that one feels immediately attracted, and I guess I just look for such individual voices rather than for building up theoretical agreement with them.

Q. Would you include Derrida?

A. Yes, I suspect that Derrida and I have wildly different interests. And I'm not sure that when I read him I read him the way he wants to be read; but he is, God knows, about as distinctive a voice as we have writing nowadays. And one has the feeling that people like Bloom and Derrida are the ones in our century who are going to be remembered.

Q. And, no doubt, yourself.

A. No, I think of myself as just a syncretist rather than somebody saying something original.

Q. Quite clearly, you and your work have been cited extensively by a wide range of scholars from numerous disciplines. While such frequent citation is undoubtedly flattering, it also increases the opportunity for misunderstanding or misrepresenting your views. Are you aware of any specific misunderstanding that you would like to take issue with at this time, that you would like to set straight? Any critiques of your work that have been off base that you might want to mention now?

A. Well, I tend to get two kinds of criticism: one from my fellow philosophers suggesting that I want to put an end to philosophy, and one from the political left saying that I'm, in effect, defending the current status quo. I tried to guard against the first objection by saying that philosophy just wasn't the kind of thing that you could ever end, but that it has quite often changed the key in which it was written and the topics to which it attended, and that you could think that a good deal of contemporary philosophy was becoming boring and repetitious without wanting to end philosophy as a subject. The leftist political criticism, I think, just reflects a genuine difference about what features of contemporary America should be attended to. I think of America as still a spectacular success story of the growth of democratic freedom, whereas my opponents on the left think of it as a racist, sexist, imperialist society. Both descriptions, I think, have a good deal going for them, but one's politics depends on which description takes precedence. So, having admitted that it's a racist, sexist, imperialist society, it seems to me it's still the best thing on offer, whereas my opponents tend to think that having said that you can sort of set it aside.

Response to the *JAC* Interview with Richard Rorty

KENNETH A. BRUFFEE

Reading the *JAC* interview with Richard Rorty makes me realize once again why I adopted him as one of my heroes ten years ago. By "him" (to make a foundational distinction) I don't mean of course the whole warty man, with whom I am barely acquainted. I mean the language of a lot of what he has written and said. Rorty seems humane and sensible. He's *menschlich*. His attitude toward America—that it is, with all its flaws, "the best thing on offer"—is one I am sympathetic to. Most of all, his language, more than that of anyone else I know, has given me ways of saying things that I have been unsuccessful trying to say myself.

Reading the *JAC* interview also makes me feel grateful to the editors for providing an occasion on which Rorty was compelled to think for forty-five seconds or so about something I had written—far more attention from that direction than I have any right to hope or expect.

But reading the *JAC* interview also makes me feel that the interviewers did me, their readers, and perhaps Rorty, too, something of a disservice in the way they framed their questions and summarized the interview.

Rorty is not a "theorist." Neither am I. Social construction is not a theory. It is a way of talking, a language, a vernacular. Least of all is social construction a "theoretical rationale for collaborative learning." It is a way of describing collaborative learning. The theory-practice dichotomy is one of the notions endemic to foundational thought that make it so constraining and so thoroughly obsolete.

Furthermore, Rorty is right, in my opinion, that talking about something and doing it "play back and forth," but that the first thing to do is to "find out whether it actually works." That description, in any case, more or less sums up my own almost twenty-year experience (good Lord!) with collaborative learning. For a decade I fiddled with it and with solutions to its practical problems contributed by the expertise I found in social group work, before I lost my epistemological virginity over it. That happened because I became increasingly and uncomfortably aware that the language of cognition could not describe in any coherent way what was going on. The language used by Rorty, Kuhn, Geertz, and that bunch could. And that was that.

In short, with all due respect to those involved, I would suggest that the foundational terms in which the *JAC* interviewers addressed Rorty, if they're representative, reveal, dismayingly, more about the stage that the conversation in composition studies is currently at than his replies reveal about either him or me.

Brooklyn College—CUNY
New York, New York

On Personally Constructing "Social Construction": A Response to Richard Rorty

JOHN SCHILB

Gary Olson's interview with Richard Rorty suggests the problems in our field's new obsession with "social construction." When Kenneth Bruffee first promoted the term, he usefully foregrounded the contextual nature of discourse. Furthermore, by invoking Rorty and other theorists, he helped composition sense its relation to other rhetorical inquiry. Yet, the boom now enjoyed by "social constructionism" threatens to obscure how notions of "the social" have historically differed. As Cy Knoblauch observed in volume eight of *JAC*, "When roving, and morally warring, bands of cognitive psychologists, text linguists, philosophers of composition, historians of rhetoric, Marxist critics, post-structuralists, and reader-response theorists all wax equally enthusiastic about 'the social construction of reality,' there is a good chance that the expression has long since lost its capacity to name anything important or even very interesting." We should find "important" and "interesting," though, the ideological differences revealed when theorists of "the social" elaborate what the word personally means to them. Rorty's *JAC* remarks offer a good test case.

The interview contains two major surprises. First, Rorty proves unfamiliar with Bruffee's "social constructionism" and, in fact, declares his notion of writing across the curriculum "a terrible idea." Bruffee can thus be accused of misleading us when he intimates Rorty and he think alike. In fact, Bruffee has often propounded a dubious Whig version of history by suggesting that all noteworthy intellectual trends converge in his doctrine. Yet, we should never have assumed that he and his favorite theorists precisely correspond. As Edward Said points out in *The World, The Text, and The Critic*, "Theory often gets modified as it 'travels' through the academy." Rorty himself appropriates Dewey by underscoring his antifoundationalism while downplaying his faith in science and his socialist politics. Our particular field has largely developed by selectively raiding others. Rather than condemn theoretical infidelity, however, we should pinpoint how composition scholars "rewrite" their precursors as well as reproduce them.

Just as Bruffee would hardly welcome Rorty's disdain for his program, so too would he share our dismay over Rorty's second astonishing pronouncement: "The idea of freshman English, mostly, is just to get them to write complete sentences, get the commas in the right place, and stuff like that." At one level, the statement merely confirms how we ourselves must trumpet our dignity. When even theorists who influence us trivialize our mission, we know we are still on our own. Yet, Rorty's declaration is symptomatic as well of problems specific to his way of thinking. Above all, he refuses to consider how he remains entrenched in the intellectual habits he scorns. In short, he practices a *de facto* foundationalism, even as he decries the official brand.

By divorcing instruction in "basic skills" from opportunities for critical thinking, Rorty affirms the mechanistic psychology that has plagued freshman English from the start. When he endorses E.D. Hirsch's "cultural literacy," he supports merely the latest version of the idea that human minds develop by ingesting chunks of data. In spinning out its implications, Rorty suggests that Hirsch advocates "historical self-consciousness" while Richard Ohmann lacks it. However, as his list and dictionary indicate, Hirsch calls not for historical explanation but immersion in terminology. Meanwhile, anyone remotely familiar with Ohmann knows he has long pressed English studies to adopt historical awareness. And as Rorty himself simplistically calls for American students to learn "the tradition," he ignores how Ohmann and other historians have identified conflicting ones.

Indeed, when Rorty comments on matters of history and politics, he hardly does so as a result of extensive, probing research. He merely capitalizes on the authority he has gained as a critic of philosophy. Although he has questioned that field's image as the ultimate "tribunal of reason," he still borrows its prestige. Furthermore, he keeps epistemology at the center of his thinking, even if only to attack it. This focus leads him to commit a fallacy that Bruffee also displays: the belief that a particular stance on epistemology dictates certain political views and judgments. Thus, both men have suggested that antifoundationalism should make one a liberal and compel one to see that America is "still the best thing on offer."

Both nurture these sentiments partly by neglecting configurations of power based on gender, race, and class. As I and others have increasingly pointed out, Bruffee's constant references to "communities" and "conversation" obscure processes of domination and struggle. His bibliographic essay on "social construction" in the 1986 *College English* significantly omits feminists (out of forty entries in this discussion of what Bruffee calls "the conversation of mankind," only three are by women), Marxists, Afro-American theorists, Third World theorists, and other analysts of power like Michel Foucault and Pierre Bourdieu. In Rorty's case, note how he trivializes the concerns of such thinkers when Gary Olson determinedly brings them up.

The language Rorty uses at these moments betrays his lingering affinity with his native field. In the name of antifoundationalism, he deflates other people's statements with a vocabulary he considers somehow more basic.

When he observes "that the idea of democratic politics and equalization of opportunities is just to fix it so that these hindrances to access are minimized," and when he concludes "that we all, Marxists and everybody else, divide the world up into the good and the bad," he rejects nuanced, rigorous, political inquiry in favor of behaviorist platitudes. Note his use of expressions like "it comes down to saying," "you can just see," "just to get them," "it's going to be primarily just a matter of," "it really comes down to," "it's just going to make it possible," "I just look for," and "just a syncretist." Such dismissal of richer vocabularies discourages exploration of how discourses can vary. Similarly, when Bruffee uses the word "community" or some form of it eighty-two times in his 1982 *Liberal Education* article and eighty-three in his 1984 *College English* one, he does not exactly cultivate heteroglossia.

Rorty sustains, as well, epistemology's penchant for tidy dichotomies. His writings often reveal a dualistic cast of mind, most prominently in their absolute distinction between "solidarity" and "objectivity," "we pragmatists" and other theorists. The contrast chiefly looming in the interview is that between "normal discourse," which high school students are to be taught, and "abnormal discourse," which is "a gift of God." Yet, as I have suggested, Rorty's sense of American history's "normal discourse" neglects the interplay of hegemonic and resistant traditions. If he wants Kuhn to blur "distinctions between science and non-science," he himself needs to ponder Kuhn's belated insight that paradigm changes can be frequent and numerous within scientific fields. In other words, we must avoid distinguishing between "normal" and "abnormal" for our own theoretical or administrative convenience. When Bruffee declares in his 1984 *College English* article that composition should teach "the normal discourse of most academic, professional, and business communities" (643), he raises the prospect of standardization by sheer fiat.

Bruffee and other "social constructionists" might also be surprised to discover strains of individualism in the Rorty interview: his statement that "I write to please myself," his admiration of "people who seem to be strikingly original." Yet Rorty has long cultivated the image of himself as a free-floating, cosmopolitan intellectual. Despite the word "solidarity" in the title of his new book, its cover is a photograph of a lone figure: Richard Rorty. And when he does invoke "solidarity," he refers to contingent theoretical alignments, not the visceral class bonding that Marxists envision. Remember, too, that when Bruffee discusses "communities," he actually summons up an academy deeply fragmented into various fields. Does the project of "social construction," then, ultimately depend on social *de*construction? To answer this question, we must keep analyzing not only the shifting dialectic of individual and society, but also the institutional conditions through which theories of it "travel."

University of Maryland
College Park, Maryland

Gayatri

Chakravorty

Spivak

Rhetoric and Cultural Explanation: A Discussion with Gayatri Chakravorty Spivak

PHILLIP SIPIORA AND JANET ATWILL

Although Gayatri Chakravorty Spivak is somewhat unfamiliar with the field of rhetoric and composition, the common concerns addressed in the following interview underscore the extent to which the boundaries separating rhetoric and composition, literary theory, and cultural criticism are shifting—and are, to some extent, illusory. Spivak's Preface to and translation of Derrida's *Of Grammatology* (1976) played a key role in introducing continental postmodern thought to the American academy. Since then, in numerous addresses, articles, and books, Spivak has been a vital spokesperson for a practice of cultural criticism rigorously informed by postmodern theory.

Spivak's concern with the shaping forces of race, class, and gender persistently refocuses critical attention onto the rhetorical—the specific circumstances of the enunciation of cultural explanations and the construction of "addressers" and "addressees." This concern with the rhetorical contexts of cultural explanations—from those generated on Capitol Hill to those produced in the university classroom—cuts across the boundary that would separate rhetoric and composition from what Spivak calls the analysis of cultural politics. In this interview, Spivak demonstrates an acute awareness of issues vital to rhetoric and composition: the problem of severing theory from practice, the strategic role of the classroom in bringing theory to crisis, and the part played by social institutions—the university in particular—in the production of cultural explanations—explanations which Spivak maintains are generated to manage crises.

Indeed, perhaps one of the most interesting suggestions Spivak makes in the following interview is her location of rhetoric, as a *techne* or art, at that very point of crisis. In her initial definition of rhetoric, Spivak at once sharply challenges the restriction of rhetoric to tropology and strongly identifies rhetoric with deconstructive theory. Recalling de Man's description of rhetoric in *Resistance to Theory*, she defines rhetoric as "the name for the residue of indeterminacy which escapes the system." Rhetoric is thus situated at a tactical point of indeterminacy, where it both looks backward to its resistance to rendering what Derrida might call exhaustive accounts and looks forward to the exploitation of indeterminacy in discursive production. The significance of rhetoric's location at that point of crisis is explicated in Spivak's discussion of rhetoric's role in the duel between theory and practice.

Spivak agrees that rhetoric refigured as a *techne*, or art, deconstructs the binary of theory and practice—not, however, by creating for itself a new place of privilege. Spivak argues that "practice persistently brings the notion of theory into crisis," and theory "just as persistently... brings the vanguardism of practice into crisis as well." If rhetoric sees itself not as creating a balance between theory and practice, but rather as "inhabiting a kind of productive 'unease,'" then rhetoric may be, as Spivak notes, a powerful ally in exposing practices that attempt to demarcate boundaries or hierarchies between, for example, creative writing and literary theory—between the "practice" of pure art and the practice of interpretation. Rhetoric thus inhabits a space of tactical indeterminacy rather than a place of strategic balance. Spivak describes this space as a point of both "persistent critique" and productive crisis—rhetoric and composition as an art of critique and invention.

Q. The term *rhetoric* has a long history of multiple definitions. Aristotle defined it as the "art of persuasion," Isocrates described it as "effective communication," and Nietzsche, Derrida, de Man and others have written about rhetoric as a tropological activity. How do *you* conceptualize rhetoric, both as an activity and as a discipline?

A. I see rhetoric as I see most other important master words in the tradition of poststructuralist nominalism. Foucault says in *The History of Sexuality* that in order to think power one must become a nominalist; power is a name that one *lends* to a complex network of relationships. In Paul de Man's *Resistance to Theory*, rhetoric is the name for the residue of indeterminacy which escapes the system. In this reading, the idea that rhetoric is tropology is not adequate to the notion that it is the name of what escapes even an exhaustive system of tropological analysis. In Derrida it would be very hard to find a definition of rhetoric that calls it a tropological activity. I think that in Derrida there is no concerted, or organized, use of the word *rhetoric* as there is in de Man. Derrida does not consistently use any master word that enables one to put together a body of definitions as something to be applied. I think the word *rhetoric* serves in the same way or does not serve in the same way in Derrida's writing. I think Derrida uses the word *rhetoric* when he's actually dealing with Greek material, but not otherwise. As for the discipline, I cannot say very much because I don't know much about its performance. I've been involved in the teaching of comparative literature, English, and, of late, cultural studies. I can't really comment on what goes on *in* the discipline of rhetoric.

Q. You are probably best known as a cultural critic. Would you give us a working definition of what you mean by cultural criticism?
A. Cultural criticism, which I am going to rephrase a little and call a "study of cultural politics," involves itself, as I understand it, with the way in which cultural explanations are generated. It seems to me that *culture* is a word which is now being used to give a sense of why large groups of people behave in certain ways. In other words, culture is being used as a description of collective agency, and these descriptions are almost always generated in order to manage various kinds of crises. So, a study of cultural politics is a study of the politics of the production of cultural explanations that are used in the academy, outside the academy, in global politics, in metropolitan politics, in national politics of various kinds, migrant politics of various kinds, articulations of majority and minority, domination/exploitation, a very wide field of managing various kinds of crises that are coming up in order to give people who act within these crises a certain way of describing what the position is. This is what we are trying to look at in the new version of "cultural studies."
Q. Your work seems to raise questions about the relationship between cultural criticism and historicism, both "old" and "new." What are some distinctions that might be drawn between cultural criticism and historicism? This is an important question in rhetoric and composition studies because of recent attention to the problematics of historiography and the role of cultural studies in the teaching of writing.
A. Historicism is something that is studied within the project of cultural studies because the production of historical narrative is an activity within the production of cultural explanations; and, in fact, explaining cultural phenomena in terms of produced historical narrative falls within the scope of the study of cultural politics of which I'm speaking. And I think it would be correct to say that all of my efforts in the study of cultural politics have, in fact, been within what I have just described.
Q. You speak of "crisis management." Is there a particular rhetoric involved in crisis management, or do rhetorical formulations always depend upon the contingencies of each particular crisis?
A. It depends upon various kinds of crisis. I don't think there is a specific kind of discourse used to manage all crises.
Q. You have been critical of the "artificial" distinction between theory and practice; and in "Explanation and Culture: Marginalia" you discuss the theory/practice binary, arguing in an endnote that Aristotle's concept of *techne* was, as you put it, a "dynamic and undecidable middle term" between theory and practice. Do you see Aristotle's concept of *techne* as a deconstruction of the theory/practice binary? If so, how does this deconstruction bear upon your vision of cultural studies?
A. I think I have really looked at some of these questions already. It's interesting that you point at the connection between rhetoric as an art, or

a *techne*—that "middle" term, which can deconstruct the binary of theory and practice. The deconstruction of something is, of course, not a deconstruction of the binary. What I think I was trying to suggest in that essay, which I don't remember very well because it was written about eleven years ago, was that practice persistently brings the notion of theory into crisis. And theory—just as persistently, and depending upon the situation—asymmetrically brings the vanguardism of practice into crisis as well, so that neither one of the two really can take "first" place. Now if the middle term is taken as creating a balance rather than a tension, then I think I would have a problem. I'm not interested in an artificial balance as much as I'm not interested in a hierarchy, a ranking between the two sides. If the middle term is something that cannot be sure of itself as either theory or practice, but finds itself inhabiting a kind of productive "unease," and every time it settles into either the theory of rhetoric or the practice of rhetoric, something on the other side beckons and says, "Look here you, you know you are dependent upon me and you're ignoring it," then I feel that the discipline of rhetoric can be an extraordinary ally in, let's say, exposing the artificial distinction between literary theory at one end and creative writing at the other end of our divided terrain. The discipline of rhetoric can be an ally, but not if the productive middle term is seen as a balance.

Q. Might considering *techne* as a middle term, however conditionally, in some way temporarily balance the tension between the privileging of either theory or practice?

A. It is quite possible, but then I would be troubled by the balancing because balancing is, in fact, too elegant a solution; it doesn't really do away with privileging but only creates a new privilege. I think that tension is productive, whereas balance is suspect. That's what I was trying to say in the previous answer. If the middle term is treated as a balance, a mediator, then a new system of privilege is created. In fact, this system of privilege is of very long standing when one thinks that the aesthetic is the medium through which practical reason and theoretical reason reach the rational will. This structuring in Kant, for example, of the access to the moral is through that middle term in itself, is in itself a kind of hierarchization. That privileging of the aesthetic sphere, which finds a remote analogy in thinkers like Habermas, does not strike a "balance" between two ends, but rather hierarchizes that "balanced space" into a privileged space. I'm much more interested in the "shuttle" between one end and the other and in the one end bringing the other to productive and real crisis rather than finding a middle space where an "apparent balance" is created. I'm not interested in choosing between balance and tensions. I'm much more interested in persistent critique.

Q. Some compositionists speak out against what they see as a new privileging of theory in composition studies. What problems do you see in this reversal of the theory/practice hierarchy? We seem continually to shift between the privileging of one or the other. Is there some way that we could possibly "mediate"—not reconcile—our differences in order to maintain a more productive dialogue in which we seek to recognize rather than suppress our differences?

A. I don't think that reconciliation is ever going to happen, frankly, because mediations are always interested. There is always a residue of either this or that side in the way in which mediations are performed. I think we should make use of the fact that our institutional system of education emphasizes committee structures, and, therefore, we should open and reopen these questions constantly. It's a great waste of time, I know, but, in fact, we should think of it as a spending of time rather than a wasting of time. It is also true that the composition—I shouldn't use the word *composition* here because it's misleading—but the constitution of our student bodies changes. It is also true that the nature of departments and their emphasis on service, and so on, quite often change with different hiring practices and philosophies of chairs, and various roles of chairs—as, for example, the chair as first among equals rather than a somewhat imperious director. So, it seems to me that much of this should actually be persistently acted out, performed in the governance of the programs in the everyday business of managing the institution. What's really happened is the construction of a theory of theory or a theory of practice, whereas the practice is actually the governance and the teaching—which is also quite informed by theories. To separate these things is already so artificial. Any mediation will always be a theory of mediation and any kind of supposedly practical mediation, that is to say the breaking down of a theory into teaching one way or the other. I don't think these are ever really going to be true solutions. I think if we acknowledge that the place of practice involves committees and governance as well as classroom practice, then we can see that we should take advantage of the way our educational system is structured and use the fact that we are not, for example, a nationalized educational system with directives coming down from ministries of one kind or another. These particular kinds of decisions should not be separated from the way we run our workplace.

Q. Speaking of the governance of institutions, do you see greater diversity in hiring practices or in the way students are treated in programs presumably oriented toward multicultural, multiracial consciousness? Do you see any progress?

A. Yes, I see it in some institutions. I think that progress is being made because if you look at recent job descriptions you will see that in our own area, English, for example, there are lots of jobs opening up in commonwealth literature and literature of the Third World, and so on. But I don't believe that this reflects anything like parity. I think there are, indeed, recruitment programs that concern themselves with minorities and ethnics. I certainly see an influence on the part of radical faculty to emphasize that hiring be more socially just. In spite of all this, however, it's still an uphill battle; it's not at all as entrenched as we would like it to be.

I would also like to say that as these things come into being, part of the proof of the success of these enterprises is to be seen also in the immense centralized opposition that one finds at the same time through all sorts of books and media programs, partly the National Endowment—Allan Bloom has become a figure to be isolated as representing the backlash—and so on. But as the emphasis on the marginal, the ethnic, the minority is gaining ground, the institution is also, in many ways, domesticating these groups so that I'm not sure that this is necessarily the reflection of any kind of resistance to the "structure." So, here again, my idea of a persistent critique of balancing is something that I would want to urge. On the other hand, when I was talking about governance, I was really only talking about the day-to-day business of running a department or program, rather than long-term policy-making. I'm saying that in those sorts of committees the question of how to mediate between rhetoric and composition, between theory and practice, depends upon the kind of student bodies that come from year to year and change from decade to decade. That is the sort of thing that I was talking about when I raised the issue of governance.

Q. Certain scholars in rhetoric and composition promote rhetoric as an epistemological act. This perspective seems dangerously close to what Derrida calls "rhetoricism," which he describes in a recent *JAC* interview as "a way of giving rhetoric all the power, thinking that everything depends on rhetoric." What are the benefits or dangers of positing rhetoric as an epistemological act?

A. I think there are dangers implicit in thinking of anything as an epistemology or thinking that epistemology is a way of thinking without limits. As I said in my answer to the first question, rhetoric is the name of that which is the limit—that which escapes, that which is the residue of efforts at "catching" things with systems. Maybe the power with which the term has been charged betrays an attempt to describe something that stands in for knowing rather than being a description of knowing.

Q. Would you say, then, that defining rhetoric as an epistemological act is an attenuation of rhetoric?

A. A domestication, a circumscription.

Q. In "Subaltern Studies: Deconstructing Historiography," you make an interesting distinction between illegitimate writing, associated with rumor and insurgency, and phonocentric writing, associated with the "authoritative writing of the law" and the metaphysics of presence which has characterized Western humanism. This distinction is particularly intriguing to scholars of rhetoric and composition in that the earliest Western rhetorics, which were sophistic, were viewed by ancient Greek philosophers as both illegitimate and insurgent; however, by the fourth century

B.C., rhetoric was an express servant of Athenian democracy and the humanist project to which it gave birth. Would you comment on the relationship of insurgent discourse to Western humanism and democracy?

A. When I was talking about rumor and how rumor works in the spread of insurgency, I was commenting on the colonial aggression which accompanied the spread of Western humanism. I was commenting on the use of Western humanism as an alibi for the development of markets and the establishment of Western democracy under imperial authority. Rumor could in fact be operative in insurgent efforts against the organized *logos*. But this requires situation-specific study. Just as people like Derrida say that they cannot speak of anything outside of Western metaphysics, I do not feel authorized to establish my critique of the imperialist field as a general theory. The moment I go outside of the imperialist field, in the neocolonial field where I do my teaching, I see the various ways in which we are complicitous with both Western humanism and so-called Western democracy. The analysis belongs to an extremely specific situation of the use of Western humanism and the establishment of Western democracy as alibis and explanations for the development and preparation of the field of operation for industrial capitalism. But outside of it, the focus changes, and the critique gets deconstructed into rumor as *techne*, the shifting *bolus* of truth.

Q. On the issue of rumor, many individuals have divided "opinion" into at least two categories: instinctive feelings, and "examined" opinion. Can a distinction be made between "informed" and "uninformed" opinion, between *doxa* and *endoxa*?

A. I was not talking about doxa, no. I was speaking, in fact, of rumor in various situations within specific imperialist contexts. From where I work, I am not a philosopher, and I'm not a historian. On the other hand, I do not think that literary criticism is a sort of "playground" of indeterminacy. Therefore, given this kind of tactical interdisciplinarity, I don't think about it in this way because when I look back on the way I read these things, I see that I'm an amateur in these three disciplines (philosophy, history, literary criticism). In the case of literary criticism, I have kind of "amateurized" myself in shifting between the empirical and the historical/theoretical and the morphological/theoretical; these lines are always moving. So, it is quite possible to see the lineaments of what might gel into what we are calling the technical use of the word *rumor* in my commentary on the operation of rumor in a very specific case. So, in fact, having said "no," I am now perhaps saying "yes" and "no"—as usual.

Q. Until recently, rhetorical theory has depended heavily on models of communication that demarcate a speaker/writer, an audience/receiver, and a supposedly autonomous message. This model has been critiqued on many fronts, and we are now faced with the task of refiguring the subject in rhetorical theory. You address the problem of the subject in "Subaltern Studies," where you describe the "crucially strategic" project of the Subaltern Studies group as that of "subject restoration," as the "strategic use of positivist essentialism in a scrupulously visible political interest." Would you elaborate on your formulation of the subject?

A. My notion of the subject, subject restoration, in that passage in "Subaltern Studies" as a strategic positivism has been appropriated especially by feminists in the United States in a way which I have found a little alarming. I did an interview with Ellen Rooney in *Differences* where I talked this out at great length. I see here a use of essentialism and then giving it an alibi with poststructuralist talk. The way I see it now is in another formula, a persistent critique of what one cannot "not" want. And what one cannot "not" want in a political interest. I now put the emphasis on the pursuit of collective agency, as secured, say, by the privative and normative discourses of constitutions (or, on a less grandiose scale, the disciplines) on the one hand, and the transformation of consciousness on the other. Notions of subject formation must bring the idea of collective agency into crisis.

Q. Judith Butler's recent book, *Gender Trouble: Feminism and the Subversion of Identity*, offers a thorough critique of both biological and cultural theories of gender as a dramatic, performative set of activities. In commenting on Butler's text, you say, "This powerful and constructive political autocritique of gender theory performs, on its way, a critique of the ethical philosophy of gender in general." How does Butler's formulation of gender as drama bear upon the notion of "women's writing" and "women's teaching"?

A. Women's writing and women's teaching, based on gender and drama, bring into play notions like performance, both in the sense of acting out and bringing about through saying, representation, and self-representation, both in the sense of standing in for and seeing oneself as metonomy in the sense of the point of agreement standing in for provisional "collective consciousness," persistently to be dissolved as a presupposition. If this seems a little cryptic, I think the best way to decrypt it is, once again, in the technology of the classroom.

Q. Many individuals who have studied and taught in universities outside of the United States, like yourself, have observed that the life of the intellectual is distinctly different in Europe than it is here. In speaking of teaching, for example, Paul de Man says, "In Europe one is of course much closer to ideological and political questions, while, on the contrary, in the States, one is much closer to professional questions." Derrida observes, "In the United States, culture or intellectual life is confined to the university more or less. In France, this is not the case, especially in Paris. Here (in the United States), the people I know, the people to whom I speak, are on the faculties. In France, it's almost the contrary: I've very few relations with colleagues or with the professors in the university." What intellectual and academic differences between America and Europe do *you* see? What rhetorical modifications do you make in addressing academic audiences versus groups comprised of laypersons, both in the United States and overseas?

A. I'm quite struck by the fact that neither of the sentences quoted from de Man and Derrida considers that perhaps some of what they are saying is dependent upon *who they are*. I can imagine that there are people in the United States who, in fact, are involved with ideological and political questions and teach at universities, although by and large perhaps it's true that Europe is much more a place broken up into small nation states with histories that began before the eighteenth century. So, to an extent, the history of the university in those places and its relationship to the state is rather different from the history of the university system in the United States, which was founded with a certain historical consciousness that was not the case in Europe. So it seems to me that it is not an "also" question. France, Belgium, West Germany, Italy, to an extent Spain, and Britain—these places are themselves rather diversified, and Derrida is at least careful enough to say that he is speaking of Paris. I feel that in the case of Derrida, it may be quite true that he is not in touch with the people and the faculties, but there are extremely universitarian people in France who work very much within the faculties. It's *the way* in which de Man relates to the university system in the United States and the way in which Derrida relates to the university system in France that comes through in those statements.

As for me, I am not a European, so when I go to European universities I am either treated as an American or as an Asian, depending upon what kind of audience is relating to me. So I really have very little to say about academic differences. I'm not a participant in European academic life. Certainly, I've taught in France some, but not as a participant in the way in which American/European intellectuals like de Man or Derrida—both powerful main figures—would teach. So, when I talk about academic situations in Europe, I am clearly talking as an observer rather than a participant. I feel quite strongly that there is a real tradition of academic radicalism in Britain, which has been both "good" and "bad" in the current context. I think in Britain there is a tendency towards universalizing British experience. I'm not saying everybody does this; obviously there are very strong cultural critics in Britain who know that this is a mistake, but radical critics in Britain quite often tend to think of their radicalism as representing more than it actually does. I think that the British situation is much more provincial in many ways, and I think the relationship between the old universities and the so-called red brick universities, the polytechnics, and so on, is much more clearly marked and at the same time sometimes not so clearly marked among the faculty because the radical people from the so-called great universities come into the so-called more public institutions. More interesting changes take place when I travel to Canada, Australia, India, the Middle East, and Bangladesh. The changes are complicated, because the negotiations of my "identity" vary from nation to nation, sphere to sphere, levels of work shading from the academic to grass roots. And much depends also on the language used—and my positioning in the great waves of gendered and classed diasporas that constitute the history and geography of our lives.

Q. You've spoken out against the emphasis on great works at the expense of other works. However, is it reasonable to assume that the corpus of any particular course, period, or genre is necessarily a "zero sum game"—that nothing can be added without a corresponding deletion? Don't those of us interested in reshaping what is taught face the difficulty of eliminating precisely those texts that are most in need of an ongoing process of critique? We're reminded of Derrida's recent comment in *JAC* on the importance of tradition: "I'm respectful and a lover of the tradition. There's no deconstruction without the memory of the tradition." Is it possible to retain the memory of tradition while reshaping what is taught?

A. I would say that it is not possible not to retain the memory of tradition while reshaping what is taught. I would also say that it is a great mistake to think that one has become an amnesiac. In fact, it is only with reference to certain kinds of memories that one constructs alternative memories. It is interesting that the issue arises today, when in transnational capitalism it no longer matters what nation-state capital is located in. On the other side is the national identity scenario: negotiated independence, national liberation, revolution/counter-revolution. The cultural explanations that are being generated are precisely attempting to undo the rupture of negotiated independence, revolution, national liberation, and so on, and construct a past with which a present and a future would be resonant, even as the idea of the division into national identities is becoming useless in the management of the global marketplace. The role of the constructing of memory in order to deal with the history of the present that is being written two ways, within politics and within economics, is now absolutely crucial.

Having said this, let me shift 180 degrees to the question about the canon—that nothing can be added without a corresponding deletion. I will move from talking about the whole world to talking about my specialty. In the English major, there is a lot of room to eliminate things. I am not against the teaching of traditional great texts, but I cannot see how this continued emphasis on single author courses has anything to do with the memory of the tradition. That is the tradition usurping the present. I'm not denying the importance of a few significant "traditional figures"; I'm simply denying the hierarchy in the kind of stratagem for eliminating the usurping of the "current" by a sort of orthodoxy—let's not even use the word *tradition*—that operates in the teaching of the English major. But that is a problem that is different from the broader problem that I think

Derrida is speaking to. I think there is great danger in pretending that the tradition simply disappears because we keep on saying "make it new."

Q. Would you give us some examples of what you have done in your own teaching to reshape what is being taught?

A. I teach everything these days with reference to the big picture. That's all; it's not a big change. For example, in a lecture last night when I was talking about French Feminism, I didn't divide my work into work on European theory and work on so-called Third World matters. I'm not an expert in the Third World, whatever that might be. I'm trained in the European and French modernist tradition, which is incorrectly taught if its imbrication with the world at large is not considered. So I'm really interested in teaching what I have been taught to teach in the "correct way," which means considering the big picture. When I'm giving a lecture on French Feminism, I also check it out with the work of an Algerian feminist who can teach and exchange with the French feminists. If I'm giving a lecture on Derrida and Foucault, I check it out with the work of Mahasweta Devi, who is almost exactly Foucault's age. She relates rather differently to the question of theory because she is basically an activist who has been an academic and is also a creative writer. In other words, the student who comes to my class to do Foucault and Derrida is obliged also to consider the texts of Mahasweta or Ife Amadiume. Teaching becomes intervention. I don't forget to look at the general critique of humanism. I don't think these things should become turf battles. I don't think that feminists of the individual rights stripe should waste their time speaking against deconstruction. To repeat, the discourse of the off-center subject should bring the discourse of constitutions to shuttling and productive crisis.

Q. In the teaching of writing in specialized courses—such as physics, chemistry, or art history, for example—do you think students should be taught to write for general audiences or should they be taught to address audiences familiar with specialized jargon, grammars, and methodologies?

A. I guess I'm a little old-fashioned about this. First of all, in any kind of a course, since writing is a tool that goes across the board, I should care if it's done competently. On the other hand, it does seem to me that it's not a very good idea to teach writing through physics, chemistry courses, and so on, because the teaching of reading cannot be done, let's say, in the "Senate house." Although we do, in fact, read the world as we are engaging in politics, you cannot, in fact, bring the training in reading into the arena where reading is something that is also done. I think there have to be places where you do nothing but the skill, and then the application of the skill develops. I'm not saying that when you teach the skill you should confine yourself to nothing but the skill itself, as a subject matter, but I am saying that when you are actually teaching, when you are actually involved in a major where the teaching of the content is important, you also must emphasize content. I don't know if this is an old-fashioned point of view, but it is certainly my conviction.

Q. In a recent interview with *Harper's*, you argued that one important responsibility of a college teacher is "to teach the young America to recognize that this is a multiracial, multicultural country." You emphasized that "the teaching of a multiculturalism should not be used in the service of some old-fashioned pieties, but is something that could work as a critical force underlying our general culture." Is there a radical pedagogy that individuals who teach writing in English departments might appropriate in meeting this particular responsibility?

A. I think if there is, it isn't a package that can be appropriated. I think work has been done at my university in the composition program. Many people are working on this in Pittsburgh, but I'm closely associated with Barbara McCarthy, a graduate student working on what such a pedagogy might be. I think that question is always directed toward the future. It's not something that exists that might be appropriated. I think it is something that might exist, that should be worked at. So I would like to end by looking forward to an indefinite future and a hope of more work rather than by making a premature closure and saying, "Yes, there it is, there is your text, there is your work, there is your book; appropriate it, then teach writing in that way."

Toward a Productive Crisis: A Response to Gayatri Spivak

JOHN CLIFFORD

An invitation to give a considered and public response to a discursive performance by Gayatri Spivak is an intellectual challenge that quickly problematizes the usual scholarly conventions for such a genre. A crisp exposition of her main ideas and an evaluation of her supporting evidence is simply not adequate to the intricate discursive strands Spivak weaves for a tapestry she eventually intends to unravel. To critique her interviews or her talks (or her essays) by the usual academic criteria of, say, clarity and coherence, would be an ironic corroboration of her call for a persistent critique of the rigidities of phallocentric discourse that is at the heart of Spivak's intellectual and political agenda. Our received notions of clarity and coherence are, she hopes, put into productive crisis by our attempts to grapple with a prose redolent with deconstructive displacements, Marxist dialectics, feminist resistances, and allusions to Third World and continental thinkers from Derrida and Althusser to Mahasweta Devi and Ife Amadiume. Readers must find their way in this interdisciplinary critical terrain with few signposts. To be lost in a detour from "subject formation" to "normative discourses of constitutions" is, I suspect, an integral part of the journey.

In Spivak's discursive universe, ideas are not vigorously asserted or rigorously defended. Instead, they are held in "productively undecidable" tension to be interrogated from a variety of postmodern perspectives. Perhaps the classic five-paragraph essay (so central to the current-traditional paradigm) with its confident thesis statement supported by three interconnected paragraphs of specific reasons, illustrations, and facts is the caricatured antithesis of Spivak's enigmatic, circuitous, tentative, and contradictory train of thought. She is, quite obviously, relentlessly rigorous in an intellectually awesome fashion, but not, most assuredly, to the measured drummer of conventional humanist discourse. There are certainly rhythms in her thought and style, but they are more likely to come from the dense entanglement of Cixous, Irigaray, Derrida, Foucault, and Gramsci. Her thoughts are not instantly accessible; nor are they meant to be, since her prose enacts her meaning. Perhaps she also eschews the plain style out of a fear of being understood too quickly, too clearly, as if real insight could be conveyed crisply in commonsensical prose. In a comparable context, William Dowling derides "the limpid style of bourgeois ideology where there is no need for obscurity because all truths are known in advance" (11). A genuine Marxist style should, he claims, produce "a dialectical shock" to force readers out of their usual and lethargic habits of mind. The goal of difficult prose is to "hear the shifting of the world's gears" (12). Somewhat less theatrically: when I read Spivak, I hear a demanding heteroglossia—a dialogic weaving and unweaving.

Her answer to the question about the relation between "gender as drama" and "women's writing and women's teaching" seems representative:

> Women's writing and women's teaching, based on gender and drama, bring into play notions like performance, both in the sense of acting out and bringing about through saying, representation, and self-representation, both in the sense of standing in for and seeing oneself as metonymy in the sense of the point of agreement standing in for provisional "collective consciousness," persistently to be dissolved as a presupposition. If this seems a little cryptic, I think the best way to decrypt it is, once again, in the technology of the classroom.

Reading this, I am reminded of Marshall McLuhan's insight that the medium is the message: Spivak is stylistically recapitulating an epistemology that needs to contextualize, to situate, to take back what has just been given, to shun generalization. This is not the linear, logocentric language of traditional scholarship. Her answer suggests that theory can only be temporarily put forth before it becomes something else under the pressure and the specificity of the classroom. Her response also suggests that ideas bring other ideas "into play," that a radically constructivist/anti-essentialist concept like gender as performance, for example, can and does act simultaneously with other, often contradictory ideas. More concretely, I think Spivak is suggesting that if a woman constructs a certain identity—say, taking a personal and nurturing stance in an intellectual debate—then that "performance" could for strategic reasons momentarily stand in for her identity. However, as Jane Gallop notes, this positing will also need to be called into question. The antipodes to be avoided are a fixed essential woman and an "oceanic passivity of undifferentiation" (Gallop xii). Here Spivak seems to be giving yet another twist to her provocative call to "take the risk of essence" in her antisexist work (qtd. in Smith 148).

In our present anti-foundationalist climate, this ongoing concern about the nature of the female subject is always controversial. The difficulties of definition are clearly foregrounded by Toril Moi's observation that any theoretical ground the essential woman hopes to stand on has already been occupied and contaminated by patriarchal ideology. There is no escape. Early American feminists, however, felt they could uncover a suppressed and authentic self by throwing off masculinist ideology, as it is manifested, for

Gayatri Chakravorty Spivak 257

example, in the canon, in objective critical methods that forbid the personal, or in the privileging of rhetorical strategies that diminish context and narrative. This pragmatic position has been roundly criticized by postmodernists such as Paul Smith for "being caught back up in the humanistic economy, the economy of the same" (137). The anti-essentialist cannot conceive of an identity (even in the case of Luce Irigaray when the female body is evoked as foundational) somehow existing outside the constraints of a particular culture in a specific time and place: "The self is always production rather than ground" (Spivak 212). And since women have always been constructed by a Western tradition dominated by males, it is unlikely Spivak would put much credence in the attempt to locate essence within a phallocentric culture. It is radical specificity that I believe Spivak is wedded to. Her chagrin at some feminists who have misunderstood her position stems from their inability to appreciate the postmodern cast of mind. For example, in a recent essay defending the virtues of the CBS style, Richard Marius invokes what he probably considers a self-evident warrant:

> As Aristotle taught long ago and as the rabbis who taught the Torah and the Talmud also believed and as the medieval Scholastics and the humanists of the Renaissance assumed, systematic exposition is defined by the law of noncontradiction. Nothing can be true and not true at the same time. (4)

On the contrary, the performance of a certain identity can be true as a strategic necessity, to support collective resistance against those structures that support fixed identities. Essence is therefore true, as in "situationally appropriate to achieve justice." But under the gaze of a historicized inquiry, nothing remains unchallenged. So essence can also be false, as in "unsupportable." The resulting internally heterogeneous subject is consequently released from those logical traps most anathema to the postmodern consciousness: homogeneity, epistemic assurance, fixity, unity, and clarity. For Spivak, Marius' law of noncontradiction is yet another masculine discursive stratagem to be undone. And if some feminists also believe they have finally established standards of truth, she is eager to register disapproval. With Lyotard, her knowledge is local, contingent, and frustratingly ephemeral.

The importance of focusing on micro-narratives is emphasized in several of her responses. Her nuanced move from strategic essentialism to a "pursuit of collective agency" is not directed primarily at global imperialism but at disciplinary discourse as it is enacted in our departments and universities. She suggests, echoing Foucault's notion of the "specific intellectual," that "decisions should not be separated from the way we run our workplace." Although the "big picture" is always in her mind, her tactics of resistance are directed at where she finds herself, doing the cultural work she does best. Her seemingly evasive response to the theory/practice binary is an example of her refusal to generalize beyond "the place of practice." Focusing on the material local practice seems wise to me. Beyond the obvious notion that current theory should inform practice, how much explicit theory should be foregrounded depends on a dramatistic evaluation of who is involved, the site, the purpose and so on. Writing an essay for *English Journal* requires the kind of practical specificity that would not please the readers of *Pre/Text*, and no one expects a basic writing textbook to be quoting Althusser. And a promotion committee at a community college must give more significance to a candidate's textbook on rhetoric than a doctoral institution would. But even the notion of what constitutes theory is problematic. If we were to use Fish's pure conception, then very little of what gets published in *CCC* or *JAC* would qualify. For some Ken Macrorie is still theory, while for others practice means applied grammatology/paralogy. The banal "it depends" can also be profound. It depends. The crucial idea here is to be the questioning subject, not the subject who already knows. Struggling effectively at work to rewrite the dominant discourse, to refigure the curriculum, and to rework received notions of subjectivity, we help to loosen the grip of the hegemonic.

Perhaps the most local gesture we can make is in the classroom, professing critical literacy. Spivak insists on teaching as intervention, as a disruption of both the conventional canon and conventional pedagogy. Her position, widely endorsed among neo-Marxists, is that as intellectuals working in institutions we cannot be beyond power, somehow freestanding in an apolitical, privileged, and isolated academic grove. We are, she insists, complicitous with the exploitative tendencies of Western humanism. Regardless of her course's ostensible content, then, a critique of the values and assumptions of our received tradition is woven into the class's day-to-day activities. She would bring other voices into the room, alternative visions, fresh perspectives from India, Africa. She would demand a confrontation with the oppositional, the counter-hegemonic, the marginal. Since it is the nature of a dominant discourse to move what it fears, rejects, or represses to the edge to achieve coherence, it is only by bringing marginal voices to the center that systems can be brought to crisis, that we can be forced to doubt our *modus operandi*. The vexed history of composition studies can provide ample evidence of how the unequal distribution of power in the English department allowed the dominant current-traditional paradigm to exile those who would speak otherwise to the edge of respectability, to the margins of influence. Spivak knows the value of the voice of the other—how it usefully mocks our fondest dogma—and demands that we admit its critique. This seems a cogent observation for compositionists as we contemplate the postmodern rhetorical canon.

At the risk of accusing Spivak of consistency, let me say that her perspective on rhetoric is compatible with her desire to undo oppressive structures/forms/discourses. Hoping that rhetoric might be more than tropology, more than hermetic pyrotechnics, she embraces de Man's notion that "rhetoric is the name for the residue of indeterminacy which escapes the system." However cogent, this is still primarily a reader-oriented view. The work of rhetoricians can certainly be illuminated by reading texts alertly and suspiciously, attentive to the excess of meaning our deconstructive, new historicist, reader-response, feminist or formalist methods can never account for. But the production of discourse—the practice of which should bring theory into crisis—deserves equal notice. The political significance of the critical rhetor has been noticed by such postmodern critics as Frank Lentricchia and Terry Eagleton but is disappointingly absent in Spivak's interview. Kenneth Burke and not de Man would have provided a more resonant model to evoke in the service of a liberatory rhetoric, one with a transformative bite, one that would be equal to Spivak's hope for a critical consciousness. From the perspective of responsibility to the "big picture," Burke's commitment to probe rhetorical alignments by first investigating our own identities as institutional intellectuals makes more political sense than de Manian indeterminacy and the problems of the individual consciousness. In shuffling her postmodern apparatus to de Man instead of, say, Althusser or Gramsci, Spivak unfortunately misses the opportunity to say something illuminating about discourse productive in university offices and classrooms. And as Lentricchia points out, Burke hopes rhetoric can undo the consequences of the tower of Babel, hopes to establish a community where the persuasive force of rhetoric would be superfluous—a self-destructive ingredient that should have appealed to Spivak.

As we might expect, her response to the question about WAC seems rather superficial. When thinkers like Derrida, Rorty, and Spivak are being interviewed for informed readers, we should probably stop asking them what they think about our specific professional concerns. Since they have not been part of our highly contextualized conversations, they lack our professional frames of references; they lack the historicized and emotional specificity that informs our contentious debates about grammar, process, evaluation, or literature. Here the voice of the other falters. Perhaps this is yet another representative anecdote about the continuing asymmetrical power arrangements within even sophisticated English departments where compositionists are expected to be knowledgeable about the literary canon from Beowulf to Barth, from Plato to Fish, while avant-garde critics seem quite satisfied being "a little old fashioned" about writing theory. Spivak would have seemed more postmodern if she had questions instead of "convictions" about composition.

University of North Carolina
Wilmington, North Carolina

Works Cited

Dowling, William C. *Jameson, Althusser, Marx*. Ithaca: Cornell UP, 1984.

Gallop, Jane. *The Daughter's Seduction*. Ithaca: Cornell UP, 1982.

Marius, Richard. "On Academic Discourse." *ADE Bulletin* 96 (Fall 1990): 4-7.

Smith, Paul. *Discerning the Subject*. Minneapolis: U of Minnesota P, 1988.

Spivak, Gayatri Chakravorty. "Subaltern Studies: Deconstructing Historiography." *In Other Worlds: Essays in Cultural Politics*. New York: Routledge, 1987. 197-221.

Talking Differently: A Response to Gayatri Chakravorty Spivak

THOMAS KENT

Michel Foucault taught us to talk about history in terms of shifting discourses rather than in terms of transcendental master-narratives. Instead of talking about history as an epic story of one kind or another—for example, as a story about our climb up the ladder of knowledge, or about our emancipation from old bad ways of thinking—Foucault asks us to think about history as changes in the way we employ vocabularies: once we talked like that; now we talk like this. In his writings, Foucault continually reminds us of the common sense observation that the world does not tell us how to talk. As Richard Rorty puts it, "The fact that Newton's vocabulary lets us predict the world more easily than Aristotle's does not mean that the world speaks Newtonian. The world does not speak. Only we do" (6). When we begin to talk about history—and knowledge, too—in terms of shifts in vocabularies, we no longer need to worry about the Cartesian or what is now called the *internalist* problem of matching up our vocabularies to something that exists outside of our own subjectivity. Consequently, we can get rid of the notion that language mediates between us and the world, for human being (human being-in-the-world) does not consist in striving for eternal truth or for ahistorical facts that exist "out there" beyond the vocabularies we employ to get things done in our everyday lives. In other words, when we stop talking about a split world—a world possessing an intrinsic nature set apart from an internal realm of mental states—and, instead, start talking about how we employ our vocabularies, we can get beyond essentialism and stop imagining that words possess a transcendental essence beyond the everyday pragmatic uses we give them.

Toward an Externalist Vocabulary

In her interview with *JAC*, Gayatri Chakravorty Spivak brings this Foucaultian lesson to life. In her responses, she refuses to employ an internalist vocabulary even when she is prodded in that direction by her interviewers. For example, when she is invited to "conceptualize" rhetoric, when she is invited to define rhetoric and reveal to us its essential meaning,

Spivak demurs. She tells us that if we really need an essentialist definition we might try on Paul de Man's anti-definition: rhetoric is a name, a name of "that which is the limit—that which escapes, that which is the residue of efforts at 'catching' things with systems." Because rhetoric is the name we give to that which we cannot name, "that which escapes" our systems for naming, Spivak reminds us that rhetoric, within an internalist vocabulary, cannot be "conceptualized" at all. By citing this anti-definition, she provides a living reminder that so long as we keep talking about transcendental categories, about conceptualizing names to correspond to things as they really are "out there," names will forever escape the systems we employ in order to pin down the meanings of names. In her responses, Spivak demonstrates that when we insist on employing an internalist vocabulary, we can never avoid the problems of skepticism and relativism. If we continue to talk in internalist terms and if we continue to insist that facts and truths exist independently of the words we employ to talk about these facts and truths, then we can never be sure that we are getting the correct facts and truths. Internalism leads directly to aporia, and so long as we hold to an internalist conception of language and meaning, we will find ourselves helplessly pursuing answers to unanswerable questions like, "How can we be sure that we have the *true* definition of rhetoric?" or "What is the *essence* of good writing?"

Spivak suggests that we would be better off if we stopped our internalist talk and started talking as an externalist, like Derrida, talks. When asked what rhetoric is, an externalist replies simply that rhetoric is what rhetoricians do. Plainly, if we insist on embracing the claim that words possess essences, this kind of response will appear to be a textbook example of tautology. However, if we stop talking about meaning in terms of a split between something in our heads—what Donald Davidson calls a "conceptual scheme"—and something outside our heads to which meaning refers, this response represents the only definition of rhetoric that we need. Within an externalist horizon, rhetoric is the activity pursued by people called rhetoricians, and, for the most part, rhetoricians talk about the production and reception of discourse in much the same way that physicians talk about healing, judges talk about jurisprudence, or physicists talk about the physical world. Of course, all rhetoricians do not talk in precisely the same way about what they do, just as all physicians, judges, or physicists do not talk in the same way, and there is no reason why they should. So when asked, "How do you conceptualize rhetoric, both as an activity and as a discipline?" Spivak's response is couched in precisely the right vocabulary. As a good externalist and Derridean, Spivak says that she "can't really comment on what goes on in the discipline of rhetoric" because she has been teaching in a comparative literature department; as a result, she cannot tell us what we rhetoricians do and, therefore, cannot define rhetoric in a very precise way. Following Derrida, Spivak refuses to employ the word *rhetoric* in an internalist way that "enables one to put together a body of definitions as something to be applied." Rhetoricians define rhetoric in their myriad disciplinary and public acts. Why should we want to "conceptualize" rhetoric?

Spivak provides another good demonstration of how to talk Derridean when she is asked about the distinction between theory and practice and whether she sees Aristotle's concept of *techne* as a deconstruction of the theory/practice binary. In her response, Spivak addresses two senses of the term *binary opposition*: the Derridean/externalist sense and the Cartesian/internalist sense. She explains that, in the Derridean sense, binary oppositions will always be with us, and we should not worry too much about them. She says that an opposition represents a continual reminder of the other, a voice within all our discourses that says, "Look here you, you know you are dependent upon me and you're ignoring it." For an externalist, then, oppositions serve to remind us of the openness of discourse, a reminder of what Bakhtin calls the "addressivity" of language-in-use. Only in the internalist sense of binary opposition do we run into the problems suggested by the interviewers' question. Only when we imagine that language constitutes a system of some sort that represents a world "out there," or when we imagine that language constitutes a self-enclosed world of its own, or when we imagine that language mediates between us and the world do we imagine that deconstruction overcomes oppositions. Spivak points out clearly that deconstruction has nothing to do with destroying oppositions, the kind of thing that internalists imagine must be going on when binary oppositions are mentioned. In the internalist sense of the term, a binary opposition comes into being only when we think of language as a system, *langue* as opposed to *parole* or something akin to this sort of bifurcation. In her response, Spivak explains that once we suppose a binary opposition to be an element of a language system, we are trapped; we can never escape the system. A term like *techne* that we employ to mediate between the opposition of theory and practice, in the vain hope that we can get rid of the opposition, only leads inexorably to other oppositions, other systems, and other "hierarchizations."

Spivak suggests (and I agree wholeheartedly) that binary oppositions have received too much press. In fact, I would like to see us stop talking altogether about binary oppositions and about language as a system, and, following the example of Davidson and Derrida, drop a vocabulary that describes language as a structure, conventional framework, system of intentional speech-acts, semiotic system, system of binary relations, and so forth. I would like to see us become strong externalists and accept Davidson's conclusion (446) that "there is no such thing as a language":

> I conclude that there is no such thing as a language, not if a language is anything like what many philosophers and linguists have supposed. There is therefore no such thing to be learned, mastered, or born with. We must give up the idea of a clearly defined shared structure which language-users acquire and then apply to cases. And we should try again to say how convention in any important sense is involved in language; or, as I think, we should give up the attempt to illuminate how we communicate by appeal to conventions.

I believe that Spivak, through Derrida's influence, arrives at this same conclusion. For example, she tells us that when we think about a problem like the relation between theory and practice we should not think of the problem in terms of a language model. Language is not a model that we can employ to settle our differences. We should not suppose that disagreements and differences in life correspond to oppositions in language; nor should we suppose that our problems can be "mediated"—as we imagine binary oppositions to be—so that we can "maintain a more productive dialogue in which we seek to recognize rather than suppress our differences." Spivak explains once again that mediations built on the model of language will be always "interested" and hierarchic. When we conceive of a language system that is motivated by binary oppositions, mediation leads to further interested oppositions, and no matter how much we yearn for an essentialist heaven beyond the cycle of mediation after mediation, we will never find relief from the system we impose on ourselves, a system constructed on an internalist model of language.

I believe that Spivak shows us a better way to talk about the "reversal of the theory/practice hierarchy" in composition theory. She tells us that we should historicize the problem and not reduce it to a question about language. She explains that theory and practice are disciplinary and institutional matters and not linguistic ones: "I think we should make use of the fact that our institutional system of education emphasizes committee structures, and, therefore, we should open and reopen these questions constantly." If, as Phillip Sipiora and Janet Atwill suggest, "Some compositionists speak out against what they see as a new privileging of theory in composition studies," we rhetoricians must settle the issue within the discourses of our discipline and our institutions. No totalizing theory of language, no epistemology in the Cartesian sense, will help us.

A Momentary Lapse

In most of her responses, Spivak talks as a good externalist should, but in one of her responses she demonstrates how easy it is to lapse into an internalist vocabulary. In their penultimate question, Sipiora and Atwill ask Spivak to address a very specific pedagogical concern: whether in specialized courses students should be taught to write for general audiences or whether they should be taught "to address audiences familiar with specialized jargon, grammars, and methodologies." Spivak responds that she might be "old-fashioned" in her views about this issue. When she employs the term "old-fashioned," Spivak displays her uncertainty about how to employ an externalist vocabulary in a discipline not her own; she confesses that she might be talking in a way that externalists no longer talk. And she is right. Spivak lapses into an internalist vocabulary when she speaks of writing as a skill that can be taught outside the discourses where writing occurs: "I think there have to be places where you do nothing but the skill, and then the application of the skill develops." According to this internalist sense of discourse production, writing is a technique (like riding a bike) that once learned can be applied automatically in many different situations. To talk this way, however, presupposes that writing constitutes an epistemological and ahistorical process and that once we internalize this process, all we need to do is apply it to different communicative contexts. As Spivak suspects when she calls her views "old fashioned," externalists should not talk this way about writing, and I would like to think that Spivak might not talk this way again if she could get another shot at the question. However, since she cannot get another shot at the question, I would like to offer (at the risk of seeming presumptuous) the kind of response that I wish Spivak had given.

From an externalist perspective, this pedagogical concern about audience begs the question about the teaching of writing. Sipiora and Atwill assume in their question that writing can be taught. For me, the question is not whether we should teach to specific or generalized audiences in specialized courses, but whether it is possible to teach writing at all. I do not believe that writing can be taught in any specialized course because writing is not a skill. Writing is not a system that can be internalized, although the scrawls we make in order to write obviously do form a system and, therefore, can be taught. However, these scrawls should not be confused with writing. Producing words and sentences does not constitute writing. Monkeys and machines produce organized scrawls, but they do not write. Writing presupposes a shared public language, so writing requires other people. Without at least one other person, there can be no language. Just as no private language exists, no private writing exists. Writing, therefore, cannot be reduced to a private cognitive process.

Hilary Putnam writes that "meanings ain't in the head"; well, neither is writing (227). An inner world of intentional mental states or of cognitive processes cannot account for writing or for any other kind of language use; instead, language use, such as writing, produces our sense of an inner world filled with intentional mental states and cognitive processes. Because we do not learn a writing system (since there is no writing "system" to learn) writing is hermeneutic and not epistemological in nature, and it cannot be separated from the public world in which we live. To write means to exist in the world. When we accept this paralogic conception of rhetoric, teachers in every course across the curriculum become therapists in the sense that they help students develop their own responses to an other, and writing becomes a collaborative and hermeneutic activity that we employ to interpret one another and, in turn, to get things done in the world.

This reply, then, resembles generally the kind of answer that I wish Spivak had given to this particular question. Of course, I believe that Spivak gave the response she did because she lapsed into internalist talk, but, in the big picture, Spivak's answer to this one question does not detract from the image she projects in this interview. In her responses to Sipiora and Atwill, as well as in her important books and translations, Spivak emerges as someone who shows us how to talk in a different way and to say more interesting things about language, literature, and culture. Clearly, her kind of talk employs a vocabulary that we do not associate readily with the vocabularies employed by most contemporary rhetoricians—vocabularies steeped in cognitivism, Kantian subjectivism, and Kuhnian constructionism. So Spivak's vocabulary—derived from a tradition represented by Nietzsche, Dewey, Heidegger, the later Wittgenstein, Quine, Rorty, and, most of all, Davidson and Derrida—often sounds strange to internalist ears.

Obviously, I believe our discipline would be better served if we dropped our internalist talk and adopted an externalist vocabulary along the lines of those provided by Davidson and Derrida. In more pragmatic terms, I believe our discipline would be better served if we talked more about discourse production and reception as hermeneutic activities and stopped talking about them—or, at least, stopped talking so much about them—as systemic processes of one kind or another. As a consequence of this shift in vocabularies, we would stop worrying about constructing totalizing internalist epistemologies and, as a result, stop worrying about reducing discourse production and reception to a body of knowledge that can be taught. Instead, we would start worrying first about better ways to collaborate and to work with others and second about better ways to structure our institutions so that the hermeneutic acts of writing and reading are not segregated in composition and literature courses where writing and reading become separated from the communicative interaction occurring in other courses within the university. In her *JAC* interview, Spivak shows us how we might begin to talk differently about issues like these, and we should listen carefully to the way she talks.

Iowa State University
Ames, Iowa

Works Cited

Davidson, Donald. "A Nice Derangement of Epitaphs." *Truth and Interpretation: Perspectives on the Philosophy of Donald Davidson.* Ed. Ernest Lepore. New York: Blackwell, 1986. 433-46.

Putman, Hilary. "The Meaning of 'Meaning.'" *Mind, Language, and Reality.* Cambridge: Cambridge UP, 1975.

Rorty, Richard. *Contingency, Irony, and Solidarity.* Cambridge: Cambridge UP, 1989.

Afterword

ANDREA A. LUNSFORD

(Re)reading in one sitting the seven interviews and fourteen responses that constitute this volume nearly gave me what my granny used to call a "splintering headache," as well as a number of provocative ways of thinking about our mutual concerns with writing and rhetoric. My nascent headache is explained first by the sheer density of some of the prose and the dizzying display of specialized vocabulary. From the "received," "subjective" and "procedural" positions in Belenky to the oblique "rhetoricism" and simultaneous "conservative" and nonconservative deconstruction" in Derrida to the "subject restoration," "strategic positivism" and "powerful and constructive autocritique" in Spivak—the essays in this volume demand close concentration, if not some outright translation. But complex ideas aren't easily (or justifiably) reducible to easy prose and are, in this case, most often well worth the effort. Second, and more troublesome by far, is the kind of one-upmanship displayed in some of the interviews and responses, an agonism characteristic of much of academic life. While a few interviews and responses offer models of the creative tension necessary for collaborative inquiry, too many exchanges smack instead of self-serving arguments, smug rejoinders, or contemptuous putdowns. Such displays of churlishness for its own sake are depressingly familiar to most of us.

Was my trip back through these pages worth the effort then? My answer is an unequivocal "yes," because such a reading can reward us with a number of important insights. While I could almost turn from page to page in this volume, commenting on provocative and insightful statements, I've chosen instead a few passages I find particularly evocative. For example, Belenky says, "People are easily locked into their own world view because they're not being engaged in hard-nosed conversations.... Without such conversations, we don't come to understand that words can communicate truths and that ideas can be developed and shaped." Until recently, scholars in composition studies were not engaged in much "hard-nosed conversation" with one another. We were too embattled from without to be hard-nosed within or to mount a rigorous critique of the truths communicated by our words or the ideas our words developed and shaped. For the degree to which the scholars interviewed here help to engage us in such hard-nosed conversation, we should be most grateful.

In her response to the Derrida interview, Sharon Crowley argues that a deconstructive reading of composition studies might ask

> why the theoretical diversity and excitement that characterize the meetings attended and journals read by composition teachers are not shared by faculty who don't teach writing, or by the culture at large, all of whom persist in defining freshman composition as a course in grammar, spelling, punctuation, and usage.

Certainly, this view of composition resonates throughout the interviews in this volume, particularly those with Derrida, Rorty, Chomsky, and even Spivak. The bifurcated view of our subject as substance/content versus formal skills is evident in these pages as well as in society at large. If we wish to challenge this binary, not to balance or mediate it but to reveal its multiple tensions, then we must do more than be engaged in rigorous critique by those interviewed here: we must also engage scholars like those interviewed here in hard-nosed investigations of the uses and functions of literacy and of the epistemological assumptions that govern their views of literacy. As Geertz says, "It's not ... even a matter of interdisciplinarity; it's a matter of being open to something outside your tradition as strictly defined."

These interviews and responses might all be read through the lens of Geertz's statement: which of these scholars, after all, is "open" to something, to anything, outside their own traditions? And how "open" are those of us in this (arguably) most interdisciplinary field of composition studies to ideas that stand far beyond our tradition, that are "other" to composition? This volume stands as one concrete answer to that question. While the interviewers sometimes have difficulty framing questions in open enough ways or in seeing beyond their own disciplinary blinders, they are clearly attempting to "open" composition and rhetoric to the frames of reference represented by philosophy, anthropology, linguistics, cultural studies, and so on. That is, this volume attempts to inaugurate one strand of hard-nosed, multidisciplinary conversation. Robert de Beaugrande comments,

> The future of the science of language lies in its potential to contribute to critical awareness and analysis, both in the sciences and in daily life.... The human race is "likely to self-destruct" less through nuclear holocaust than through the uncritical thought and discourse ... that justify complacency, self-interest, and inequality.

The questions explored in this volume—What does it mean to write, to be a writer? (How) can writing be best learned and taught? Whose interests are served by current constructions of language and writing? Who is (and is not) allowed to write? How should we define knowing at the end of the twentieth century?—are questions whose answers have all-too-real consequences. Juxtaposing the answers offered to such questions by thinkers representing a variety of perspectives highlights how much is at stake in asking and answering those questions. This volume cannot, and should not, offer answers; rather, it seeks to illuminate the questions and to engender wider conversation regarding them. Thomas Kent claims that we should

> stop worrying about constructing totalizing internalist epistemologies and . . . about reducing discourse production and reception to a body of knowledge that can be taught. Instead, we [sh]ould start worrying first about better ways to collaborate and to work with others and second about better ways to structure our institutions so that the hermeneutic acts of writing and reading are not segregated in composition and literature courses where writing and reading become separated.

"Hard-nosed conversation," "theoretical diversity and excitement," "being open to something outside," "collaboration"—such phrases exist as part of the powerful terministic screen this volume presents. The literate acts of reading and writing are not well served by narrowness, isolation, or bureaucratic institutionalization characteristic of most of our educational homes as well as of our disciplinary languages.

The interviews and essays in this text demonstrate the rich elusiveness, the cultural complexity, and the hermeneutic challenge posed by widely varying constructions of literacy; they call out to us to be open, to collaborate in continuing the hard-nosed conversation animating these pages.

Ohio State University
Columbus, Ohio

GARY A. OLSON teaches in the graduate program in rhetoric and composition at the University of South Florida, where he also edits the *Journal of Advanced Composition*. Besides publishing articles in such journals as *College English*, *College Composition and Communication*, and *Liberal Education*, Olson has edited and coauthored several books and textbooks, including *Writing Centers: Theory and Administration* (NCTE, 1984). Recently, Boynton/Cook published his *Advanced Placement English: Theory, Politics, and Pedagogy* (co-edited with Elizabeth Metzger and Evelyn Ashton-Jones), and Allyn and Bacon published *The Gender Reader* (co-edited with Evelyn Ashton-Jones).

IRENE GALE teaches composition and technical writing at the University of South Florida, where she also serves as Associate Editor of the *Journal of Advanced Composition*. She has published articles and reviews in *WPA: Writing Program Administration* and *Teaching English in the Two-Year College*. Currently, she is completing a book on critical thinking and another on dialogic theories in composition.